RASCHHOFER · POLITICAL ASSASSINATION

HERMANN RASCHHOFER

POLITICAL ASSASSINATION

THE LEGAL BACKGROUND OF THE OBERLÄNDER AND STASHINSKY CASES

MCMLXIV

PUBLISHED BY FRITZ SCHLICHTENMAYER

TÜBINGEN

Translated from the German by Ernst Schlosser, London

Printed by Carinthia, Klagenfurt (Austria)

TABLE OF CONTENTS

PREFACE TO THE ENGLISH EDITION

The English as well as the French edition of the book has been considerably enlarged by adding the problems of the "Stashinsky case" compared with the original German edition. On August 12, 1961, one day before the Berlin wall was built, escaped Bogdan Stashinsky, then a member of the Soviet Secret Service, with his wife to West Berlin, where he appeared before American authorities. He admitted having killed two people by order of his superiors — one of them beeing actually in charge of the office of the Deputy Prime Minister of the Soviet Union — in Munich with a recently developed gas pistol. The victims, Lev Rebet and Stefan Bandera, had been leading Exile-Ukrainians. The Americans submitted Stashinsky to the German authorities. The whole complex of his confessions was tried at the Federal Supreme Court in Karlsruhe. The trial verified point by point Stashinsky's confessions which at first had seemed to be quite improbable.

The facts proved in the trial are significant in two ways. On the one side there is a connection with the facts of the "Oberländer case" which has given the title to the German edition. The communist propaganda had charged the former minister of the Federal Republic of Germany to have provoked the assassination of Bandera and hereby eliminated a possible witness of his alleged war crimes in the Ukraine. The facts recorded by court prove this impeachment to be a false and malicious accusation by a political enemy.

The result of the Stashinsky trial has, however, further significance. A communist state may, according to Lenin's doctrine, make use of all means to maintain its power and to abolish its foes. The statements made by experts during the trial showed that, on the one hand, the communist government of the Soviet Union has abandoned the former practice of having executed terror actions, such as the assassination of political enemies, by order of the Secret Police. They showed, on the other hand, that murder by order of state authorities still continues to be a means of the communist struggle against the opponents of the Soviet System (only the commanding authority seems to have changed) *.

---

* Karl Anders, "Mord auf Befehl", Tübingen 1963, p. 76: "A careful investigation by the American Central Intelligence Agency (CIA) indicates that, in the NATO-countries and Latin America, between 1956 and 1962

These facts are meant to be emphasized in the English Edition by the terms "public enemy" and "political assassination". The term "public enemy" does not meet, however, the real issue of the phenomenon, because the determining significance is the opposition to the communist system. After making this clear, the use of the term "public enemy" in this study may, however, be appropriate.

Murder for political reasons does not only exist in our era, whether it relates to outstanding individuals — from Julius Caesar to Kennedy — or to entire groups or nations. Extreme hate has never shrunk from violent removal of political foes.

The examples examined in this study base upon a particular presupposition, i. e. the function of law as an instrument of class struggle developed by the philosophy of Marxism-Leninism and put into practice by the soviet-communist countries. For them law laid down in statutes is an instrument of political power in order to secure communist authority and to fight against their enemies.

The communist claim of power does not tolerate neutrality. Those who think otherwise become foes of the system, become "public enemies". Believing in its victory over the whole world, the communist system seizes its opponents not only inside, but also outside of the borders of the communist countries. That means that the leader group of a communist country can declare anybody a public enemy and draw consequences of different severity.

The communist version of the "Oberländer case" has found worldwide publicity. Its purpose was to dishonor not only an expert in questions on Russia and the Soviet-Union, but also the Federal Republic of Germany and its government.

The claim of the English edition is to give interested foreign readers the opportunity to form their own opinion by studying the original sources.

---

16 politicians have probably died no natural death, but have been killed by hydrocyanic acid with a gas pistol — like Dr. Rebet and Stefan Bandera.

The Bandera case had exerted an influence upon CIA to have the death of some 150 politicians examined who so far had been supposed to have died a natural death. Even if the number 16 might be too high, this investigation by CIA has proved that the Soviet Secret Service has ordered and executed further political assassinations."

PREFACE

For a considerable lenght of time, the 'Oberländer Case' has served to fill the columns of both the German and the foreign press. The chief bone of contention during the newspaper controversy was whether a man with an allegedly dark political past — a past that stood under the shadow of membership and active work in the National Socialist Party — was suitable for holding political office, particularly that of a minister, in the Federal Republic of Germany. Additionally the dispute was deepened substantially by foreign official quarters becoming parties to it. The Soviets asserted, apparently on the strength of massive witnesses' reports, that the Minister had been guilty of horrifying war crimes. Judgment passed on him by a court in the Soviet Zone of Germany seemed to confirm these accusations.

Also in the Federal Republic, political opponents of Professor Oberländer have tried to prosecute him through the criminal courts, by laying an action against him with the Public Prosecutor. This has led to a criminal investigation being started against him by the *Oberstaatsanwalt* (Chief Public Prosecutor) at the *Landgericht* (District Criminal Court) in Bonn. But careful scrutiny under the Rule of Law of the various points alleged against Oberländer led to a double finding: On the one hand, no *prima facie* case could be made out against Oberländer of having committed any war crime. On the other hand, much more was found — it was shown that his attitude during the time in question was completely contrary to the convictions of the Nazi Party and to Nazi practice; that Oberländer tried, with great personal risk, to persuade others to support him in this attitude; and that, insofar as he was able to act under his own responsibility, he lived up to what he preached.

The judgment of the Soviet Zone court has evaluated evidence in a way that does not stand up to the formal process of investigation under the Rule of Law. This court also alleged that International Law was violated, and it claimed to be fit to sit in judgment on the case in question by appealing to questionable notions of international law. Therefore, the legal side of the Oberländer Case poses a number of fundamental questions about the nature and the purpose of Law and Courts of Law on the territory of states built on the basis of Marxism-Leninism, and about fundamentals of contemporary International Law.

The second basic question connected with the Oberländer Case will be dealt with here only briefly.

A large number of men, most of them aged between forty and sixty, at one time joined the National Socialist Party in good faith and became politically active in its ranks. Is that sufficient reason for excluding them, on principle, from public life, or from holding certain offices? Many foreign critics of the Federal Republic of Germany accuse our state of employing 'many former Nazis', and thereby implicitly, and without any reservation, accept such reasoning. This, however, is highly problematical, and a clear answer to that question is, in fact, of immense importance. Those who have been members of the Nazi Party, and who worked in it and for it, must clearly answer the question whether they have gone over to the camp of Democracy and of the Rule of Law from pure opportunism, as clever trimmers, or from insight and inner conviction. Are they simply turncoats or truly changed men?

Once the question has been put like this, it is clear beyond all doubt that not only the group of former Nazi members will have to answer it. Also the German Communist Party aims at the creation of a revolutionary Dictatorship. If, therefore, membership and activities in the Nazi Party by themselves, no matter why the membership was acquired, and how the ex-Nazi acted, when he was still a Nazi member, shoud always preclude permission for being politically active in a free political community and under the Rule of Law, the same restriction must be applied to former members and active militants of the Communist Party, both for reasons of state security and under the fundamental postulate of equal rights for all citizens.

The court files of the Oberländer Case are an important contribution to the hitherto unwritten history of the tragic destiny suffered by the young generation which came to the Nazi Party because it saw in it a force that could help them to attain their aims and longings bound up with the interests of German minorities in the East and across the German frontiers. Almost without exception, all these men and women quickly became basically opponents of the doctrine and practice of the NSDAP. In the proceedings of the Soviet Zone court, this clear opposition of Oberländer to focal points of the Nazi doctrine and of the Eastern policies of the Nazis has not only not been accepted but denied by every available method. Among other things, this shows the true motives of Eastern campaigning against Oberländer. They form part and parcel of a broad offensive staged by the Communists against the Federal Republic and against all its leading personalities whom they deem sufficiently important and dangerous.

When official quarters suggested to me to start upon my investigation, the result of which is this book, I have also scrutinized the objection against my person as a possibly interested party. The reason for this is the fact that I belonged to the Bergmann unit between the spring of 1942 and the autumn of 1943. As such, I took part in the fighting in the Caucasus and in the Crimea, and I belonged to the group of persons against whom an investigation for war crimes was started.

However, the suggestion that I start this work was received by me only after this investigation had been closed, and when its result, based on a thorough examination of the evidence, was long known. The files of the investigators in the cases of the Nachtigall and the Bergmann units were no longer "live" material for police investigation and judicial examination but had entered history as documentation. I received permission to study the papers in the files only after the judicial proceedings had ended. My personal involvement in the events did not and could not influence the findings produced by the investigations, but these, in the event, gave no reason for any objections of mine. I could not have wished for any different picture from that which the completed investigation produced, and this enabled me to re-examine the facts with the instruments of historical and legal science unemotionally and without prejudice. Naturally, I have to admit that it gave me particular satisfaction to be able to contribute, by elucidating in a scientific way the entire complex, to the restitution of honour for my German and foreign comrades, who had served in those units, and whose reputation had been dragged down into the mire for so long.

Bernt von Heiseler has written an appreciation of the public morality shown by the treatment of the Oberländer Case, and I cannot do better than using his words as a conclusion of this preface. B. von Heiseler reminds his readers of the shameful treatment of Colonel-General von Fritsch by Hitler, and continues:

'And now we have arrived at a juncture — as I see it — where such a cause does not affect any longer only the honour of a single individual, be he called von Fritsch, Oberländer, or by any different name, but the honour of all of us.'

'If public opinion in any state permits calumny to reach its aim without any effective correction, then this state loses the firm ground beneath its foundations. It is not only the honest name of those who hold public office which goes unprotected, so that every habitual toper in the pub may say: "Very well, he who dips his fingers into the political saucepan should not be surprised if he gets dirty." — No, also the "regular" in the beerhouse will be affected; it is everybody's personal affair if no retribution hits those who falsify the words of a persecuted person, so that they seem to mean the opposite, as was done in the case of Oberländer. Personal honour is a basic human right. No state will ever be without fault, but whether it has remained healthy depends upon its capacity for establishing the law and for protecting it. That means: the State must offer all its citizens the chance to defend their honour, and it must protect its citizens against the harm done to them by libel and calumny, if such an attack is proved to be libellous and untrue. It requires but little thought to appreciate the truth of this observation.

'If the community tolerates our honour to go unprotected, calumny soon becomes a weapon used for personal and professional ends as well. This statement of mine does not refer to future worries, since we have witnessed in the past how, in thousands of cases, personal competitors who could not be beaten through superior efficiency were liquidated by means of informing against them and libelling them, both in 1933 and in 1945. Such habits destroy all active life, all energy for confidently joining in a fair contest, in the entire nation. The case of Oberländer is only a highly important and extreme example for the general and widespread canker that eats up our public life.'

I

SHOW TRIAL VS. CRIMINAL INVESTIGATION METHODS UNDER THE RULE OF LAW

It is very unlikely that there has ever been in legal history another case started against one defendant only which was dealt with in two separate proceedings dealing with the same incriminating facts, and resulting in completely opposite findings. The first of the two has ended in sentencing the defendant (in his absence) to hard labour for life, whilst the second did not go beyond the stage of a judicial enquiry resulting in the declaration that for none of the proffered accusations a *prima facie* case has been made out, so that there was no reason for an indictment. On the basis of the first accusation, the defendant was

> sentenced for multiple and continued acts of murder, for multiple and continued instigation of others to the commitment of murder, for continued membership in associations formed for the purpose of committing crimes against human life, and for continued appeals to others to commit crimes, to hard labour for life [1].

In the text of this judgment, the Court emphasized that it considered the death sentence to be applicable and just, but following special considerations, it decided to commute it into a life sentence. The second judicial authority has found these extreme accusations, consisting of numerous, alleged criminal acts, in all their particulars as being without foundation. For this reason, the proceedings were quashed [2]. On the one hand, the death sentence, commuted into life imprisonment, and final and complete moral condemnation of the defendant, on the other hand, total moral rehabilitation of the person in question.

The rare case of two completely incompatible findings by two judicial bodies, basing their decisions on virtually identical facts, and sitting practically at the same time, has occurred in the proceedings taken against Professor Dr. Dr. Theodor Oberländer, then Federal German Minister for Expellees, Refugees and War Victims. The first was the result of a criminal investigation and prosecution brief prepared by a Public Prosecutor's Office *(Staatsanwaltschaft)* in the Soviet-occupied Zone of Germany, and of the ensuing judgment pronounced by the Supreme Court of the so-called German Democratic Republic (G.D.R.). The second was the outcome of a criminal investigation carried out by the *Oberstaatsanwalt* (Chief Public Prosecutor) of the *Landgericht* (District Court) at Bonn.

How can we explain the flat contradiction between the two findings? How was it possible that two different judicial bodies have assessed identical facts and the same person in such contrary terms? It is a well-known everyday occurrence that higher courts often judge the same facts differently on appeal, that findings of guilt or acquittals are overthrown, or that the severity of the punishment is mitigated or increased. It is also rare for a judge's bench to arrive at unanimous verdicts, though it is admissible only in Anglo-Saxon law for the minority on the bench to publish its minority opinion with regard to the judgment itself or to the reasons adduced for it, together with that of the majority. The International Court of Law [3] and (in Germany) the Supreme State Court of Bremen [4] have adopted this form of procedure. But it is not for such reasons that the results of the two criminal investigations were so totally different in Berlin-Pankow and in Bonn. On the contrary, Pankow's complete condemnation of the defendant is based on fundamental differences in the established notions of Law and of the tasks and scope of the judicature. Later, we shall have to discuss the basic ideas on Law and Judicature prevalent in the Soviet realm, and thus also in the Soviet-occupied Zone of Germany. Here it is sufficient to recall that the Soviets, basing their legal theory upon the ideas of Marx and Lenin, consider *the Law to be the will of the ruling class translated into statutes and legal prescriptions*, so that *the Law mirrors the policies of the class ruling the legislating State.* In our case, it is of importance that this relationship between State and Law becomes visible, *not only through form and content of applicable statutes but also in the process of their application.* Membership of a particular class or political opposition, under this system, are equivalent to guilt, and the severity of punishment depends on the intensity of the opposition. It has been stated, with complete justice, that Soviet legislative and legal principles are being, in the full sense of the term, *slavishly copied* by the German Soviet Zone.

If we consider the Pankow proceedings on the basis of these principles, all sense of mystery vanishes. The purpose of the Pankow trial was to hit an enemy. The proceedings of the Soviet Zone against Professor Oberländer are, and will remain, one of the classical examples for the subordination of Marxist Law and Justice to the intentions and purposes of Marxist policies.

But is the totally different result of the Bonn Prosecutor's investigation not the outcome of political pressures, too? Could the West German investigating magistrate dare to subject to his impartial scrutiny a man who held one of the highest public offices? Was he not a member of a political party which, at that time, had an absolute majority in the Federal Parliament? Did this majority not everything in its power to protect him and cover him up? Can we take the Bonn investigation seriously, or was it some sort of pseudo-judicial window-dressing? But if we go into the case more deeply, we cannot pretend that Professor Oberländer was, in the event, not brought before a criminal court only because he was a government minister then, and because the ruling political party took him under its wings. Viewed from the standpoint of party politics, it is much nearer the truth that his own political party dropped him like a hot potato. In fact, the party to which he still belongs, did not rally behind him at all. Only a few years before his 'case', Oberländer had joined the CDU (Christian-Democratic Union) after the split of the *BHE (Bund der Heimatvertriebenen und Entrechteten,* commonly known as 'Expellee and Refugee Party', but since re-named as *GDP*, or *'Gesamtdeutsche Partei'*, meaning All-German Party), of which part went over to the CDU. It is well known that Oberländer had not only friends in the CDU. Whatever the reasons may have been, also newspapers of so-called party friends directed violent attacks against Oberländer. The minister had ample opportunity to test the truth of the saying: *May God protect me against my friends, for I am fully able to protect myself against my enemies.* Thus, even the actual position of the minister within his party did not create any temptation — otherwise conceivable — to tamper with justice for political ends. But those who want to explain away the results of the Bonn investigation as political skulduggery leave out of consideration two other powerful influences: the legal conscience of the investigating magistrates, and the political power of a parliamentary opposition. Critics of this type, on the one hand, unjustly suspect the integrity of the Public Prosecutors in the Federal Republic. Article 46 of the Federal Constitution bases the rights and duties of members of the Federal Diet upon the Rule of Law and upon parliamentary tradition. Members of the Diet enjoy immunity from prosecution, which means that they cannot be incriminated or arrested for any punishable offence without Parliament granting permission by lifting the privilege of immunity. Proceedings taken against Professor Oberländer under the Rule of Law (in the cases *'Nachtigall'* and *'Bergmann'*) were started after the left-wing *VVN (Vereinigung der Verfolgten des Naziregimes,* i. e. 'Association of Victims of the Nazi Regime) had laid information against him with the Public Prosecutor. As Professor Oberländer was a member of the Federal Diet, the examining magistrates, during their investigation, prepared their application under Article 46 of the Federal Constitution for the lifting of his immunity, submission of this application depending on the results of the investigation. Careful study of the files and papers collected and examined during the investigation allows of no doubt that the Federal Diet would have received an application for lifting Oberländer's immunity in case suspicion had coagulated into a *prima facie* indictment.

Everybody who has perused the files of the investigation must return from this study with the highest respect for the circumspectness, the scope and the watchfulness of the methods used for clearing up the case. We will have to say more on this subject later.

But apart from the good faith and conscience of the examining authorities, there were other, political forces which would have prevented any tampering with the law. Under democratic conditions, based on the Rule of Law, it is not only the conscience of the examining magistrates and public prosecutors that safeguards the legal integrity of criminal investigations and prosecution procedures. Additional guarantees are the existence of a parliamentary opposition and of a free press. Does anybody seriously believe that the powerful opposition in the Federal Diet was not willing and able to enforce, by its action in parliament, the lifting of Professor Oberländer's immunity and subsequent prosecution if the investigation had dug up sufficient evidence for it? In a totalitarian dictatorship, ruling power is unlimited, and law courts have no genuine freedom to evaluate the facts on record. Every opponent of the regime against whom a prosecutor has received his brief is sentenced in advance. The show trial is a fixed institution of the government machinery. This institution did not fail to carry out its task in Oberländer's case. On the other hand, numerous verdicts of courts in the Federal Republic — e. g. the sentences passed on the former Free Democratic member of the *Bundestag*, the ex-general Hasso von Manteuffel, und against Field Marshal Schörner — have proved the independence of West German courts of law. And even the Bonn investigation against Professor Oberländer declared it to be conceivable that individual members of the *Nachtigall* unit may have taken part in the anti-Jewish atrocities of June 1941 in Lwow, though it justifiably sees a difference between these acts, if they can still be proved, and the responsibility of Professor Oberländer for them. If such atrocities can be proved, they were committed by individuals of their own volition, against given instructions and orders, and thus outside the responsibility of their military superiors in international law.

The reasons for calling the proceedings against Professor Oberländer in the Soviet Zone a show trial [5] are a number of considerations, which all lead to the same result. The first of these is the timing of the trial. If the extremely serious crimes of which Oberländer was accused had been actually committed by him in Lwow and in the Caucasus, it can hardly be understood that the accusers have waited nearly twenty years before bringing them before a court. Precisely because of their extraordinary seriousness, it will be shown later in detail that the prosecuting authorities of the countries where the crimes were allegedly committed must have known the events and those responsible for them already twenty years

years ago — that is, not long before the extraditions of the first alleged German war criminals to Poland and the Soviet Union took place. In particular, the trial in the Soviet Zone accepts as credible even the most fantastic and unlikely stories of witnesses, because, as the court says, the acts of which Professor Oberländer stands accused are of

> such brutality and cover such a wide field that their reconstruction after a relatively long lapse of time makes no extraordinary claims upon the faculty of human memory [6].

If such a long memory is supposed to exist in witnesses who were not resident in the places where the crimes allegedly took place but passed only through them, it can be taken for granted that the resident population of such places ought to remember them even better. The witness, Aleskerov [7], asserted that Professor Oberländer ruled over the Northern Caucasus as an all-powerful and much-feared governor, who appointed all the holders of administrative offices, e. g. local mayors, police superintendents, and gendarmery commandants. If we accept it as a true fact that Professor Oberländer was in such close and daily contact with the resident population, we must also assume that his name and that of the unit under his supposed command would also have engraved itself indelibly on the memories of the survivors, and in indissoluble connection with the horrible crimes of which they are accused. The same would be the case in Lwow. Not later than at the end of the war, but more likely during the reoccupation of these areas by Soviet troops, the inhabitants of these districts would have been quick to report such crimes, and we may be sure that, if this was the case, criminal proceedings and sentences would have followed such depositions immediately. This unsolved paradox has been the subject of a discussion of the alleged crimes of Oberländer and the *Nachtigall* unit by a source of particular importance: a periodical published by exiled Poles compiled a documentary report on the Lwow atrocities of the summer of 1941, and this report stressed the fact that a truly appalling crime of that period, the butchering of a group of Polish scientists, which plays a permanent role in the propaganda of the Soviet Union, of Communist Poland, and of the German Soviet Zone, had already been dealt with and cleared up in the Nuremberg Trial against the Chief War Criminals. According to the admissions of the sentenced criminals, the mass murder had been committed by a special unit of the Security Service *(Sonderkommando des SD).* The Polish description underlines the special significance of this document and adds:

> ... during the Nuremberg Trial, nobody asserted that Oberländer and the *Nachtigall* battalion had been responsible for these crimes [8].

Therefore, if it took almost twenty years until a communist court started proceedings against Professor Oberländer, and if the court chosen for starting them lay neither in the Soviet Union nor in Poland but in the German Soviet Zone, this must have special reasons. Also this can be explained by the basic Marxist-Leninist postulate that the Law and the application of the law are the instruments of politics. Investigations carried out under the Rule of Law have proved that the crimes of which Professor Oberländer has been accused for the period when he was in the Caucasus were pure invention. The investigation of the Nachtigall case, under the same conditions, has made it indisputable that several thousand inhabitants of Lwow had been murdered, by order of the Soviet authorities, some of them in the most cruel way, before the German Army entered Lwow. Both the populations of the North Caucasus and of Lwow well remember the conditions and events of that time. If the Soviets had staged a show trial in the places where the alleged crimes were committed, this might have led to incalculable risks for the smooth running of the court proceedings. On German soil, this was not to be feared, and at the same time, a trial in a court that was a stranger to the countries and witnesses of the events in question was a reliable instrument for staging the planned main effect in terms of political propaganda.

For it was not, in fact, the defendant, the individual Oberländer, who was to be found guilty of the crimes which were alleged to have been committed by him twenty years ago as an army first lieutenant or captain. The Soviet Union was in no way interested in the person of Oberländer as a human being, nor did the politically-steered jurisdiction of the Soviet Zone care for him. It was his high office, the member of the West German Federal Government, who had to be charged with unimaginable crimes. The Minister was well known as an expert on the Soviet system and as an opponent of Soviet communism. When the court held its sittings in the Soviet Zone, Oberländer was member of a government against which, and against whose chief, Chancellor Adenauer, both the Soviet Union and the Soviet Zone have been carrying on an unceasing war of calumniation. If they had succeeded in smearing a member of this government by a verdict on his allegedly bestial and criminal past, it would not have been only a political opponent who fell — also his government would have been severely discredited for tolerating such a man within its ranks. These speculations are not mere figments of the author's imagination, for they formed part of the actual court proceedings. In the transcript we read:

> The Public Prosecutor's Office *(Staatsanwaltschaft)* is convinced that not only the defendant, Oberländer, has been in the dock, but with him that system of Bonn, under whose wings the murderer, Oberländer, has sought again protection last week against the will of the people and the wrath of the public [9].

To be continued thus:

> Twenty-five years ago, the chief of the *BDO (Bund Deutscher Osten,* i. e. "Rally of the German East") and the *VDA (Verein für das Deutschtum*

im Ausland, i. e. "Union of Germans Abroad") was busy with the same sort of work. To-day, he has returned to it as minister of the Adenauer Cabinet... *In the interest of Peace, the organizer of the Fifth Column must be rendered harmless.* Oberländer always was, and has remained, a criminal, who has become socially acceptable only by being a member of the Adenauer Cabinet, and holding command in the *Landsmannschaften* (organisations of German Eastern expellees), mobilizing them for aggression against the East [10].

In the Preface of the shortened transcription of the trial in the Soviet Zone, the same argument appears:

> Adenauer kept Oberländer after the Committee for German Unity *(Ausschuss für Deutsche Einheit)* had proved at an international press conference, held in Berlin on 22nd October, 1959, from the original files that his minister was, and is, one of the chief instigators and practicians of fascist war and extermination policies. Adenauer continued to protect Oberländer even after the Committee for German Unity had made known to a wider public the documents proving Oberländer's crimes at the beginning of February, 1960, in its "Brown Book", *"The Truth About Oberländer"*.
>
> What sort of a government is that, if its chief keeps silent for seven years about the murders of a cabinet member, about which he knew all the time? A government which covers up these crimes, and which in the face of irrefutable proofs for his guilt assures the minister of their special confidence, as happended officially on December, 1959, and in January, 1960, in the Federal Diet [11]?

And further:

> The behaviour of the Adenauer government is characteristic for this system of clerical militarism which intends to leave the fascist past *undigested,* because it is planning new wars of revenge and new acts of aggression. For this purpose, it needs the old forces, who have led Germany already twice to the brink of disaster. With their aid, the Bonn government intends to provoke a third mass murder of the nations, this time using atomic weapons [12].

The carefully thought-out terms of the accusation alone are sufficient proof that the Soviet system is not interested in a particular human being, but in the minister of a government, who has to be rendered harmless as an opponent of the Soviets. It is the Adenauer cabinet and the holder of ministerial office who are to be hit by such proceedings — carefully staged for prearranged results in a show trial. To serve this purpose effectively it was of course highly expedient to select the Suppreme Court of the Soviet Zone as the venue of the trial. For propaganda purposes, court proceedings held in the Caucasus or in Lwow would have been much less effective and valuable, apart from the risk of calling as witnesses, and admitting to the public galleries, residents of the area, who know the accusations to be false. Even a totalitarian system cannot completely exclude highly embarrassing incidents under such adverse local conditions. On the other hand, the Soviet-occupied Zone of Germany offered itself as the best available platform from which the Federal Republic's direct opponents were able to speak.

The communist campaign against Oberländer, reaching its climax in the verdict of the East Berlin court sentencing the 'defendant' to hard labour for life (which the Communists describe as a 'mitigated' sentence, illustrates the nature and tasks of Soviet communist jurisdiction.

In addition, it shows the significance of the political identification of certain people with a legal type described here, for reasons of simplification, as 'enemies of the state' [13].

Describing of a given person (or group of persons) — in our case it is Oberländer — as 'enemy (enemies) of the state' is a decision reserved to high or even the supreme political authorities. Once this decision has been made, it becomes binding upon courts of law. Court proceedings then have only the task to transform the 'enemy of the state' legally into a criminal.

However, enemies of the state can also become the targets of direct violent action, both inside and outside Soviet territory. To tear the veil of secrecy from such usage has been one of the most important achievements of the trial of October 1962 before the Federal High Court in Karlsruhe against the former Soviet citizen Stashinsky. The trial, at the same time, illustrates the connection between methods of violence and political calumniation.

On October 15, 1959, the exiled Ukrainian politician, Stepan Bandera, had died in Munich under circumstances which immediately aroused suspicions of murder. Before the open grave, a high Greek Catholic (uniate) priest in his funeral oration pointed to the Communists as the probable directing agents behind the suspected crime [14]. Authorities of the Soviet Union and the German Soviet Zone immediately accused the then Minister Oberländer that he had caused the crime. Thus, *Krasnaiva Svezda,* the newspaper of the Soviet Ministry of Defence [15], wrote that Bandera had entered Lwow during the war with the Nachtigall battalion and had known too much of the events connected with this event and of the rôle played by Oberländer in them. Oberländer allegedly intended to get a witness to his crimes out of the way. *Komsomolskaya Pravda,* the paper of the communist youth organisation, copied these attacks. Under the headline, 'Accident or Murder?', it published a cartoon showing Oberländer standing near Bandera's coffin, saying: 'He was a good Nazi, a pity only that he knew slightly too much about me.'

The true murderer, the Soviet citizen Stashinsky, fled to West Berlin on August 12, 1961, and surrendered first to the American and then to the German authorities. He admitted to have killed Bandera by order of the Soviet Secret Service, and also to have murdered the Ukrainian author, Lev Rebet, in Munich on October 12, 1957.

Whereas Soviet propaganda tried to smear Oberländer with the crime and the responsibility for it, the Soviet Zone press agency *ADN* published a different explanation of the killing of Bandera. The Judgment of the German court comments this version as follows [16] : —

> ... In the Soviet Occupation Zone, a propaganda action was started on October 15, 1961, with the untrue assertion that the exiled Ukrainian, Myskiv, murdered Bandera by order of the Federal German intelligence service on October 15, 1959, and that Myskiv himself later fell victim to an assassination. Towards the end of October, the Federal German intelligence service monitored a number of radio instructions of the Soviet Secret Service addressed to one of its agents in Germany, which requested the recipient to report on the effects of the Myskiv propaganda wave and on the possible need for continuing it.
>
> Actually, Myskiv was in Italy on the day of the murder, the 15th of October, 1959, and he died on March 27, 1960, from proved natural causes.

The text of the Judgment then continues [17] : —

> This propaganda action, which was clearly started by request of the Soviet authorities in the Soviet Occupation Zone, was designed to charge Federal German intelligence service with responsibility for the killing of Bandera. Thereby, communist propaganda committed one of its typical psychological errors. It is a widely-known trick of this propaganda to turn inside out certain important events, by crying 'stop thief!', thereby actually revealing its own habits and customary methods involuntarily.

Another false report spread from the Soviet Zone may serve as additional proof for the calculated methods of inventing and broadcasting such calumnies: During the campaign against Oberländer in the Soviet Zone, a report appeared that the former officer-in-command of the Nachtigall unit, Dr. A. Herzner, had died 'recently' in mysterious circumstances [18]. As in the case of Bandera's death, it was hinted that Oberländer had used middlemen to kill Dr. Herzner as an awkward witness who knew too much about Oberländer's alleged crimes.

Dr. Herzner's widow, Frau Käthe Herzner, wrote a letter to the Berlin RIAS radio transmitter, dated November 2, 1959, describing the true circumstances of her husband's death. According to Frau Herzner, her husband had frequently told her of the events in Lwow, and had always emphasized that cruelties and crimes had already been committed before his unit reached Lwow. Of these atrocities, he spoke with all signs of revulsion, both orally and in letters to her. It was equally untrue that Dr. Herzner died 'recently under mysterious circumstances'. Actually, he died already on April 3, 1942, in the Hohenlychen military hospital, from the after-effects of a war injury, and he was buried with all military honours on April 9, 1942, in the 'Heroes' Cemetery' of Potsdam. Frau Herzner also informed the Chief Public Prosecutor *(Oberstaatsanwalt)* of the Bonn Land Court of these facts.

Already the criminal investigation carried out at Bonn had resulted in the finding that Bandera did not come to Lwow with the Nachtigall unit, as the Supreme Command of the *Wehrmacht (OKW)* had called him to Berlin. That means that he did not know personally of the alleged events happening in Lwow.

The Judgment of the Federal Supreme Court, which is based upon its own investigations and on the admission of Stashinsky, produced further proof that the orders causing the assassination of Bandera (and of Rebet) were issued by Soviet government departments, which then tried to pass on the responsibility for them to Oberländer.

The trial against Bogdan Stashinsky made it clear beyond all doubt that Oberländer had nothing to do with the Bandera affair, because highly placed Soviet authorities issued the orders to kill Bandera, and this finding is therefore of high material importance. The methods used by high Soviet officials, revealed by the trial, pose the question of the relationship between politics and law in the contemporary Soviet communist system.

Since the end of the Stalin era, the international discussion on whether the Soviet system is undergoing a fundamental change has never stopped. There are many signs for a deep change taking place within Soviet *society*. But it is quite a different question whether, and to what extent, the Soviet *government system* is undergoing important changes, especially whether the Communists's traditional opinions of the relationship between State authority and Law are affected by the transformation. The reasons given by the Federal High Court for its verdict are of eminent significance for the answers to several sides of this question, as the judgment had to evaluate these problems when weighing the criminal nature of Stashinsky's actions. In its comment, the Court states that, in this field, there is 'much new territory to which criminal law and criminology have devoted little research' up to date. The Court assumed that in cases like that of Stashinsky, there is none of the usual personal motivation in the development of such crimes committed by official order. The recipients of such orders 'carry out their assignments under the influence of political propaganda, or under the pressure of higher authority, or similar factors emanating from their own state.' The source of origin 'for the *motivation* of such crimes, of the forces impelling the agent, are not the recipients of such orders, *but the holders of State authority*' [19]. In view of this finding, the supreme German court has also discussed the question whether the changes observed since the end of the Stalin era have also affected the field of these crimes. But it found proved only a change in the chain of command for issuing such criminal orders, and not a general dropping of the claim justifying the use of such methods by present-day Soviet communist state authorities.

The Court also found it proved that such criminal orders were carried out not only on Soviet state territory but also on the territories of foreign states. These findings of a Supreme Court invest the murders, caused by a foreign state, committed against Rebet and Bandera with high significance in international law.

The criminal investigation against Professor Oberländer in Bonn, and the East Berlin trial against him, both offer profound new knowledge about Soviet communist legal theory and legal practices. The trial against Stashinsky uncovers the possible consequences that may be inferred from the basic idea that there is such a criminal type as an 'enemy of the State', or an enemy of the system, which are the underlying determinants in both cases. These consequences are therefore also enormously important for the question whether the Soviet communist system has undergone true and fundamental changes since the death of Stalin.

FOCAL POINT OF THE INVESTIGATION — ACCUSATIONS BY THE SOVIETS

Our investigation has its focal point where we compare the judicial proceedings taken against Professor Oberländer, on the one hand, before the Supreme Court of the Soviet-occupied Zone of Germany with those opened, on the other hand, by the Chief Public Prosecutor *(Oberstaatsanwalt)* of the Bonn *Landesgericht* (District Court). This means that the accusations made against the former German Wehrmacht units, Nachtigall and Bergmann, must remain in the foreground. In addition, we have to scrutinize the assertion that Professor Oberländers' military service as an officer of the reserve can be considered as a direct and decisive contribution to making practical preparations for aggressive war against the States of Eastern Europe. This part of the charge ist of central importance for the entire court proceedings in the Soviet Zone. If this particular part of the charge is accepted, the Soviet Zone court may be considered as the right and proper place for passing judgment upon Professor Oberländer; if it is rejected, that court has no jurisdication. The investigations started in Bonn against the Nachtigall unit were undertaken on the basis of information laid by the *VVN (Vereinigung der Verfolgten des Naziregimes,* i. e. "Association of Victims of Nazi Persecution") on July 31, 1959, with the Central Office of *Länder* Judicatures at Ludwigsburg (a central office collecting charges against Nazi and war criminals), which passed the information on through official channels to the Public Prosecutor at the Bonn District Court. *VVN* asserted in its report to the Ludwigsburg office that the Nachtigall unit, whilst it was quartered in Lwow, took part in the massacre of three thousand members of the Polish intelligentsia. Already during the first night after German troops occupied Lwow, the Nachtigall Battalion allegedly shot hundreds of citizens of the town of Lwow, among them many Jews.

The investigations against the Bergmann Battalion, which was commanded by Professor Oberländer, were based, in part, upon further information laid by *VVN* on April 6, 1960. This information contains the same accusations as were published one day earlier (April 5, 1960) in Moscow at a press conference, which used the findings of a Special Soviet Commission. This Commission had used especially the depositions of some former members of the Bergmann unit, of Caucasian nationality, who are now residing again on Soviet territory. Another part of the Commission's findings derive from a former member of the unit reporting to the Soviet police on July 30th, 1960, because he felt his honour affected by alleged libels against the Bergmann unit, and demanded his legal rehabilitation.

A report on this press conference was published by the "*Pravda*" on April 5, 1960, which means, one day before *VVN* sent in its report to the Ludwigsburg office. The *Pravda* report was published on page 6 of that paper under the headline, "Oberländer's Bloody Misdeeds — Press Conference for Soviet and Foreign Journalists". Following the official translation made by order of the Public Prosecutor's Office at Bonn, the text of this report runs, in part:

> Theodor Oberländer, Minister of the Federal Republic of Germany, committed appalling crimes during the Second World War. Irrefutable proofs for his crimes were produced during the press conference for Soviet and foreign journalists, which had been called by the Extraordinary State Commission for Verifying and Investigating the Crimes of the German-Fascist Bandits for April 5.
>
> The numerous press representatives who were assembled in the October Hall of the House of the Trade Unions were handed information collected by the Extraordinary Commission, which was signed by its Chairman, N. M. Shvernik, and by its members present at the press conference, namely W. S. Grisodnbova, Hero of the Soviet Union, T. D. Lysenko, Member of the Academy of Sciences, Nikolay Metropolitan of Krutitsa and Kolomna, and the Leading Secretary, P. I. Bogoyavlensky.
>
> The information handed to the Press contains the observation that both foreign and Soviet newspapers have published recently evidence for Oberländer's crimes, which were committed by him on parts of the territory of the Union of the Socialist Soviet Republics that were occupied by the German fascists for some time. In connection with these publications, the Extraordinary Commission received numerous statements and depositions of Soviet citizens, which contained descriptions of the most aggravating crimes committed by Oberländer and demanded the opening of criminal proceedings against him. The Extraordinary Commission has charged the proper authorities with opening an official investigation. During this investigation, many witnesses were heard and documentary evidence was collected, which all prove that Oberländer is guilty of the misdeeds committed by him.

The information issued contains the allegation that Professor Oberländer had formed and trained *Special Punitive Units* in order to use them for criminal actions on the territory of the U.S.S.R. One of these allegedly was the *Nachtigall Battalion.* It is stated that the Nachtigall unit was one of the first German troops that marched into Lwow during the morning of June 30, 1941.

> As a result of the investigation it was found that several special groups received the order to exterminate people who had worked for the Soviets, and also persons of Jewish and Polish nationality. According to witnesses' depositions, the Hitler bandits shot dead masses of peaceful citizens, women, children, and old people after abusing and maltreating them. The Nachtigall bandits annihilated a large group of well-known Polish scientists, among them Bartel, Boi-Zelenski, Lominki.
>
> It was ascertained that members of the Nachtigall Battalion and special groups of that unit used brute force against Soviet citizens in the villages of Zloczow, Satanow, Yusvin, and Mikhampol, and shot them.

The report then deals with the *Bergmann Unit,* and says:

> During the autumn of 1941, Oberländer was appointed commander of a special battalion, which was named Bergmann. It consisted of prisoners-of-war. Oberländer and his close collaborators then started travelling through prisoner-of-war camps, and criminally disregarding international agreements and principles of warfare, they threatened the men kept in these camps, who were incapable of resistance through hunger and torture, with death if they did not join the Bergmann Battalion, and later took the oath on Hitler. It was Oberländer himself who administered this oath. The period between September, 1942, and January, 1943, when the Bergmann Battalion operated in the Northern Caucasus, was filled with acts of brute force against the population, pilfering, and atrocities. In the vicinity of Naltchik, the professional bandit, Beshtokov, head of a sub-unit in the Bergmann Battalion, especially raged like a madman. Under instructions of Oberländer, Beshtokov's helpmates shot down the population, they robbed and pilfered, they burned down houses, and sent the stolen property to Germany. A large part of the stolen goods was intended for Oberländer personally. During the second half of October, Oberländer shot, by his own hand, fifteen Soviet citizens who were imprisoned in the jail of Piatigorsk. The Extraordinary Commission considers it as proved that Oberländer has committed crimes against peace, war crimes, and crimes against humanity.

The report then quotes allegations by witnesses, which will be dealt with when we discuss the proceedings before the Supreme Court of the Soviet-occupied Zone of Germany. It ends with the statement that,

> ... after the press conference, which had lasted for almost four hours, the press representatives viewed with great interest the exhibition staged in the October Hall of the House of the Trade Unions. They saw numerous photographs and other documents which bear witness to the misdeeds of Oberländer in Lwow and in the Caucasus.

However, the report contained no hint that another Soviet Commission on War Crimes had already dealt with the murder committed against a group of Polish scientists during the summer of 1941, and had come to a completely different conclusion about the persons who ordered this assassination, and the person who carried it out. This earlier conclusion had been presented to, and accepted by, an Inter-Allied Military Tribunal. This fact, which is highly important if we want to judge the credibility of the accusations against Professor Oberländer, is only mentioned here but will be discussed in another context.

All this means that the prosecution and court verdict in the Soviet Zone find Professor Oberländer guilty of two separate groups of war crimes. Commitment of the first group ist not localized, whereas the second one ist supposed to have been committed in certain circumscribed localities — on the one hand in Lwow and the surrounding Western Ukraine (Galicia), and on the other hand in the Northern Caucasus.

The prosecution and verdict consider Professor Oberländer's activities during peacetime, when he was an officer of the reserve and was active in '*Abwehr II (Ausland)*', i. e. Counter-Intelligence abroad, to have been non-localized criminal acts of extreme gravity. They also state that the accused person's political activities after the war represent a direct continuation of his pre-war policies. All of this is described as preparation of aggressive war against other states [20]. Those alleged crimes which are localized would be conventional 'war crimes', i. e. violations of the international laws of war, committed by the agents of a power engaged in war, and affecting citizens and property of the enemy state. On the other hand, the nonlocalized crime, alleged against Professor Oberländer, is supposed to fall under the questionable legal term of 'crimes against peace'.

This part of the charges (which the prosecution assumes to be proved in regard to the Second World War) is of crucial importance for the proceedings taken in the Soviet Zone, because it is the reason under which the Soviet Zone court claims that it had jurisdiction over a crime (committed whilst Oberländer was still in Germany), with which the further alleged crimes said to have been committed in and near Lwow, and in the Northern Caucasus, are knitted into an indivisible whole. The case for the prosecution states that Professor Oberländer has

> supported effectively the fascist policy of aggression, whose purpose was the extermination and enslavement of the Eastern European peoples by ideological, psychological, and subversive, as well as pogrom, activities, and thus has taken part in annihilating the lives of innumerable human beings [21].

In this context, the prosecution claims that Professor Oberländer's professional position as director of the Institute for East European Economics in the university of Königsberg (which he held jointly with his professorship there), and also his honorary work as East Prussian provincial chairman of the *Verein für das Deutschtum im Ausland (VDA*, i. e. Association for Assisting Germans Abroad), and as President of *Bund Deutscher Osten* (League for the German East), were part and parcel of his criminal doings. It is held that he used his position for organizing the Germans living in foreign countries in *associations for the preparation of putsches and subversive acts* against other sovereign states. The verdict agrees with the prosecution in all its points, both with regard to the general and the particular charges. The judgment states that the criminal has, from the advent to power of Hitler,

> ... actively, and in a leading position, collaborated both in preparing and unleashing, as well as carrying out, Germany's imperialist aggression during the Second World War [22].

The questionable legal notion of a *crime against peace* will have to be discussed more extensively later. But what was the look of historical and political reality, compared with this sweeping generalization, which is not supported by any evidence?

To find an answer to this question, we have first to examine the assertion that activities as an '*Eastern research worker, (Ostforscher)* have made Professor Oberländer, in themselves, a person punishable under the penal law of war. There is, naturally, no doubt that the professor was one of the many men and women who devoted their knowledge and energies to clarify the situation in which different nationalities in Europe, and especially in Eastern Europe, whose frontiers have been overlapping during many of the past decades and centuries, have found themselves — nationalities which, independently of changing state borderlines that were fixed by international treaty law, have been constantly contesting their settlement areas one against another. This contest, which German writers have been describing for nearly one century now as '*Volkstumskampf*' (the fight for maintaining the substance of nationhood), could be observed in Europe along almost all the nationality borders since the period in which modern national consciousness was born. Its main cause is the fact that state frontiers, which have been drawn according to dynastic, hereditary, military, or political, but very rarely according to national, settlements, almost always cut across the dividing lines between different nationalities. '*Volkstumskampf*' was being waged not only along the German nationality borderlines. In all places where national majorities and minorities battle for landholdings, places of employment, trade and commercial positions and organizations, the right to use their own languages, the dominating positions in administration and education — to name only some of the most important stakes — this struggle can, and could be observed as part and parcel of the daily routine, similar to that between the adherents of different religious denominations, especially where such communities live in insolubly intermixed settlements (as, for example, in India and Pakistan).

To get a lively picture of this process, it is only necessary to remind the reader of the nationality struggles in Tsarist Russia, especially between the Russian and the Poles, or between Russians and Caucasians; in the old Austro-Hungarian monarchy; in the Turkish Empire; of the quarrel for Alsace-Lorraine; of the fights between Walloons and Flemings, or between Germans and Poles.

The research institutes and associations of the German Reich, which are now quoted and accused by the Soviet Zone court as inherently criminal, were only some of the small stones in the vast mosaic of innumerable institutions belonging to many different nationalities, who have been active in all frontier areas.

If we accept the decision of the Soviet Zone court that Oberländer's, and all other interested parties', research activities directed to other nationalities, and all care for one's own nationality engaged in a contest with other groups, were serving the preparations for an aggressive war, we must also put in the dock retrospectively for at least sixty years almost all the European governments, most research activities, all the churches, the business communities, etc., of all nations, unless they succeeded — as they did in Switzerland — in reconciliating the divergent national interests under one unifying idea of a federal state.

Those who brand political and scientific concern for other nationalities, and the defence of one's own nationality's right to exist, as an *aggressive* and criminal activity are distorting reality, and are at the same time leaving the realm of any positive criminal law.

The history of nationality struggles in Europe has not yet been written, especially not that of its German sector (neither that under the Hohenzollern Empire, nor under the Weimar Republic, nor in the Third Reich.) The Court of the Soviet Occupation Zone, which itself accepts the Oder Neisse Line, in violation of new international law created by the Potsdam Conference, as a final and binding settlement of frontiers, throws out the child with the bath water by slandering all the *German research activities into Eastern questions (Ostforschung)* since the last war, which labour to make a scientific contribution to the history of Eastern Europe, in order to analyse and understand the past, and draw from it guiding ideas for the policies of the future, that can only be built upon all interested parties shedding their former narrow and nationalist views. Such work pursues a genuinely scientific mission of a high order, no matter what the regime in the Soviet Occupation Zone lets its scribes write, and it judges adjudicate, about it.

If the findings of that court contain, on this subject, political verdicts of a general nature, believing to be able to draw such conclusions from primitive and distorting generalizations about past events of the twenties and thirties for the present century, this will only confirm that marxist justice flows from the principles described at the beginning of our investigation.

Besides, the legal aspects of this complex problem are determined by the following rules: —

(1) Article 9 of the Constitution of the League of Nations provided for the revision of "treaties that have become inapplicable", and of "such international arrangements whose maintenance was liable to endanger the peace of the world." The situation created by the Treaty of Versailles, and by the new frontiers fixed by it in the Polish Corridor and in the Free City of Danzig, as well as the conditions in Lithuania after that state had destroyed the Memel District's autonomy, were acknowledged to be striking examples of such dangerous arrangements, even by wide non-German circles. Research into such problems, and into questions of nationality connected with them, which tried to make out a case for revising the said arrangements, were completely justifiable and legitimate within the framework of the League of Nations and its era.

(2) One of the examples for the complicated legal problem posed by the subject of "Eastern Research", which was simplified and assessed — by prosecution and verdict — exclusively on the basis of its political aspects, which were described by the court, has been given by the following decision of the American Military Court in the so-called Wilhelmstrasse Trial: —

> As long as there are no treaty obligations to the contrary, it is permissible to support political movements on the territory of a foreign state, to keep up relations with the leaders of such movements, and to support them — also by subsidizing them financially — in order to strengthen a movement whose final aim it is to further an annexion of territory without a breach of International Law. Only if such acts are committed in the knowledge that they are to become part and parcel of future acts of violence that have been carefully planned, and that they are to be followed, if necessary, by a war of aggression or by a military occupation, these acts are punishable, and jurisdiction lies with the present Court... The present Court has power to adjudicate upon definite, clearly defined crimes but not upon such questions of morality which have nothing to do with the *prima facie* cases of breaches of International Law. (Heinze-Schilling, *Die Rechtsprechung der Nürnberger Militärtribunale,* i. e.: Jurisdiction of the Nuremberg Military Tribunals; 1952, p. 161).
>
> The enforced return of the Memel District to Germany was not made a subject of the prosecution by the International Military Tribunal.

(3) Neither *VDA (Verein für das Deutschtum im Ausland,* i. e. 'Union of Germans Abroad') nor BDO *(Bund Deutscher Osten,* i. e. 'Rally of the German East') stood accused before the International Military Tribunal as allegedly criminal organizations. Besides, the Nazi Party decided already in 1937 to depose Professor Oberländer from his honorary offices which he had held in these organizations.

On the one hand, the case for the prosecution has never been fully made out in the Soviet Zone, and on the other hand, political hostility and a one-sided political slant in the description of facts, are both striking features of the verdict, in so far as it deals with the problem of *Eastern research,* and this makes the proceedings in the Soviet Zone part of a political show trial.

Similar observations can be made about the treatment of Professor Oberländer's military activities before the war. It is possible that his deep knowledge of Russia, and of other parts of Eastern Europe, may have been of use to the military authorities for drawing up their war plans, but the attempt to transform the work done by a lieutenant, or first lieutenant, of the reserve, who was called to the colours temporarily, into active and responsible preparations for waging aggressive war, without ever trying to prove that, and how, a subaltern in the *Abwehr* (Counter-Intelligence) could have actually influenced the government of the Reich and the High Command of the Wehrmacht, is completely futile. *

What these facts signify for the question whether the court in the Soviet Zone had jurisdiction will be dealt with later. Those of Oberländer's alleged crimes which are tied to definite localities comprise, among others, his work within the *Nachtigall* and *Bergmann* units. The verdict has the following to say about the *Nachtigall* unit: —

> This battalion was recruited, trained, and *led by him* when it was used for taking part in the attack against the Soviet Union. [23]

---

* I have asked Professor Oberländer to enlighten me in more detail on this point. He answered by the following letter: —

Bonn, March 6, 1962.

Dear Mr. Raschhofer,

When you started to collect material for your book, you asked me whether, during my service with *OKW-Abwehr,* I ever came across advance information on the preparations for the war against Russia. I should like to say the following on this subject: —

In the spring of 1938, *OKW-Abwehr* asked me to start an investigation into the causes for the failure of the armies of intervention — Koltchak, Denikin, Yudenitch, Wrangel.

In making this investigation, I came to the conclusion that these armies failed less for military reasons than because they were beaten in the field of revolutionary warfare, as they disregarded the liberties of the non-Russian nationalities, and also did not leave the peasants in possession of the land they had taken over from the landowners. For me, the result was clear: Any disregard of these problems would only be to the profit of the Bolsheviks. On March 1, 1941, I heard in the *OKW* (High Command of the *Wehrmacht*) at Berlin of the alleged need for an armed struggle against the Soviet Union. On hearing this, I referred to my article on 'The Red Army', which I had contributed to the book, ‚*Die Welt in Gärung*' (World in Ferment) by Haushofer, Fochler, and Hauke. I had written this article already in 1937, and I had warned in

According to the text of the verdict, the Nachtigall unit marched into Lwow during the morning of June 30, 1941, when it was commanded by Oberländer. By order of the defendant, so the verdict continues, his unit committed mass slaughter and pogroms against communist officials, and against Jewish and Polish parts of the population.

The verdict also alleges that the Nachtigall unit and its alleged commander, Professor Oberländer, were guilty of murdering a group of Polish professors during July, 1941 [24].

And finally, the verdict also takes over two different groups of accusations of fact that had been made against Professor Oberländer's activities as the organizer and commanding officer of the Bergmann unit, which had been recruited from among captured Caucasian Soviet soldiers in 1942 [25]. In detail, the verdict alleges: Oberländer organized conditions in the p.o.w. camps in such an inhuman fashion that prisoners were made willing to join the Bergmann unit. Prisoners who had volunteered but had proved unfit for service were allegedly killed. Members of the unit who had decided not to fight against the Soviets when the battalion was taken to the battle front were allegedly maltreated, and put to trial, which had been illegally rigged by Oberländer. They were sentenced to death or put into a concentration camp. When in the Caucasus, Oberländer is said to have carried out an even more cruel recruitment campaign in the p.o.w. camps behind the front. He allegedly committed

---

it against underrating the Soviet Union. SS circles therefore had dubbed me 'the red professor'. Furthermore, after the Nazi Party had abandoned, about the month of September, 1937, the aim of liberty for all nationalities, for which it had stood for many years, and had embraced opposite policies after the campaign in Poland, I had given a warning against a war against Russia to Admiral Canaris, because such a war could not be won without a nationality policy built upon liberation from bolshevism, and without an agricultural policy based upon private property of the peasant farmers. The Admiral gave me the order to write a short memorandum containing my fears, which was to be treated as strictly secret *(streng geheime Kommandosache)*. These qualms of mine were based, in the first instance, on my observations in occupied Poland. Within a short time, extreme tension had arisen there between the occupying power and the Polish population. I expressed my fears that the same might happen regarding the relations between the Wehrmacht and the population of Russia. In the second instance, I emphasized that the Russians have a tradition of partisan warfare. Canaris showed this memorandum to Hitler. On July 25, 1941, he told me at Yusvin in the Ukraine that he failed to convince Hitler of the correctness of my theses.

These views of mine, which I held already then, can be proved both by my article in the book by Haushofer, Fochler, and Hauke, and by my various memoranda.

With my best regards,
Yours,
(signed) *Th. Oberländer.*

fantastic cruelties against civilians, among them also women, and among other things, he had masses of Jewish citizens and enemies of Hitler from among the civilian population of the Naltchik district shot.

In the following pages, we shall examine these allegations on the basis of the court files of the investigation and the order for quashing the proceedings, which were made under the Rule of Law. These produce, with the aid of convincing evidence, a completely different picture.

FOOTNOTES

[1] Verdict of the Supreme Court of the so-called German Democratic Republic, p. 1. The text of this verdict was published as a supplement to the periodical, *Neue Justiz*, 1960, No. 10. Quotations are from this text.

[2] Orders for Quashing the Investigation, made by *Oberstaatsanwaltschaft* (Chief Public Prosecutor's Office), Bonn.

[3] Statute of the International Court of Justice, Article 57.

[4] Rules of Procedure for the State Court of the Free Hansa City of Bremen of March 3, 1956 (Law Gazette, 1956, p. 35), Article 13, Paragraph 3.

[5] *Über den Begriff des Schauprozesses* (What is a Show Trial?).

[6] Verdict, p. 16.

[7] *Kurzprotokoll* (Abstract from the Minutes) of the Proceedings before the Supreme Court of the so-called German Democratic Republic, p. 121.

[8] The Order for Quashing the Proceedings in the Nachtigall Case quotes literally part of this Polish assessment from an exile source, p. 60 *passim.*

[9] *Kurzprotokoll,* p. 184.

[10] *l. c.,* p. 185.

[11] *l. c.,* p. 7.

[12] *l. c.,* p. 8.

[13] The term, 'enemy of the state', is imprecise, because the true holder of political authority in the Soviet system to-day is — as is shown further below with the aid of Djilas' analysis — not the State (and the machinery of the state) but exclusively the Communist Party. This means that the opponent of the Soviet system, who is meant by the term, 'enemy of the state', can be better described as an 'enemy of the Party', or an 'enemy of the system'. What Communism really wants in this context is to destroy all the opponents of the Soviet communist system and of its doctrinal basis which, as Djilas was able to show, form an inseparable unit up to the present day.

[14] *Stimme der Freiheit,* December 1961, p. 8.

[15] *Stuttgarter Zeitung,* Oct. 23, 1959.

[16] Judgment, B II 3 b.

[17] Judgment, *l. c.*

[18] e. g., *Berliner Zeitung,* Oct. 20, 1959.

[19] Judgment C II 1.

[20] Verdict, p. 10.

[21] *Kurzprotokoll,* p. 11.

[22] Verdict, p. 3.

[23] *l. c.,* p. 11.

[24] *l. c.,* p. 12.

[25] *l. c.,* p. 13 *passim.*

II

THE NACHTIGALL UNIT (The Nightingale Battalion)

The main Content of allegations made by the Soviets and in the Soviet Occupation Zone consists of accusations against two volunteer units of the German Wehrmacht which were formed by foreign nationals *(Nachtigall* and *Bergmann).* What the Nachtigall unit supposedly did was the following, according to the Soviet Zone proceedings [1] : —

> Jointly with the notorious fascist and racial ideologist, Professor Hans Koch, Oberländer, in the beginning, organized the Nachtigall battalion, using for this purpose the units of the Ukrainian terrorist and chauvinist, Bandera. As its military commanding officer, he drilled this battalion in the service of fascist ideology, indoctrinating it with anti-communism, antisemitism, and hatred against the intellectual strata of the East European nations.
>
> Utilizing his experiences of many years as a counter-intelligence officer working for the Sabotage Department of the Wehrmacht High Command, he trained the Nachtigall battalion in carrying out sabotage and disruptive work, pogroms and assassinations. Command authority over the battalion lay in the hands of the then First Lieutenant, Oberländer, who, of all the German officiers, was feared most.
>
> Oberländer headed the murder battalion Nachtigall when this unit attacked the Soviet university town of Lwow during the hours of the morning of June 30, 1941. Under his leadership, the members of the Nachtigall battalion started pogroms against the Jewish population, and a systematic extermination campaign against the leading representatives of the town's intelligentsia, using for this purpose lists of names which had been prepared in advance.

How the Unit was Formed. Its Commanding Officers, the Principles of their Selection and Training.

The first essential question — who was the Commanding Officer of the Nachtigall Unit? — has not been answered by the court of the Soviet Zone, as far as the published information about the proceedings there permits us to judge, on the basis of its own investigations but by simple reference to a literary source, and this answer was wrong.

The verdict of the *Supreme Court* of the Soviet Occupation Zone takes over the allegation of the prosecution that the Nachtigall unit was commanded by Oberländer, in the following words [2] : —

> In the Nachtigall unit, the defendant held authority of command.

This assertion is based on a quotation from a report written by the

Eastern Europe Institute in Munich on the relations between Germany and the Ukraine between 1934 and 1945, whose author is a certain Ilnytski. This report calls Professor Oberländer 'Supervisory Officer and German commander of the Nachtigall group' [3]. In addition, the verdict believes to be able to interpret in the same sense a passage from a report, which was written by Professor Oberländer himself (dated Nov. 11, 1943). This report stated that he had been given orders to *train and make military use* of a Ukrainian unit [4]. When the Soviet Zone court heard witnesses' evidence, witness Melnik, however, told the court that the commanding officer of the battalion was a German named *Herzen* or *Herzner* — and not Oberländer [5]. The printed Abstract from the Minutes of the Proceedings *(Kurzprotokoll)* does not allow us to judge whether the court in any way investigated this essential question, on which much of the decision about responsibility for the alleged crimes depends. By the investigation carried out under the Rule of Law, however, this question has been thoroughly cleared up, and an unambiguous answer to it was found in a statement of the former commander of the First Battalion of the Training Regiment *Brandenburg,* to whom the Nachtigall unit was subordinated. This man is still alive. His highly important deposition has been printed in our Appendix [6]. Beyond the fact that this deposition enlightens us about the fact that Oberländer did not serve as commander of the unit but was seconded to it as some sort of adviser for special questions of the foreign members of the battalion, its other features deserve our particular attention, for it describes the principles which were used in the selection of officers for the Nachtigall unit. It also highlights the general attitude aimed at by the leaders of that unit, which was made the basis of orders given to the subaltern officers and n.c.o's: Indirectly, this also implies an assessment of Oberländer's political opinions, in particular of his Eastern policies, by his military superiors, in the last instance by Admiral Canaris. This again makes this deposition a touchstone for the likeliness or unlikeliness of the truth contained in the accusations against the unit, which relate to its activities in Lwow. The author of the deposition is F. W. H., former commander of the First Battalion, Training Regiment *Brandenburg.* In the spring of 1941, the Head of Department II of the *Amt Ausland Abwehr* (Counter-Intelligence Office, Foreign Countries), Colonel von Lahusen, informed F. W. H. that a unit of foreign legionaries, consisting of West Ukrainian volunteers, was in process of formation in Silesia. This unit was to serve under witness F. W. H. in case war should break out with the Soviet Union. It was not intended to use this unit much for fighting purposes but more for propaganda to impress the population of the Ukraine. Witness discussed details about the subdivision and the appointment of officers for the Nachtigall unit with the proper quarters, i. e. with his superior officers. It its clear from the deposition that it was Dr. Herzner, and not Professor Oberländer, who was appointed to command the Nachtigall unit, and precisely the description given of Dr. Herzner's personality is of the highest importance. The reasons adduced for the spirit in which the training of the volunteers was to be carried out, and for the selection of Dr. Herzner, point to the political intentions of the organizers of the unit, and to the desired attitude that was taught of the unit, which was in complete and stark opposition to the crimes alleged against it in Lwow. Witness reported that it was he himself who arranged for the appointment of First Lieutenant Dr. Herzner, whom he knew privately and officially well. Herzner died after a war injury, during the war, at Hohenlychen. Witness made the following statement about Dr. Herzner's character:

> First Lieutenant Herzner belonged to the political circle of periodical, *Der Nahe Osten* (The Near East). He was an officer of the reserve in the Infantry Regiment No. 9 in Potsdam. From the outbreak of war, he had worked for *Amt Ausland Abwehr,* and to judge by his character and political attitude, he was himself sufficient guarantee for me that the Nachtigall Battalion would not do anything against the intentions and inclinations of Admiral Canaris, Colonel von Lahusen, and myself. Dr. Albrecht Herzner was a practising Christian and an officer *who, for many years, had taken an active part in the resistance movement.* In September, 1938, he was concerned in the formation of the commando unit *(Stosstrupp)* recruited in Berlin which was intended to accompany and support Infantry General von Witzleben during his action, which was planned like a *coup d'état,* against Hitler for the prevention of the Second World War. In addition, I arranged for the appointment of the former Imperial Austrian officer, *Rittmeister* (cavalry captain) Erwein Count von Thun und Hohenstein, as company commander in the Nachtigall unit. This officer was also one of my personal friends. Count Thun was an Austrian nobleman in the best sense of the word.
>
> During those days, I also completely regrouped my own personal staff, *so that I was enabled to take direct influence on the methods of fighting, and the behaviour towards the civilian population, in the Eastern territories which were to be occupied.* [7] *

This deposition by a witness appears to us of crucial significance for judging the truth of the accusations agianst the entire Nachtigall unit, and in particular against Professor Oberländer. The Officer in command of the unit was a man who, for years, had been actively concerned with organising the resistance against Hitler, and who took part in 1938 in forming the commando unit to be used for carrying out a coup against the Führer, and for accompanying the leader of this coup, General von Witzleben. That the coup did not take place was due to the developments in international politics. Herzner's active hostility against Hitler was not in doubt for all who knew about him. Also the mention of Dr. Herzner's membership of the political circle round the magazine, *Der Nahe Osten,*

---

* Italics, except in the case of foreign words italicized, by the witness.

is most revealing. This magazine had developed a *neo-Prussian* programme already before the Nazi era, which demanded a return of the political foundations of the Prussian Kingdom into a modernized form. The leading intellectual of this circle, Hans Schwarz, was therefore diametrically opposed to the ideas both of the nation-state and the racial ideology of National Socialism. For the area where Germans and Slavs live, side by side as nighbours, Schwarz advocated a new territorial order following a modern design akin to the supra-national Prussian monarchy. [8] If a man from such a group was entrusted with the command over a military unit formed from Ukrainian nationals, this implied a programme and a political attitude to which it was tied, and by which the orders given to it were determined, a central feature of which was the strict admonition issued to its subaltern officers and n.c.o.'s immediately before the start of the Russian campaign *to act always humanely*. In this context, the description given by the witness of Professor Oberländer and other officers serving with that unit are of special importance.:

> In May 1941, I paid my first visit to the Nachtigall battalion at the Neuhammer exercise ground. I talked with the German and Ukrainian leaders of the battalion, and as far as I remember, this was also the time when I first met Professor Oberländer. To my knowledge, Oberländer had been seconded to the battalion on the request of Colonel S. in a special mission. Professor Oberländer had been in the service of *Amt Abwehr* for some time already. He spoke Russian and Ukrainian. He was known as a man who knew conditions in the East, and had been charged with the double mission to look after the political interests of the Ukrainian volunteers, and to advise me about topical Eastern questions which came into my purview. I may add here that, as long as First Lieutenant, Professor Oberländer, served under me — which was from about March or April 1941 to the end of August 1941 — I have never heard any antisemitic remarks from him, nor did ever come to my knowledge even the slightest violation of the orders given to him in the clearest fashion that all prisoners and civilians were to be treated humanely.
>
> When I talked to the German and German-speaking Ukrainian leaders of the battalion immediately before the start of the Eastern campaign, I admonished all my subordinates most strictly, and even begged and beseeched them, always to act with humanity.
>
> I remember that one of the companies of the Nachtigall battalion was under the leadership of Lieutenant M., who was a man with a deep political interest, and he confirmed, in a conversation with me, that he was of the same opinion with me politically.

In this connection another factual statement contained in this deposition deserves of our attention. Witness relates that he sent his personal driver (during the first days of the German military occupation of Lwow) — this man is now living as a jeweller in Hamburg — to Admiral Canaris with several reports describing the chaotic state of affairs in Lwow. These reports contained, among other things, complaints about the atrocities committed by German "Special Staffs" and also, in some cases, by German troops. With this basic attitude of witness, it is completely convincing when he answers the interrogating official of the public prosecutor who questions him that never during the time when the Nachtigall batallion, First Lieutenant Herzner, or the sub-units of the batallion directly, which would have authorized, or even mentioned, shootings, maltreatment of persons, or pillaging of property. Witness always did all in his power to investigate the conditions under which the batallion operated, in order to prevent atrocities and injustices. At no time did he receive any reports about such atrocities having been committed. The evidence given by this witness, which has been accepted, with good grounds, by the investigators under the Rule of Law, is of crucial importance for arriving at a true assessment of the intentions of the military leadership which led to the formation of the Nachtigall unit, of the expectations which it harboured, and of the staff policies which it followed in order to carry out its programme of action. Evidently, the deposition is that of a most important witness, for it is more than likely that the military high command did not only examine the fitness of Dr. Herzner as unit commander, which was based for them, last but not least, on Dr. Herzner's political attitude towards the Nazi Party. In addition, they certainly also reviewed the character and attitude of the second man who was given the not unimportant task to act as liaison officer and political adviser on a battalion consisting of foreign nationals. The military high command seems to have been satisfied with its arrangements after it had been decided to appoint the then First Lieutenant, Dr. Albrecht Herzner, to the post of unit commander, and Oberländer to that of liaison officer. Authority of command over the unit, thus, lay in Dr. Herzner's hands. It would have been completely inconceivable if, in contrast to the motivation for the selection of officers for the Nachtigall batallion — as described by witness — the superior command had chosen a man to be liaison officer who did not correspond, in his attitude, with the overall directives, whose execution was to be secured by careful sifting of the available officer material.

The final conclusion, drawn by the German investigation under the Rule of Law in answer to relevant questions, runs as follows: —

> The relatively small staff of the Unit consisted of: The then First Lieutenant, Dr. Albrecht Herzner, deceased on September 9, 1942, in Hohenlychen through the effects of a war injury, was the officer in command of the unit; then First Lieutenant, Theodor Oberländer, was the liaison officer between the Ukrainian unit and the *Training Regiment Brandenburg*, also the *Amt Ausland Abwehr;* the evangelical parson, W. M., had the rank of warrant officer, and the Greek Uniate parson, D. J. H., a Ukrainian, served as a chaplain to the unit, without German officer's rank.
>
> Information laid also accuses Professor Hans Koch (who has died in the meantime) of war crimes. Professor Koch was not at any time a member of the Nachtigall battalion. He had been sent to Lwow in a special mission by

the *Amt Ausland Abwehr* immediately after the town's occupation, in order to establish contact with the leaders of the Ukrainian liberation movement. Lieutenant, Baron Voelkersam, who is also accused of crimes, had never been seconded to the Nachtigall unit. Baron Voelkersam, an officer of the *Training Regiment Brandenburg*, has died during the war.

All this proves: —

(1) Professor Oberländer did not hold command over the unit. Oberländer was liaison officer, in an advisory capacity;

(2) Power of command over the Nachtigall battalion lay in the hands of First Lieutenant, Dr. Albrecht Herzner;

(3) The officers of the unit were selected with a view to obtaining personal guarantees for an attitude of humane understanding to be shown towards the population of East European countries.

ATROCITIES IN LWOW; THE TIME WHEN THEY WERE COMMITTED

MOTIVATION AND GUILTY PERSONS

During a period which apparently extended over the days before and after the occupation of Lwow by the German forces (June 30, 1941), certainly several thousands of the inhabitants of Lwow, of Ukrainian, Jewish, and Polish nationality, were murdered. The prosecution in East Berlin asserted, and the verdict in the Soviet Zone accepted the allegations to the full, that these murders were committed chiefly by German troops, and that the Nachtigall unit was, in large measure, responsible for these misdeeds, when it was allegedly following orders of Professor Oberländer, who has been wrongly called its commanding officer.

The investigation carried out under the Rule of Law, after extremely careful research, came to a fundamentally different conclusion. On the basis of extensive enquiries, it shows, using also the files of the Inter-Allied Tribunals in Nuremberg, that, on the one hand, the *Einsatzgruppe* (Special Action Unit) of the *Reichssicherheitshauptamt* (Chief Security Office of the Reich, i. e. Gestapo Headquarters) made arrests, and committed killings, in great numbers among the Jewish population, and also among leading Poles, apparently after careful selection and preparation, shortly *after* Lwow had been taken. On the other hand, the enquiries also supplied incontrovertible proof that many murders committed against the inhabitants of Lwow had alredy taken place before Lwow was occupied by the Germans. These earlier atrocities may have become, very probably, the emotional cause for reprisals against the likely murderers, after the town had changed hands.

The investigators made it evident that responsibility for these earlier atrocities lies with the Soviet authorities. This means that the investigation under the Rule of Law discovered two separate periods during which murders and other atrocities were committed, and of which each had different political and psychological motives.

The basis for these discoveries is an examination of the fundamental political realities in Galicia and Lwow from the time of the First World War, when especially the tensions arising from the life together on a narrow space of Ukrainians, Poles, and Jews played their part. It became clear to the investigators that frequent changes of political authority over this territory also affected the position in which each of the different nationalities found itself. Only in this way was it possible to work out the time-sequence of successive phases of violence, and to find the persons and authorities responsible for each single one of these.

Regarding the Nachtigall unit, the investigators came to the firm conclusion that the battalion definitely did not take part in acts of mass violence or in the killings. They emphasize that the Nachtigall unit was under strict orders and instructions to show exactly the opposite behaviour. In extreme cases, the investigators deem it possible that individual Ukrainian members of that unit — against instructions and orders received — may have taken part in some of the atrocities, but further enquiries have reduced the likelihood of such happenings to a minimum. With regard to the person of Professor Oberländer, the investigation under the Rule of Law did not arrive even at a suspicion of his participation.

The Nachtigall Unit and the Mass Murders Committed in Lwow, as They Were Treated by the Soviet Zone Investigators

The Nachtigall unit took part in the occupation of Lwow on June 30, 1941. It has been accused of having played a big part, under the leadership of Professor Oberländer, in the mass atrocities against the Jewish population of Lwow during the first days of July, which will be described later.

Evidence for the alleged criminal acts of the Nachtigall battalion in Lwow, shortly after the capture of the town, consisted mainly of the following witnesses' statements: —

> Shpidal, as a witness, reported [11] about his special military training in a Ukrainian camp at Brandenburg. He met there men who were later sent to the Nachtigall unit. He met them again on the *second or third day* after the capture of Lwow, after he himself had been sent to serve in that battalion. He was told in Cracow that the Ukrainian nationalists had prepared lists of names of people who were to be liquidated by force. He was billetted

in a building where Ukrainian nationalists were shooting civilians in the courtyard. He insists that he has clearly seen these shootings, and he observed that members of the Nachtigall unit took part in the shootings. Three persons who took part in the shootings were met by him later, and they were acquaintances of his from a camp at Brandenburg. He also stated that German officers took part in the executions by shooting.

Melnik, as a witness [12], directly accused Professor Oberländer. He heard Oberländer's name for the first time on June 29, on the way to Lwow. On June 30, members of the battalion told him that a leading Ukrainian member of the unit, Shukhevitch, and Oberländer had given them lists containing names of persons to be arrested. They continued by telling witness that, following the lists, they had shot the persons shown on them. After about six or seven days, Professor Oberländer told the battalion, which had been called out on parade, that its mission had been carried out as expected, so that the unit would be now transferred for carrying out differents tasks. According to the same witness, more shootings took place in Satanov, a place in the Western Ukraine, again according to lists issued by Shukhevitch and Oberländer.

Another witness, a woman named Kukkar [13], stated that in the early morning of July 7 she looked from the window of her flat on the first floor of a house and saw persons being shot. A group of German officers who had stood by at the shootings shortly after walked up to her window and remained standing underneath. The officers looked upwards, and the face of one among them remained in her memory. In 1959, she saw a picture of Oberländer, and 'at the first glance, I recognized the officer who stood under my window at that time and looked me in the face.' Witness affirmed that she was able to identify this man after almost twenty years.

Witness Reiss [14], at the time under review, was under arrest at Lwow. and in prison and had seen victims of cruel atrocities, whom he knew personally. He succeeded in escaping from prison. An Ukrainian friend from his youth later told him that a special unit, consisting of Ukrainians and Germans, had marched into Lwow, which had been given the task to *clear up (Ordnung zu schaffen) the town of Jews and Bolsheviks.* He could not make any statement about the person of Oberländer.

Nor do the statements of witness Makarukh [15] contain any hint about Oberländer's personal activities. On the other hand, Makarukh stated that troops of persons led to the execution grounds were guarded and accompanied by Germans and Ukrainians in German uniforms.

Witness Sulim [16] stated that he observed from his flat the killing of members of the Polish intelligentsia in the evening of July 3, and also a number of other, particularly brutal happenings. He also witnessed that German soldiers, some of them with yellow and blue stripes on their uniforms, guarded a large procession of arrested persons (about 800) on June 30. He asserts that members of the Nachtigall unit took part in pogroms in Lwow.

Witness Hübner [17] had arrived in Lwow as a member of an advance unit, and he belonged to a company of security guards. From the guard room on the first floor of a house, he could see a fire brigade headquarters with a tower. People were driven into this tower through rows of soldiers who were beating them. Their victims were forced up the stairs and pushed through a window to jump into the courtyard. Those who were not dead after their fall were beaten to death in the yard. A group of German officers was looking on and called upon the soldiers to beat their victims. Witness asserted on the basis of a picture, which he had seen in a newspaper in 1959, that one of these officers was Professor Oberländer.

Witness Stein [18] reported about acts of violence committed by Ukrainian military units and Ukrainian civilians. He emphasized that, on July 1, he was stopped several times by armed men in German uniform, who were not, however, German soldiers but men who spoke Polish or Ukrainian. According to witness, the main perpetrators of the pogrom were civilians from Lwow who wore blue and yellow armbands.

Witness Pankiv [19] reported that, on the third or fourth day after the German capture of Lwow, he visited a Ukrainian military unit. Whilst he talked to members of this unit, a German officer passed on his way, and his acquaintances told him that this was First Lieutenant Oberländer. Another acquaintance told him that he (the acquaintance) took part in acts of violence against members of the Polish intelligentsia, and that Oberländer had played a leading part in organizing these atrocities.

CRIMINAL INVESTIGATION UNDER THE RULE OF LAW

Political Conditions and Nationality Problems in the Galician (Western Ukrainian) Area. The Effects of the German-Soviet Frontier and Friendship Pact. The Impact of the German-Soviet War.

The investigation under the Rule of Law begins by describing the tasks assigned to the Nachtigall unit. In doing this, ist unterlines the political and psychological fundamentals, which determined the attitude of the unit's members, following this up with a description of political and national conditions in the Galician area [20] : —

> According to orders received, the Nachtigall unit was operating under the authority of the commander, First Battalion, Training Regiment Brandenburg, the then Major H., who is now working as a journalist and writer. The unit's main task was, in the case of war against the Soviet Union, to achieve a propaganda effect among the Western and Eastern Ukrainians, of whom part were in opposition to the Soviet authorities, and also — if necessary — to assist the fighting troops in capturing strategically important points, through their knowledge of the country, the local conditions, and the language. The Ukrainian members of the battalion were in sympathy with the aims of the Ukrainian national movements, which worked for an independent Ukraine.

Such sympathies were based on the political history of these areas and of the nationalities living there. These areas were the subject of fierce fighting especially during and after the First World War. These conditions served as a background and forcing bed for the bloody events of Lwow. After the disappearance of Tsarism in Russia, the *Eastern Ukraine* had formed a separate state early in 1918, and after the dismemberment of Austria-Hungary, also the *Western Ukraine* became independent but was immediately claimed for ist own by the revived Polish state, which called this part, *Eastern Galicia* (after Halycz, or Galycz, a medieval principality, a mixed Western Russian-Polish state with a short life). The Eastern Ukrainian national government was driven out by the Soviets, and its territory was merged in the Soviet Union. The Western Ukrainian administration was suppressed by the Poles, and its territory was annexed to the Polish Republic. These acts of pure power politics deepened the political gulf between the Ukrainians and the Poles, and between the Ukrainians and the Soviet Union, which had been in existence before, and the mixture of nationalities living in the area contributes to an increase in the national tensions. The report of the West German investigators goes into the details of this situation [21] :

> On the soil of the Western Ukraine (East Galicia), there were five different nationalities living together. The largest group were the Ukrainians with 62.3 per cent of the total, then came the Poles with 26 per cent, and the Jews with ten per cent, whilst both the Germans (Volksdeutsche) and the Russians were under one per cent each. In Lwow, the capital city of the Western Ukraine, the shares of the Poles and Jews were higher, so that each of the above-named, big nationalities represented about 30 per cent there. The Polish central government in Warsaw, after its formation, pursued a policy of forced Polonization of the Western Ukraine. The reaction of the Ukrainian part of the population was an early formation of parties and movements which tried to defend themselves against this policy by legal means, but also the setting-up of revolutionary nationalist underground groups, of which OUN *(Organisation of Ukrainian Nationalists)* was the most important one. The main aim of this movement was always the formation of a free and independent Ukrainian national state.
>
> The Ukrainian part of the population, especially the Ukrainian nationalists, were hostile to the Jews, for historical reasons that cannot be clarified further here. This anti-Jewish feeling found expression in the so-called Petliura Movement which, shortly after the end of the First World War, when the Western Ukraine had been declared independent, organized a pogrom against the Jewish part of the population. Tensions between these two national groups remained in being, though latent, also during the period of the Polish administration in the Western Ukraine, and through the events of 1939, they were intensified.

The events of July, 1941, can only be understood against this historical and political background. Sudden changes in the political sovereignty over this area, which happened after the outbreak of the Second World War, were stoking up the political dynamism in this hotbed of tension. The comment of the investigators under the Rule of Law to this development runs thus [22] :

> After the outbreak of the war between Germany and Poland on September 1, 1939, German troops entered the Western Ukraine and, until Poland capitulated, had reached the suburbs of Lwow. Through the arrangements of the so-called *German-Russian Frontier and Friendship Treaty* of September 28,

1939, the Western Ukraine (East Galicia) was declared to belong to the Russian sphere of interest up to the river San, and the area was occupied by the Soviet Union. The incorporation of the Western Ukraine into the Soviet State was greeted by most of the Jews residing there with a feeling of relief, in part even with enthusiastic joy, because the Galician Jews knew of the Nazi regime's attitude towards Jews, and were afraid of its effects upon them in case the Germans occupied the Western Ukraine. Only the Zionist Movement looked upon the Soviet regime with some concern. In fact, the Russians, soon after they had taken over administrative power, suppressed the Zionist Movement and the use of the Hebrew language. On the other hand, Jews, in so far as they showed sympathies for Communism, obtained some political influence, which up to that time nobody had thought possible. Jews, during the period between 1920 and 1939, had never been able to enter the civil service, but now they were admitted to important administrative posts, since also some leading officials of the Russian administration were Jewish.

The *German-Soviet Treaty of Friendship* [23] of September 28, 1939, had not only immense territorial and international political consequences, by opening to the Soviet Union — at least temporarily at the time — the road into the eastern parts of Central Europe. On the spot, e. g. in Eastern Galicia, it also led to revolutionary changes in the distribution of power between the various local groups. For example, the Polish nation ceased to be dominant, as it was persecuted by the Soviets. Pressure upon nationalist Ukrainians, who likewise were hostile to the new order, increased in line with the intensification of Communist dominion over them. On the other hand, non-Zionist Jews were, for the first time, favoured citizens, whereas their Zionist coreligionists soon joined the ranks of the persecuted. The report of the investigators describes this state of affairs [24] : —

In line with the gradual sovietization of the country, measures taken by the new authorities are directed especially against the Polish part of the population, and at the same time also against the Ukrainian nationalist movements, who stand for national independence. As time went on, the series of arrests against the Polish intelligentsia, and of leaders and members of the Ukrainian nationalist movement, became a daily occurence. Side by side with these measures, large actions of resettlement (deportations) to the interior of the Soviet Union took place, which hit especially all the former Polish civil servants and former members of the Polish military forces, also all the Polish citizens who had fled, during the war between Germany and Poland, from Western Poland to Galicia, and all so-called *capitalists* (factory owners and important merchants of all nationalities). After the outbreak of the German-Soviet war on June 22, 1941, a new wave of arrests occurred, directed mainly against suspected followers of the Ukrainian nationalist movement — for shortly after the first aerial bombings of Lwow through German war planes, the Ukrainian nationalist movement started active resistance in the town. Russian troops, on their march through Lwow, were the targets of Ukrainian sharpshooters — members of the Ukrainian underground movements who fired from church towers and house roofs.

This description is based upon reports by former Polish, Jewish, and German inhabitants of Lwow, which agree in all materialpoints. A particularly revealing Polish report will be quoted later.

The outbreak of the war between Germany and the Soviet Union led to a new reversal of fortunes. Poles in Eastern Galicia had nothing to hope for in the new situation — on the contrary. This is also the case of the Jews, even more so, given Hitler's attitude towards them. The only favoured element are now the Ukrainian nationalists; they believe that their hour has struck. The more active amongst them are trying to influence the commencing military struggle. Ukrainian resistance fighters are giving battle to the Soviet troops in Lwow.

The Soviets retaliate by numerous arrests. Especially the prisons in Lwow are full to overflowing. *This is the situation to which the first days of July and their events are the direct reaction.* The investigators have to report on this [25] : —

> Political prisoners, mainly Ukrainians, were housed in three prison buildings in the town of Lwow — the town lock-up in Kazmierzowska Street (also known as Brigidki Prison), the provisional prison in the NKVD headquarters in Lonskiego Road, and the military prison in the Zamarstynow quarter of the town. Through mass arrests, all the prisons were overcrowded. In many of the bare cells, that contained not a stick of furniture, up to sixty prisoners were kept.

And now a new act of Soviet violence brings the already very tense situation to boiling point. The outbreak of war between Germany and the Soviet Union apparently threw the Soviet rear immediately behind the front into indescribable chaos, especially the entire traffic organization breaking down completely. Deporting the imprisoned Ukrainian nationalists to the Russian interior had already become impossible, as the retreat of the Russian troops had paralysed all transport. When the German advance neared the town rapidly, the leadership of the Communist Party gave orders for an act of direct terror. The NKVD Chief of Lwow was instructed to liquidate all the Ukrainian nationalists who were held in the town's prisons. This order will be discussed later. The investigaters' report gives the following description: —

> During the days between June 24 and 27, 1941, both criminal and political prisoners, who had been pushed into the prison cells, were brought out. Most of them were Ukrainians. The were shot or beaten to death. Their corpses were deposited in the cellars of the prison buildings, some of them were drenched with petrol and burned. The cellar entrances were then bricked up. During the night between June 27 and 28, 1941, the prison guards left Lwow with the last Soviet troops.

In addition, the enquiry under the Rule of Law is able to supplement this description by a graphic witness's report of Jewish origin: —

M. G., Jewish, now living in the Federal Republic of Germany, had fled in the spring of 1941 from the Jewish ghetto in Kielce (Poland). When he crossed the frontier into Soviet-held territory, the Soviet authorities had arrested him, and he witnessed himself the events between June 22 and 28, 1941, as an inmate of the town prison in Lwow. According to his statement, some prisoners had tried to break out from the prison during one of these days, but this attempted flight had been prevented by the Russian guards in the prison yard through salvoes from sub-machine guns, with bloody losses to the prisoners. The prisoners believed, when no food had come to them one day, that the prison guards had already abandoned their posts and had fled before the advancing Germans. After the prison guards had restored order in the prison, and had repaired the broken-down doors, *witness G. saw during the following days that successive groups of Ukrainian prisoners were taken from the cells, never to return.*

Already during the morning hours of June 28, 1941, the Lwow population, worried about the fate of their imprisoned relatives, flooded the prisons and liberated the prisoners that were still alive in their cells. The town prison (Brigidki) had been put on fire by the retreating Russians. The crowd put out the fire, and it tried to enter the bricked-up cellar doors, where the murdered prisoners lay. A small number of the corpses could be brought out from the cellars and laid out in the prison yard for identification.

Another witness, a certain W., whose brother had been arrested for reasons that had nothing to do with politics, and who had been imprisoned in the town lock-up, had hurried to this prison immediately after the last Soviet troops had left Lwow. Members of his family accompanied him. In the prison yard, he met his brother, who had in the meantime been let out from his cell, and he witnessed himself how the first corpses were carried from the cellars of this prison.

The investigators under the Rule of Law summed up their findings on this point as follows [28] : —

At this time — during June 28, 1941 — when the surviving prisoners were liberated from the Lwow prison by their relations and other citizens of the town, and the first corpses of murdered prisoners had been found, not a single German soldier had yet entered Lwow.

When the German troops eventually entered the town, they became witnesses of a situation not of their making. In the investigators' words [29] : —

This situation was met by the first German troops, who entered the town on June 30, 1941. Among them were parts of the First Mountain Sharpshooters' *(Gebirgsjäger)* Division, viz. *Gebirgsjäger* Regiments 98 and 99, Mountain Artillery Regiments 79 and 111, also advance units of the 68th Infantry Division, The Territorial Sharpshooters' *(Landesschützen)* Battalion No. 258, advance guards of the 53rd Artillery Regiment, and the Nachtigall Battalion. Information about the massacre of the prisoners had been passed on to some of the troops already in their marching quarters near the borders of Lwow. Moreover, the crowds of Lwow citizens whom they met in the streets immediately told them of the murders. The commanding officers of the fighting units that advanced into Lwow and the Field Kommandantura, which was soon established, arranged for the collection of the prisoners' corpses to be continued from the three prisons. The corpses that were found were first laid out in the prison yards, so that the population of Lwow could identify them. Soon after, they were given a mass burial. In some of the prison cells, it proved impossible to advance through the heaps of decaying corpses; these cells which lay in the prison basements were disinfected with chlorate of lime, and again bricked up. Estimates made by the persons employed to evacuate the corpses amounted to about 3,000 persons killed. *Among these corpses, they also found the bodies of four German airmen who had been captured by the Russians.*

Large numbers of the soldiers belonging to the above-named units (officers, n.c.o.'s, and men) were eye witnesses to the finding of the corpses, and quite a number of them took photographs of the scenes, of which some have been put in as evidence. *Statements of former Wehrmacht soldiers, who have been heard as witnesses, were partly based on notes they had made at the time in their diaries, or on descriptions given in their letters home to their families, and these leave no doubt whatever that this mass killing of prisoners in the Lwow prisons took place before the German troops entered Lwow.*

All this means that is has been consclusively proved that

(1) During the final phase of Soviet dominion over Lwow, when the German-Soviet war had already broken out, persons opposed to Soviet rule, mainly Ukrainian nationalists, had been arrested in great numbers. Most of them were placed in the three prisons in the town of Lwow;

(2) When the breakdown of transport in the Soviet rear made it impossible to deport them to the Russian interior, the Communist Party leadership ordered their assassination. The number of people murdered has been estimated by the persons collecting the corpses at about 3000;

(3) The murders had been committed before any German soldier had entered Lwow.

This result of the investigation establishes the incontrovertible fact that prisoners housed in the prisons of Lwow had been murdered during the days immediately preceding the capture of the town by the German Wehrmacht. It is worth while to examine the sources more closely which have led to this conclusion. The pieces of evidence can be broken down into three groups. There are contemporary reports of German Wehrmacht soldiers who became eye witnesses of the conditions in the Lwow prisons when they entered the town; these can be supplemented by official investigation reports of German Army authorities. Secondly, there are reports made by people who, at the time, were living in Lwow; and thirdly, there are other statements of value as evidence. On the following pages, we print a selection of statements from each of these groups. All of them are important, but special weight must, of course, be ascribed to the statements of Jewish witnesses. Among them, there are depositions made on oath in Bonn by three surviving Jewish witnesses, who now live in Israel, from which we publish parts that are of particular relevance to our own investigation.

REPORTS OF EYE WITNESSES

Mass Killings before the German Wehrmacht occupied Lwow

(a) German Eye Witnesses

We start with the deposition of an evangelical chaplain to the Wehrmacht, Pastor H. [1] : —

H. reports that he was travelling to Lwow, together with his Roman Catholic colleague, R., a few days after the German occupation of the town. They met girl secretaries of the Lwow university, who spoke fluent German, and who told them the following: —

'They told us that the Russians, already for weeks before the war against Russia, had sent armed groups *(Kommandos)* into the houses of Ukrainian nationals who arrested the inhabitants and placed them into the prisons of the town. All these Russian armed groups had been led by Jewish inhabitants of Lwow. Later, the Russians evacuated their prisoners continuously in sealed railway goods trucks eastward from Lwow. When the final battle for Lwow was approaching its end, and it was no longer possible to send away the prisoners remaining in the prisons, the Russians put them all to death, often in a particularly atrocious manner. They then poured petrol over the bodies and set fire to them ... The main interest dominating these, and other, talks, with Ukrainians was the constantly repeated question about the future of the Ukraine: Shall we be free, shall we be independent? As in this conversation, so always also in later talks we had with Ukrainians during these first weeks, we noticed deep confidence in the Germans.'

Another German witness, St. [2], who is now a *Baurat* (architect with a university diploma), made the following statement: —

Being a traffic expert, he was given orders for July 1, 1941, to reconnoitre whether parts of his division (the 71st Infantry Division) would be able to march through Lwow. St. underlined the fact that his party was greeted in a highly friendly fashion by the population of Lwow when they drove through the town, and occasionally bystanders threw flowers into his car. He then observed that a big crowd was lining the roads, with a space in between, on the way leading to the entrance of a prison: —

'Through the rows of people lining the streets, other people were chased through, both men and women, older and younger persons. These were apparently Jews. At any rate, the German soldiers who stood there looking on said so. Some of these soldiers stood together in groups, as also we did, and looked upon what happened, others gave me the impression as if they were posted there in order ot keep back to a certain extent, the rows in which the population lined the streets. As far as I remember, these guards were dressed in German Army uniforms. Some of the civilians were beating the people who were chased through the space in the middle of the roads, a few of them using canes and sticks for this purpose. A number of the civilians tried to tear off the clothes that their victims wore — I recall a young woman whose only cover was a torn shirt. The soldiers who looked on, and also those who formed a chain to hold back the population, did not take part in these atrocities. I had the impression that the persons who were running from the blows were driven towards the prison gate. I did not see any soldiers who took part in this chase, nor any civilians who accompanied the victims of the beatings as guards — at least I cannot remember this. When I asked the soldiers standing round near me what happened here, I was told that the population were pulling the Jews from their houses in order to exact retribution for what the Jews had done here under the Russian occupation.

Witness then entered the prison yard. According to what he saw, prisoners were no longer maltreated in the yard, they were permitted to look after the injured among them. He was told that there was still another courtyard further in the back, which he entered: 'We found there many corpses, laid out in rows on the ground, men and women. They made a horrible impression on us. Often their clothes hung in tatters. In some cases, the eyes of the bodies had been gouged out, breasts of some women, and the private parts of some men, had been cut off; but I looked at only a few of these corpses. I had the impression that these people had been dead for more than two days — my belief was founded upon the fact that I had seen dead bodies several times before, during the war (during the campaign in France). My impressions were supported by what the soldiers present in the yard told me. They said that the dead were inhabitants of Lwow whom Jews of Lwow had betrayed to the Russians at the beginning of the Russian war, and the Russians had murdered them before the Germans took the town.

People asked us whether we wanted to go down to the prison cellars. There, too, thousands of dead bodies could be seen. We tried to descend by the basement stairs but we gave up because of the bestial smell of rotting corpses.'

Former members of the Nachtigall unit have produced a number of sworn statements, of which we quote some: —

A former officer [3] reports that he went to the Brigidki prison, accompanied by an Ukrainian soldier of his unit, but they entered only the prison yard where a large number of corpses, dressed in civilian garb, lay on the ground. However, on two of the bodies, he also recognized parts of the uniform of German airmen. He did not enter the prison building as already the view offered by the bodies lying in the yard was too terrible. From the wounds shown by the corpses, it was clear that these people had been killed by having been shot in the back of the neck. Even though the weather was very hot, it could be seen that these bodies had been dead for several days already. This was confirmed by the Medical Officer of the Battalion. Witness then learned that about 2,500 dead bodies had been found, most of them Ukrainian but also some Poles and Germans *(Volksdeutsche).*

On the behaviour of the Nachtigall unit: —

'To begin with, I may state with confidence that all members of the Nachtigall unit, although they knew of the ferocious murders committed by the Soviets, by whom also some of their own relations had been killed, kept perfect discipline. I have never seen or heard anything of illegal or criminal acts committed by members of my unit against inhabitants of Lwow. In order to report the full truth, I should like to mention a particular incident in this context: When I returned in my car from a visit to the Metropolitan, in which also Captain Koch, First Lieutenant Oberländer, and the chaplain of our unit had taken part, and drove to my local billett in the second car behind Professor Oberländer and Captain Koch, Captain Koch stopped his car to talk to a Ukrainian from our unit who apparently had been involved in an altercation with a civilian. As I had not been able to see exactly what had happened, I asked Professor Oberländer upon my return to the billett what had been the matter. Oberländer told me that this Nachtigall soldier had picked a quarrel with a passer-by trying to force him into doing something. The soldier had been sternly admonished and instructed again that he had to be absolutely correct in all his dealings with the citizens of Lwow.'

The former Greek-Uniate chaplain to the unit, Dr. J. H.[4], now priest to the Ukrainian community in Munich, who had been a professor of philosophy in the Theological Academy at Lwow until 1939, made the following statement: —

The entire unit had been formed from anti-bolshevik Ukrainians, altogether about 300 men. About half of these had passed the *Abiturium* (university entrance examination). Witness describes Professor Oberländer's position as that of an A. D. C. to First Lieutenant Herzner for establishing liaison between the German military authorities and the Ukrainian unit. The aim of the Ukrainians was the liberation of the Ukrainian people from Russian-Bolshevik rule. The Ukrainians had the hope to become the nucleus of the future Ukrainian army. The German leaders of their unit had sympathies for these aims. Witness emphasizes that discipline in the unit was extremely strict. It is true that *some* of its soldiers, whose home-town was Lwow, were given leave to visit their families and relations but none of the members of the unit were for example, allowed to take part to the meeting on the night of June 30, 1941, when Ukrainian independence was proclaimed from the floor of the hall: —

'I can state with absolute certainty that our unit was never given orders to make arrests, or even to carry out raids with the aim of liquidating certain groups of the Lwow population. I also do not know of a single case in which any member of the unit had committed an act of violence of any sort against citizens of Lwow.'

The tale told by M.[5], an evangelical pastor, who was a soldier (not a chaplain) in the unit, runs as follows: —

I believe I can state with confidence that no member of the Nachtigall unit ever took part in atrocities against the population when under orders. The personality of the officer in command, First Lieutenant Herzner, whom I knew more intimately, was sufficient guarantee against the unit committing any acts of violence. First Lieutenant Herzner was one of the members of the officers' circle round Prince Wilhelm of Hohenzollern. I do not know exactly for how long the First Battalion Brandenburg was billetted in Lwow, but from talks I had with its commander, Major H., I knew that he thought very badly both of the eastern policies of the German government, and of the atrocities committed by the *SD* (Security Service, a subdivision of the Gestapo) in the rear areas, and made no secret of this. One such talk with the major took part about one month later in the joint billett of the Brandenburg and Nachtigall officers at Yosvin, when we lay in front of Vinnitsa.

The following important statement was made by one of the platoon leaders in the Second Company, the former *Feldwebel* (Master-Sergeant), K., who is a sales agent to-day in L., during a libel suit which is pending before the Fulda *Landgericht* (District Court). The statement was put at my disposal by the Attorney-at-Law, Will, of Fulda.

K. states that he was given orders to occupy a certain object in Lwow, viz. the gasworks. He was able to enter the town without being engaged in any fighting. With one platoon, he approached the gasworks cautiously, and with some of his men he climbed over the wall. In the courtyard, they were met by workmen, who told him in German that the Soviet Commissar had already gone away but his wife was till there. When K. entered Lwow, he witnessed individual acts of violence being committed by civilians, apparently against Jewish inhabitants of Lwow. The gasworks were handed over to him without any trouble. He then assembled his entire platoon on the grounds of the gasworks and issued strict orders that no member of the platoon was allowed to leave the gasworks.

Questioned whether he had granted leave to any Ukrainian soldiers of his platoon whose home was in Lwow or near the town, K. answered with a definite No. He remembers that some soldiers had asked him for leave, but he took the view that he had no authority to grant leave. If a general order was issued to that effect he might be enabled to permit leave but he did not feel able and willing to make this decision for himself.

K. goes on to state that, in a street extending in a straight line from the gasworks, he saw Jews being maltreated. He intervened with the help of members of his unit in order to stop these acts of violence. In addition, he let the Jewish inhabitants of that street and of the neighbourhood take refuge in the gasworks. He had them fed and employed them at light work. In this behaviour, he was led by the conviction that the German Wehrmacht had the obligation to maintain peace and order. He then issued an order that no Ukrainian member of his platoon was allowed to leave the gasworks without his own special permission, and without a German to accompany hin. This order covered the Second Platoon of his Company, which was under his leadership. Later during the day, about twenty or thirty Jews, most of them old people, came to the gate of the gasworks to beg protection. He admitted these people to the courtyard, too. Protection to the Jews in the gasworks was given until the unit marched out of Lwow. As far as he remembers, some days after, he heard Jews saying in Lwow: *German soldiers with bird on arm not good, without bird good* (the 'bird' was presumably the Nazi eagle badge). K. also remembers that First Lieutenant Oberländer issued oral instructions about the necessity to treat the civilian population well. K. himself told his unit that blameless and loyal behaviour was expected — and this was an order. K. states: When he and his platoon first approached the gasworks, they noticed a penetrating and repulsive smell. He believed that this was the smell of gas, but was told later that this was the smell of corpses. The smell was so strong that it was not necessary to know where the prison was, as one needed only to follow the smell to find it. The Jews he admitted to the courtyard, who had been given work of some sort, were sent home in the evenings. They were told with great precision that he was not in a position to admit more Jews, since he was obliged to restrict his protection to those only, and mainly old people, who lived in the street leading from the gasworks to the town. When his unit left after some days, two Jewish girls had climbed on one of his motor lorries, and inspite of their insistent begging, he had to pull them down. The girls had offered to remain as Wehrmacht helpers with his unit because they felt safe there.

K. also states that he can say with certainty that his platoon was not engaged in any fighting, so that not a single shot was fired. This was also true for the rest of the battalion, as far as he knew.

In addition, K. reports that before his joining the *Reichswehr* (German army) he was Chief Clerk to a Jewish attorney at Breslau, and when he left this employment to enter the *Reichswehr*, this happened on completely friendly terms.

After the German capitulation, K. was a prisoner of war in the Soviet Union. There he was forced to give a thorough description of all the phases of his military service before and during the war. In this context, he also informed his interlocutors about his service with the Nachtigall unit. The Soviet authorities, at that time, seemed not in the least interested in this.

R., another German witness, who had belonged to the Nachtigall unit [6], gave the following descriptions, among other things he reported: —

The companies of our unit marched into Lwow, singing Ukrainian songs. The population noticed the singing; people welcomed the soldiers frantically, and also threw flowers at the soldiers. R. describes then a speech made by the Metropolitan to the Nachtigall unit, and to the masses of people assembled round it.

'When we were standing there, the Ukrainian leader of our unit, who had not been given German military rank, was told by the people surrounding us that his brother had been shot only the day before by the Russians. I talked to him myself when I saw him crying. The entire unit, as far as I know, took part in the burial of the murdered man, one or two days later.'

Witness then states that the entire Nachtigall unit obtained billetts, two or three days later, in a large building in the centre of the town. From there, a number of individual sentry units were detailed. The remainder stayed in their quarters at their usual company fatigues and drill.

'I can take it upon my oath that the Nachtigall unit was never detailed for any missions against groups of the Lwow civilian population during these days, until we left Lwow on July 6, 1941. Nor did I see or hear anything of individual members of the unit, on their own initiative, committing any atrocities against civilians. I will add here that Ukrainian members of our unit wore German army uniforms — as we did — but without any badges of rank, etc. However, the Ukrainians' uniforms were marked on the shoulder straps by yellow and blue stripes.'

R. continues: —

‚After we had left Lwow, the Ukrainian members of our unit heard that their aim — which was the creation of an autonomous Ukrainian state — would not be granted, as the Western Ukraine was to be incorporated in the "*Generalgouvernement*" (the Nazi name for the larger part of Poland that was not directly administered as part of Germany). As I could see for myself, they were very depressed and sad about this news, and they believed the aims of their struggle to be lost.'

Another German witness [7] who served with the Nachtigall unit, and who now belongs to the *Bundeswehr* (Federal German forces), stated: —

Witness mentions the joyous reception of the unit by the population of Lwow. He emphasizes that the unit was kept under military discipline in Lwow, and that the so-called 'small service' (fatigues) was carried out even more strictly among the Ukrainians. Only in very exceptional cases, as far as he remembers, members of the unit were given town leave.

'I am able to take it on my oath with great confidence that the Third Company, to which I belonged — and it is only for that company I can bear witness — never received during the time it remained in Lwow any kind of order for an activity directed against certain groups of the Lwow population. I can also state with complete confidence that neither of the two Ukrainian platoons of my company, for any motive whatever, has ever undertaken activities of this type. If individual soldiers took part in acts of violence, I should certainly have heard about it.'

The statement made by a German soldier of the unit, W. B. [8], is important in various ways: —

W. B. states that his unit got to hear very quickly that the Russians had killed, before their retreat, the persons from among the Lwow population whom they held imprisoned in their various prisons. Witness himself did not visit these prisons but one of his comrades told him of undescribable scenes when relations of the murdered people identified the bodies: —

'From conversations with Ukrainians who spoke German (many of them had been students) I gathered that some of the Ukrainian volunteeres, too, had lost relations through the murders, and that a number of the assassinated persons had been found by them. The Ukrainians were deeply shocked by their discoveries.'

Witness remembers that some of the Ukrainian volunteers, whose homes were in Lwow, absconded from the unit and never returned: —

'With complete truth I am able to state that the Nachtigall battalion was never used for any measures to be taken against the civilian population during its stay in Lwow. I have already pointed out that we were completely inactive whilst waiting for the continuation of our eastward march. I should never have come forward as a witness if my conscience had been in any way troubled.'

Witness goes on to describe how the Nachtigall unit later advanced in the rear of a *Gebirgsjäger* Division, which had forced the break-through to Vinnitsa, and he states: —

'The fighting morale of the Ukrainian, by that time, had already been greatly weakened because of the political decisions of the Reich leaders about the creation of a Ukrainian state and a Ukrainian army. Whilst advancing towards Vinitsa, the unit lost a fair number of Ukrainian soldiers through desertion. These may have, with great likelihood, returned to their home towns and villages. The whole battalion was then taken back from Vinnitsa to Neuhammer.'

Shortly after, the Nachtigall unit was disbanded. That it had such a short life makes it so difficult to write its complete history as — in contrast to the Bergmann unit — there remained no veterans' association to keep up the unit's tradition.

The responsible German Army authorities, too, made an investigation of the events in the Lwow prisons. For us, it is sufficient to quote a report of the Army Field Police Group of July 7, 1941. Its Report No. 1 runs as follows [9] : —

On Monday, June 30, 1941, a few hours after the end of street fighting in Lwow, after German troops had captured the town, the Group entered its streets, which in several places were still on fire. All parts of the town population took part in vivid exclamations of joy and relief.

The investigations about the Lwow massacre led to the following results: —

In three prisons in Lwow, mountains of male and femal corpses, which were horribly mutilated, were found. Among them were bodies of very young people, even of children. The three prisons were situated as follows: No. 24 b, Kazimierzowska Street (the political prison of the GPU); No. 1, Leona Sapiehy Road (the main GPU prison, under *Prokurator*, i. e. the Public Prosecutor); No. 7, Zamartynowska Street (Criminal Prison, and GPU barracks). The number of the persons slain could not be precisely ascertained, as in the hot weather the smell of corpses pervaded whole quarters of the town, and the Epididemiological Service of the Police objected to further work at collecting individual bodies. Very soon, in advancing into the cellars, we found a layer, composed of a viscous mass, into which the corpses had congealed. In the first-mentioned prison, bodies were stacked four or five deep on the cellar floor. Some of the cellar doors had already been bricked up by the Russians. A large number of the bodies must have been buried in this way already some time before war broke out, since putrefaction — as stated — had made great progress then. The number of people killed in the whole town of Lwow may be estimated at about 3,500.

In the second of the prisons named above, the impression gained on the first day after entering the city was: From the service wings of the prison, which were situated on the ground floor looking out on a courtyard surrounded by a wooden fence, one body after the other was carried into the yard. In this case, there was no doubt that the victims had been murdered only a few days before our capturing Lwow. The cellars in question had ceilings that were splashed with blood, and in a room which had apparently served for interrogations the floor was covered with a layer of dried blood that was 20 centimetres (about 8 inches) deep. The bolshevik hangmen had literally waded in blood.

In the prison yard, mass graves were found in two places, and the bodies buried there were lifted out, to be laid out in rows, so that their relations could identify them. The Medical Officer present, who had the rank of general *(Generalarzt)*, however, objected to this procedure because most of the victims were already unrecognizable, and their relations ought not to be shocked unnecessarily. All those who have seen the horribly mutilated bodies, and had to witness the terrible scenes when relations, as did not happen often, recognized the dead, had to support the *Generalarzt's* view. Only in very few cases, people were able to identify the bodies, and in these the remains were handed to the families for private burial. This leads to the surmise that many victims came from the country-side surrounding Lwow. This conclusion is supported by the fact that to this day country people are crowding in front of the prison, demanding to be shown their relations who had been arrested months ago. It might also be assumed that there are many families in Lwow who do not yet know that their relations, who have disappeared, are no longer alive, for the crowds who reported for identification of their dead were relatively small, and they did not correspond with the number of victims. Military medical officers, who examined the bodies, stated it to be unlikely that the cause of death had been shooting. From the prison in Leona Sapiehy Street, ten bodies were taken to the Forensic Academy, for post-mortems to ascertain the causes of death. Generally, all these bodies showed heavy and multiple injuries that had been caused by blunt instruments. Many of the women had been raped, their breasts had been cut off. Also the private parts of males had been the objects of bolshevik perversion. From the faces of the dead that were distorted as if by spasms, the torn clothing, and other signs, it can be seen that the arrested persons have undergone appalling tortures. All of them had been literally bludgeoned to death, and doctors were also of the opinion that some of them had been suffocated under the mounds of corpses. In the other prisons, dead prisoners were found whose arms had been pinioned together with the feet behind their backs, which warrants the conclusion that they were cruelly tortured. Everywhere on the door jambs of the guard's rooms near the gateways that lead into the prison, extensive traces of blood can be seen.

Less than one per cent of the dead were Jews; it is said that these were Zionists. It is possible to break down the victims of the bloody terror in Lwow into groups of people suspected of political activities, of being capitalists, and criminals, and also people already sentenced. To this must be added members of the Ukrainian and Polish intelligentsia, as well as those who were arrested by the GPU only after the outbreak of war. During the last few days before the Germans entering the town, also about sixty Polish and Ukrainian students had been arrested ...

(b) Jewish Eye Witnesses

The following statements and depositions have been made by Jewish eye witnesses of the pogrom in Lwow.

The first witness [19] was a student of music in Lwow at the time. Today he is a member of the editorial staff in the Jerusalem broadcasting studios.

Witness describes how he queued up for bread in front of a baker's shop, on the day of the German occupation, and continues: —

Whilst standing in the queue, I saw posters being fixed to a wall very near of me. Being curious, I went over to the posters, which were wirtten in both Ukrainian and German. They were signed by a "*Ukrainian National Committee*", or similarly, which welcomed the victorious German Wehrmacht, and gave expression to the hope that a free Ukrainian state would be set up. Some phrases have stuck in my memory. They ran as follows: "Long live Adolf Hitler and Stepan Bandera! Death to the Jews and to the Communists!" When I returned to the waiting queue, we were told that there was no bread left. The waiting customers dispersed. On my way home, a civilian suddenly stopped me. He wore a yellow and blue armband. He demanded to see my passport, and after a lengthy cross talk found out that my passport showed that I was registered as a Jew. He then hit me in the face with his fist, and blood began to pour down over my face. The blow made me feel very dizzy. Then, other civilians with blue and yellow armbands appeared. They forced me to hold my arms behind my back and led me to a gateway, where a number of other Jews stood. I guess, there were between twenty and thirty there. From there, we were driven by some guards — all of them civilians with blue and jellow armbands — towards the centre of the town, to the Brigidki prison. We had to march two by two. The nearer we came to the Brigidki prison, the thicker became the crowds. These civilians attempted to mob us, and many of them beat us with various instruments. The guards who marched with us tried to push back the other civilians so that we could proceed on our way. When we arrived at the gate of the Brigidki prison, very many people had assembled in the road which is very wide there. We saw beaten-up and dead Jews, who had been chased to the Brigidki Prison before us. Also here, the civilian crowd rained blows upon us. I myself was hit several times, and I was soon sticky with blood all over. In front of me, I saw a small child being held by his feet and his head swung against the wall, the child's blood dripping over me. In the gateway of Brigidki Prison, two rows of German soldiers in fieldgrey uniforms and with their steel helmets on their heads held back the crowds in order to keep the way into the prison open for us. The soldiers did not take part in the beatings and other maltreatment.

When I finally arrived in the prison yard with the other thirty, I saw already a great crowd of Jews assembled — I estimate they were about 1,000, who filled almost the entire space. I soon saw that some of the Jews in the yard were busy bringing out corpses from the prison buildings. I immediately joined a group which used a rope to pull litters carrying corpses through the cellar windows. After a while, I saw more clearly what happened there. A number of Jews worked in the cellar, putting the dead bodies stored there upon litters, and other Jews had to pull these litters from the cellars with ropes. Another group had to take the litters to the rim of a large hole dug in the ground of the prison yard, where the bodies were laid out in rows in front of the pit. The various groups of working Jews sometimes changed their jobs, so that I also had to enter the cellars. The corpses were already in a state of advanced putrefaction. In some cases, when we tried to lift them, arms or legs were torn off. It was impossible that these were freshly killed human beings. I had the impression that among them there were Ukrainians, Poles, and also some Jews. It was evident that these were prisoners whom the Russians had shot before their retreat from Lwow. The Jews working in the prison yard were guarded by a group of soldiers in German uniform. They wore steel helmets and field-grey dress. I estimated the number of these soldiers at about thirty. Part of these soldiers marched up and down in front of the mass of the Jews huddled together. Others sat or stood lounging on the side of the courtyard. They apparently changed jobs ever so often with their comrades who kept guard over us. The guards wore gas masks, as the stench of corpses, and also the smoke of the burning building, were extremely strong. One of these soldiers, whom I passed by accident suddenly took off his gas mask and said (almost with these words) in Ukrainian: "Look what you have done", pointing with his hand to the corpses. We — that is I and the other Jews beside me — were highly surprised to be addressed in Ukrainian. When I looked at the soldiers more closely, I noticed that they wore blue and yellow markings on their uniforms, as far as I remember, on the lapels of their collars, and also on their steel helmets.

Witness is being corrected: —

According to all previous investigations, members of the Nachtigall battalion wore only blue and yellow piping round their shoulder straps.

Answer of Witness: —

It is conceivable that my memory is now slightly at fault in this detail, but I remember clearly that they wore blue and yellow badges.

Witness E. B.[11], born in Lwow, now resident in Jerusalem, studied philosophy at Lwow university fourth semester — i. e. half-yearly term, which means that he was before the end of his second year as a student), when Lwow was captured by German troops. He made the following statement about the facts he observed: —

Lwow was a town of mixed nationalities. Roughly one third of about 150,000 inhabitants of Lwow were Jews. Most Jews of the town were Jewish nationalists. Zionist groups were highly active. I myself was a member of the Zionist youth movement. More than one third of Lwow's population was Polish, the remainder Ukrainian. Already under Polish rule, there were Ukrainian groups working for an independent Ukraine.

Leaders of the Ukrainian nationalist movement had been arrested and tried in the Polish courts. According to my experience, the Jewish part of the population endeavoured to keep a neutral distance between the two other nationalities. Drawing upon their experiences after the First World War, the Jews of Galicia remembered the Petliura movement, and this caused them to be reserved against Ukrainians, however, only towards Ukrainian nationalists. When the Russian administration took over Galicia, the Jews felt some relief, for they knew of the attitude and measures of the Nazi system against the Jews, and had reason to fear them. Soon after the Russians had assumed administrative powers, they suppressed all Zionist groups, and this was a bitter personal blow for me. In addition, they prohibited the use of the Hebrew language. However, Jews were allowed to study. Under Polish rule, no Jew could enter the administration as a civil servant or a public employee and this was different under Russian dominion. Both Jews and Ukrainians were now admitted to administrative posts. As the official languages, Ukrainian and Russian replaced Polish. Up to the outbreak of the war between Germany and Russia, many deportations were carried out by the Russian authorities. By this "resettlement", all Polish State officials, members of the Polish Police and the Polish Army, also Polish and Jewish refugees who had fled to Lwow during the war between Germany and Poland, and all so-called capitalists of all nationalities were affected. I heard also of arrests of Ukrainian nationalists and, in some cases, of members of the Zionist organisations that were carried out by the Russian NKVD. Among the persons arrested, there were also some I had been friendly with. From my own knowledge, I cannot state that a bigger wave of arrests had started after the outbreak of the German-Russian war on June 22, 1941.

Already at the beginning of the Russian occupation of Lwow between 1939 and 1941, the Soviets had set up a military organisation which they called the militia. The militia consisted largely of Ukrainians, though also some Jewish citizens were members. Only Russians were officers in the militia. The militia was uniformed in olive-green trousers, a rather dark blue Russian military tunic, and a Russian military cap with a red rim. This is the uniform as I remember it now. Whether my memory is correct in all details, I can, of course, not say now with certainty, as almost twenty years have passed since. Members of this militia (of course only Ukrainians) who had torn off their Soviet uniform badges, and civilians with yellow and blue armlets, went from house to house in our road and brought out Jewish men, women, and youths. Our own house was left in peace, as our Ukrainian caretaker, who stood in the doorway, told the searchers that no Jews were living in his house. I saw with my own eyes from our window how Jewish men and women were taken from houses opposite. Those who resisted were pulled out into the street by force. After the militia had left our road with the Jews they had herded together, people told me that the Jews were informed they would be set to work.

About the fate of the arrested Jewish citizens, I can report only from hearsay. Already on the first or second day after the event, I heard from Polish and Ukrainian neighbours that the Jews from our part of the town were taken to the military prison in Zamartynow street. On the way there, they were heavily beaten both by the escorting Ukrainian militia and the civilians who crowded after them. Near the gate of the military prison, a large crowd had assembled, and through this the Jews were chased to the gate. They again received a beating there. In the prison, the Jews were forced to wash corpses that had been stacked there, and to load them on carts for taking them away. Also there, the Jews that were put to work were abused and maltreated, and a great number of them died under this torture.

These reports were confirmed by a number of Jewish youngsters, who had succeeded in slipping away from the other Jews who were herded into prison. These told me that some relations of mine, an uncle, an aunt, and their two sons, who all lived in Balanowa Street, had also been torn from their flat, and not returned. They never came back after that. The only thing I could learn about them was that they had been chased to the Zamartynow Prison, with other Jews. The same informant told me that German officers and privates were in the military prison, looking on whilst Jews were maltreated and killed. They took photographs of the scene. I have never heard of German soldiers having taken an active part in this massacre.

Witness A. G.[12], university-trained engineer *(Diplomingenieur)* from Altenburg in Germany, who had lived in Poland from 1938, and in Lwow from 1939, now resident at Ramat-Gan, Israel, made the following statement: —

My family and I were informed of the German military occupation of the town by the caretaker of our house, who was a Pole. He came to the cellar to tell us. Upon hearing this, we returned to our flat upstairs. During the first day after this, nothing happened in our house, though we heard that in other parts of the town some measures had been taken against Jews. The next morning, Ukrainian auxiliary policemen turned up in our house. They were members of the militia, which had already been set up by the Russians. The militia was led by Soviet officers, and most militia men were Ukrainians, though some Poles and Jews were also among them. Militiamen wore a dark blue military tunic and riding breeches with high boots. They took from our house five young male Jews — I was one of them — and together with other young Jews from neighbouring houses, we were led to the Auxiliary Police Station, not far from our street. There we were herded together with other Jews who had already been brought in. At the Police Station, I also saw civilians wearing a yellow and blue armband, which marked them as auxiliary policemen. The militiamen had told us and our families that they came to put us to work. About 70 or 80 of the arrested Jewish men were marched under militia guard to the Russian NKVD buildings in Lonskiego Street. Already on the way there, civilians abused us and spit at us. In the NKVD building we were taken to the interior courtyard. A larger number of Jews were already assembled there. They had to take corpses from an open pit, and to load them on waiting carts. I have to add to the foregoing that at the gate of the NKVD building we were handed over by the Ukrainian auxiliary policemen to a group of members of the Wehrmacht. This group had about platoon strength (between forty and fifty men). The soldiers wore field-grey German uniforms, steel helmets, and carbines. From the orders they gave us, I immediately recognized them as Ukrainians; they were certainly no Germans. Among each other, and to us, they talked fluent Ukrainian only.

(c) Polish Eye Witnesses

A Polish witness, W.[13], who was interrogated at Bonn, is now a resident of Hamburg. He gave a description of what he saw in Brigidki Prison shortly after the departure of the Russians: —

In one of the prison wings, we looked into a number of cells — perhaps twenty of them — and in all the cells we noticed on every wall, except that where the door was, a large number of bullet holes in three or more rows. The floor boards, in some places, had been torn open. In the open holes, and also under the boards which we lifted, the soil was red and moist by having been drenched with blood... When we passed through the prison, we were told that most the prisoners had been killed by the Russians, but in none of the cells did we see corpses lying about. The bodies of the killed — as several signs had indicated to me before — had been taken from the cells some days earlier. When we returned to the courtyard, we were met there by a big crowd of people in high excitement. We saw some men of the fire brigade and other persons breaking open the bricked-up entrances to the prison cellars. As soon as a passage had been opened, men of the fire brigade, with gas masks, went down and soon brought up the first corpses, which they laid out in the prison yard. Some of the bodies were dressed in torn clothes, or only in shirts. However, their faces were still recognizable. We looked only at some of the dead and then returned home.

During the two days of which I have spoken I never saw any German soldiers, either in the town or in Brigidki Prison. Rumours about the discovery of corpses circulated in all Lwow and also in the suburbs. Other people from Lwow told us that about 2,000 inhabitants of the town had been killed, principally members of the intelligentsia. I also heard that other corpses had been found... in the building of the NKVD, but not as many as at Brigidki. NKVD headquarters had been there, and they kept there only those prisoners who had been arrested for offering resistance to the Soviet authorities. Such prisoners did not stay there for long but were sent elsewhere.

Witness underlines the fact that he heard of Jews being shot by Germans only in 1942/43, but he knew that great wrath against the Lwow Jews filled the population, as Jews hat cooperated with the Russians, und had at times laid information against Poles and Ukrainians with the Russians. Of the existence of a Nachtigall Battalion he knew nothing at the time.

Another Polish commentary is contained in a documentary report published by the Polish exile magazine, *Kultura* (Paris, 1960, No. 1 and 2). Naturally, testimony given by Poles is of almost equally great importance as that of Jews. The author of the report, Boris Lewitzki, used for this report both his own and the experiences of other Polish eye witnesses. This is his report, in parts [14] : —

As is well known, the German-Soviet war began early in the morning of June 22, 1941. Three million German soldiers advanced across the Soviet frontiers and met with hardly any resistance. Nevertheless, it must be mentioned that isolated Soviet units opposed the German advance with a desperate effort, and thus were able to slow down the quick progress of the German offensive of the first day. The German Wehrmacht entered Lwow not before June 29 at 3.15 a. m. After Stalin's death, several official Soviet voices have even accused the dead dictator and his closest advisers of having been taken by surprise by the German attack, inspite of precise advance information and warnings reading them. Therefore, in all the areas along the Soviet western frontiers, complete chaos began to rule immediately. *After the outbreak of war, the security authorities in Lwow received orders from Moscow to evacuate the political prisoners eastward at any price. As it proved impossible to follow this order, shootings of prisoners started already on June 22.* After the futile attempt of prisoners to flee from Zamartynowka Road, the shootings were speeded up. From a person who, at the time, was one of the prisoners, I obtained the most precise description, which I am reproducing here in its crucial parts. Already during the first days after war had begun, the prisoners were sorted into political and criminal cases. Most of the criminals were released. Not later than on June 22, the NKVD began to take men out of their cells without their belongings, and two days later, the same procedure started with the women. The first executions were carried out along the wall of the prison chapel, and later in all the court-yards of Brigidki Prison. In order to save their life, some of the prisoners stayed in their cells, not giving an answer when an NKVD guard called them out by name. When the Germans began to approach the town, the guards went over to liquidate all the prisoners left in the cells, using for the purpose sub-machine guns and hand grenades. These killings lasted until June 28. In the prison in Zamartynowka Road, only two prisoners were shot who were there already on the day when war broke out. All Lwow citizens who had been arrested after the beginning of the war were taken to the NKVD remand prison in Lonski Street. A bloody massacre took place among them, too.

In their majority, the prisoners were of Ukrainian nationality, but there were also many Poles among them.

That mass shootings had taken place in the Lwow prisons in those tragic days of June was known all over the town and its surroundings. Despair and worries led the population to look upon Hitler's soldiers as saviours. It is neither a lie nor an invention of propaganda that Hitler's armies, on their march into Lwow, were greeted by the terrorized people — both Ukrainians and Poles — with feelings of relief.

Identical observations were made by a German company commander who stated about happenings in Brigidki Prison: —

When I went to Brigidki Prison for the second time, I saw that quarrels had broken out among people in the streets. When I asked what was the matter, I was told that people were abusing the Jews who had drawn the hatred of the remaining population upon themselves by cooperating with the Russians and informing about the Soviets' victims to them. However, I witnessed only isolated incidents. Among other things, I remember that a boy with an injury to his left temple was carried into the yard of Brigidki Prison. I could see that he was dead. I witnessed how the *Field Gendarmery* (Military Police), which had been given orders to seal off the prison against the outside, restored order.

When I went to Brigidki Prison for the third time, Jews were working there at carrying corpses form the cellars and laying them out in the prison yard. The yard was under guard of the Field Gendarmery. As far as I remember, a Field Gendarmery captain had already arranged for the prison being hermetically sealed against the street.

Upon questioning, Witness answered: —

'Neither on the first nor on any of the following days did I see Ukrainian soldiers in German Army uniforms in Lwow ... Especially in Brigidki Prison, I met only soldiers of the *Gebirgsjäger* Division, who could be recognized by the Edelweiss badge on their left arm, and Field Gendarmes. I never knew that there was a German-Ukrainian unit among the troops marching upon Lwow.'

EXECUTIONS OF POLITICAL PRISONERS — A PLANNED ACT OF LIQUIDATION?

The descriptions from Polish sources are clearly of particular value in englightening us about the events: They give a graphic picture of both the Lwow Ukrainians' and the Poles' reaction to the arrival of the German Wehrmacht. They contain the immensely important pointer to an order issued by Moscow to transfer all political prisoners to the interior of the Soviet Union at any price. As this proved impossible — the Polish description continues — shootings of prisoners started already on June 22, that is, full eight days before the German Wehrmacht entered Lwow. This implies that the massacre of the prisoners cannot be treated as a measure that was planned by Moscow from the very beginning. If that can be proved, the inference is that the Soviets would have preferred to keep their prisoners alive. But another, extremely weighty statement of a witness raises certain doubts against that assumption. This witness appeared in Bonn during the investigation under the Rule of Law, and made and signed a statement. Its complete text, with name and origin of the depositor, forms part of the files of the investigation, but what this witness had to say makes it impossible to give any hint as to his identity. The witness is a former Soviet citizen who, some months before the outbreak of the

German-Soviet war, came to Lwow. There, he was in close personal contact with a leading personality in the Lwow NKVD. This man told witness that, at the beginning of the German campaign against Russia, a new wave of arrests had started, for which lists of people to be imprisoned had been prepared beforehand. It was impossible to deport these prisoners as the outbreak of war destroyed all semblance of a functioning traffic organisation in the Western Ukraine. On the evening of June 23, witness was told by his NKVD acquaintance that German troops had arrived at a distance of about 30 kilometres (18—19 miles) from Lwow. The Soviet authorities believed that parachutists might be used against the town, and that ground troops might attempt its encirclement from the east. *Witness then states that the men in charge of the Lwow NKVD received an order by telegram to annihilate all prisoners belonging to the 'great (i. e. higher) intelligentsia'. The telegram was signed 'N. Kh.' It made the officers in charge of the NKVD personally responsable for the execution of the order.*

According to witness, the annihilation of people in prison was carried out between June 24 and 28. Later, witness was told that the number of prisoners killed amounted to about 2,800, among them 200 Germans. This statement is extremely significant, because it supplements the above-quoted Polish and Jewish testimonials. It may explain, at least in part, the fact that no proceedings against War Criminals were opened at Nuremberg because of the massacres and pogroms of June, 1941: The population of Lwow knew too much about the liquidation of prisoners by the Soviets, which were the immediate cause for the acts of violence that followed later.

After the Occupation of Lwow by German Troops

The first German troops entered Lwow in the morning of June 30. They were greeted as liberators, as is shown, for example, by the Polish statements quoted by us. The new political situation gave rise to two separate movements: The forces of Ukrainian nationalism became feverishly active. Already on the evening of June 30, a *constituent assembly* was convened, and in this assembly, the free and independent Ukrainian Republic was proclaimed. The primate of the Ukrainian Church, the Metropolitan of Lwow, on July 1 approved and welcomed this decision. As an instrument of the revolutionary executive, Ukrainian civilians were banding together to form a Ukrainian militia, whose badge was the yellow and blue armband. It put itself at the disposal of the Ukrainian national movement.

On the other hand, Ukrainian civilians started to commit acts of violence. The report of the investigators gives the following description [15] : —

... Already before noon on June 30, 1941, Ukrainians were engaged in fierce rioting against the Jewish part of the town's population, and this led eventually to a pogrom, which had tragic consequences for the Jews. However, such pogroms had not been unknown in the earlier history of the Ukraine. According to witnesses' statements, the probable causes for these riots were, apart from the permanent tension between the two national groups, especially the firm belief held by the Ukrainians, whether justly or unjustly, that their Jewish neighbours had been partly responsible for the arrests of many Ukrainian nationalists, as Jews had cooperated with the Soviet authorities and, in particular, the NKVD. The horrible discoveries of many corpses, which were the remains of Ukrainians that had been killed in the Lwow prisons, raised the emotional turmoil among the Ukrainians to a climax. It may also be assumed that the Ukrainians knew of the anti-Jewish attitude of the Nazi regime, and therefore believed to ingratiate themselves with the new authorities by their anti-Jewish excesses.

Anti-Jewish measures started simultaneously in several parts of the town during the morning of June 30, 1941. They had their main effect in those quarters of the town where Jews predominated, e. g. in the Zamartynow suburb in the north. Ukrainian nationalists, among them many members of the abovementioned Ukrainian militia, according to the results of the investigation, did not only start, but also were most active in carrying out, the pogrom. Groups of Ukrainian nationalists and militia members, accompanied by Ukrainians of the lowest social groups who took part in the campaign for selfish motives (pilfering), did not only patrol the streets of the town to search for Jewish victims but they also entered Jewish houses and flats by force. All Jewish men who could be found, and in some parts of the town Jewish women and children, too, were taken away with the explanation that they were needed for forced labour. Any attempt to resist was immediately put down by brute force. The Jews that had been grabbed from the streets and houses were taken to collecting points under armed guard. Marching the Jews to these collecting centres often offered the militia guards, and also the civilian crowds of Ukrainians assembled in the streets, an opportunity to beat and maltreat the Jewish prisoners, in some cases severely. The crowds used for this purposes sticks, canes, and other instruments, and they also threw things at the procession of Jews. From the collecting centres, groups of Jews were led, without regard to their individual social status, to places where they had to perform various low and menial tasks, often without suitable tools, e. g. to sweep the streets, to pick up glas splinters with their bare hands, etc. When they did this work, the Jews were also exposed to crude abuse and violence by a raging mob. In other parts of the town, however, the Jews were used for definite jobs of work and not physically maltreated.

The worst treatment, however, was meted out to those Jews who had been dragged from the collecting points, or straight from the streets, to the three prisons in the town. There, they had to collect the corpses of prisoners. What happened there, will be described in detail later.

The pogrom that had broken out on June 30, 1941, continued with even greater ferocity during the following day, July 1, 1941, and came to an end only on the third day after the German capture of the town, when the First *Gebirgsjäger* Division formed a local *Kommandantura* on July 2, 1941, after reports about the pogrom had reached the Staff of the 49th Army Corps. Colonel W., the officer commanding *Gebirgsjäger* Artillery Regiment No. 79, was appointed town commandant, according to the statement made by

Lieutenant Colonel K.[16], then Captain and II a (Staff Officer Supply) in the divisional staff of the First *Gebirgsjäger* Division. By suitable decrees and measures, Colonel W. was able to restore outward order in Lwow.

Through a description found in the diary of a dispatch rider to the German *Gebirgsjäger* Regiment No. 98[17], the state of affairs in Lwow is graphically shown: —

> In the streets, there were huge crowds milling about, from which groups were formed from time to time, as it appeared, arbitrarily, which hunted for informers, traitors, and stool pigeons, who had been guilty, actually or allegedly, of delivering over anti-communists to the cruel mercies of the Soviets. The raging mob, among whom I did not see any people in uniform, nor any men carrying firearms, committed crude acts of violence. Because of the overcrowding of the streets, I was not able to observe details but I saw several gangs of civilians breaking down house doors, and I heard cries for help from several floors of these houses.
>
> Proceeding to the battalion, I again passed the above-mentioned prison building, and I saw rows of men and women standing in the prison gateway, and hitting with sticks, planks, and their bare fists, etc., other human beings, whose clothes were torn and who were smeared with blood. These victims were chased along by other civilians and forced through the gateway into the wide prison yard. There, they were forced to sit down on the ground and fold their hands over their heads. I did not go to the prison again or enter the prison yard at a later time; therefore I do not know what happened to the people herded together there. As we were told later, they were apparently employed for collecting and burying the bodies found in the prisons.

The investigation carried out under the Rule of Law has produced an objective analysis of the political and psychological situation in Lwow (and East Galicia) up to the outbreak of the German-Soviet war. This situation was determined, and changed, by the outbreak of war, which suddenly reversed the relationship between the various political factors of life in the area; by the mass arrests of Ukrainian nationals through the Soviets; by the killing of the prisoners — political prisoners only, for the criminals were released; by the publication of these crimes after the flight of the Soviet authorities, by the revived national aspirations and hopes of the Ukrainians — all this contributed to an emotional and political combination which gave rise to mass violence against the Jews of Lwow. Weighing carefully all available testimony, there can be no doubt that this mass violence was indeed a pogrom, identical with earlier forms of mass brutality against Jewish people in Eastern Europe. One of its most characteristic features is the very anonymity of riots directed against any national minority, and in particular against Jews — there is no directing authority which claims responsibility for them (which does not exclude the existence of seditious leaders). In the case under discussion, there was obviously another contributory cause, whose importance may even have been preponderant, namely the belief of the masses that they acted in a just cause by avenging, through a form of summary justice, the horrible mass murders committed against Ukrainian nationals by the Soviets, for which sympathizers with the Soviets, who were also shown favours by them, were then punished by the pogrom.

This assumption is confirmed by the statement of the Jewish witness, J. [18], who told us that one of the soldiers near whom he stood in the prison yard took of his gas mask, and suddenly said: 'Look what you have done!', pointing with his hand to the corpses lying there.

The same picture is presented by the diary notes of a member of the German Wehrmacht [19]. This soldier, a dispatch rider, passed by one of the Lwow prisons and saw bleeding people in torn clothes being chased into the prison through two rows of civilians who kept on beating them. He then says: —

> There were thousands of Lwow citizens forming this crowd. The town had just been taken by us, and there was as yet no trace of a German authority enforcing order. It was obvious that these crowds had taken justice into their own hands and tried to avenge themselves.
>
> I must, in any case, emphasize that nowhere did I see a single German soldier taking part in these riots — there was not a single person in uniform among these gangs of bruisers, terror groups, and wild crowds of people. Nor did I get the impression that these acts of revenge were committed under any sort of leadership or outside guidance. They arose completely spontaneously out of the midst of a fanatically excited, embittered, and disgusted Lwow population.

The Jewish statement appears to provide proof for the emotions of the Ukrainians who believed that enormous crimes had been committed against their co-nationals, whilst the German witness points to one of the basic motives for the mass acts of violence: *Revenge and Lynch Justice.*

Through the impartial and detailed analysis of events, and their motivation, contained in the investigation results obtained under the Rule of Law we get a sensible explanation for the acts of violence that occurred in Lwow during the first days of July, without making it necessary to interpret them as due to the presence of German troops, or even to their participation. This alone makes nonsense of one of the central parts in the verdict of the Soviet Zone Supreme Court, which alleges a planned and organised massacre committed by the Nachtigall unit on the responsibility of Professor Oberländer. Acts of violence, which did occur, were, on the contrary, proved to have been direct mass reactions to the mass killings committed by the Soviets, whose victims had been mainly Ukrainian nationals but also Zionist Jews, all of whom were held in the prisons of Lwow.

Atrocities in the Lwow Prisons After the German Wehrmacht Had Taken Lwow

Another series of questions of fact remains to be answered now: Did members of the German troops, which had in the meantime entered Lwow, join in the atrocities that had already started? And if so, was this the case with units of the Nachtigall Battalion, or with some of its members? With some exceptions that will be mentioned, nobody so far has asserted that members of the German Wehrmacht played any part in the riots and brutalities that took part in public. However, some credible depositions speak of the presence of members of the Wehrmacht within the prisons, and assert that such soldiers took part in maltreating people, in some cases even in a leading rôle.

Under the Rule of Law, these questions have been examined with the greatest care. The investigation was divided up into three separate enquiries for each of the three Lwow prisons.

Statements and depositions of witnesses continually repeat the observation that only civilians, or civilians marked by blue and yellow armbands (militia), were concerned with breaking into houses, arresting, and taking away Jewish inhabitants of Lwow. With the exceptions to be discussed, no witness has reported about Wehrmacht soldiers having committed acts of violence in public. Witnesses' testimony almost exclusively charges civilians with the observed crimes. We are giving some examples: —

Witness T. [20], a former general staff major, states that on July 1 'Jewish inhabitants were chased through the town by civilians.' — Lance-Corporal S. of the *Gebirgsjäger* Regiment No. 98 observed 'civilians chasing Jews through the streets, others pulling Jews from houses, and dragging them to the town lock-up'.

There is a particularly precise statement on this subject by *Hauptwachtmeister* (Staff Sergeant) S. [21] of the Artillery Regiment (Special Purposes) No. 201. Also the former lieutenant, witness S., of the 211st Infantry Regiment, describes 'the two rows of people' through which 'old and young persons, apparently Jews, were chased'. He adds that 'neither individual Wehrmacht soldiers, who were looking on, nor the unit in German uniform which blocked the way to the prisons took any part in the maltreatment of people'. — The Jewish witness, B., states that *units of the Ukrainian militia* were taking Jewish men and women and youngsters from their houses; this is confirmed by witness G., who, together with two other Jews from his house, was taken by the same militia to the Police Station, which was 'occupied solely by Ukrainian militia, among whom there were civilians with blue and yellow stripes round their arms'. — Also the Jewish witness, J., was stopped in the street by a civilian with a blue and yellow band round his arm, who took him away to a group of other Jews, who were already arrested; on the way to the prison 'the civilians tried to mob us and beat us with various instruments'. The guards escorting this procession tried to push back the civilians, but in front of the prison gates, civilians again gave them a beating. Witness mentions, too, that in the gateway leading to the prison rows of German soldiers were posted, who wore field-grey uniforms and steel helmets. 'Those soldiers pushed the masses back, in order to open our way into Brigidki Prison. The soldiers did not take part in any acts of violence against us.'

Only two other witnesses have alleged that raids against Jews were carried out not only by civilians and Ukrainian militia (meaning, civilians with blue and yellow armbands) but that also soldiers in German field-grey uniforms, who spoke Ukrainian, took part in them.

Under the Rule of Law, the investigators have carefully and extensively scrutinized these allegations. As its point of departure, their report takes the following situation [22] : —

> Following the investigations about the course taken by the pogrom against the Jewish group among the inhabitants of Lwow, which lasted from June 30 to July 2, 1941, and which seems to have reached its climax on July 1, 1941, it appears to be certain that atrocities *taking place outside the three prisons* were caused by the Ukrainian civilian population, and the Ukrainian militia, only.

With regard to statements of witnesses, G. [23] and R. [24], that differ from this finding, the report of the investigators says [26] : —

> Statements of witnesses G. and R. point to the conclusion that — at least on June 30, 1941 — individual soldiers of the Nachtigall battalion took part, on their own, in the raids upon Jews in the town. In contrast to all other Jewish witnesses interrogated, there are certain, not unimportant, reasons for not believing these two witnesses to be fully credible.

These reasons for doubting their credibility are based upon the following arguments [26] : —

> Witness R., in the first instance, had answered questions put to him by a journalist in Tel Aviv for the periodical, *Die Tat,* about his experiences in Lwow. The written text of this interview does *not* mention that witness himself was affected by the atrocities of June 30, 1941, and was dragged to Brigidki Prison. According to this text, witness also stated that, at the time, he knew nothing of a certain Nachtigall Battalion, and of an officer of this battalion named Dr. Oberländer. But the same witness later stated in the columns of the Israeli newspaper, *Yedioth Akharanoth,* that Professor Oberländer bears responsibility for the annihilation of the Jews in Lwow during the Second World War. He even declared his readiness to take this statement on his oath as a witness. *However, when he was cross-examined by the Public Prosecutor and the Examining Judge in Bonn, he no longer insisted on this assertion.* His further statement that the two or three soldiers in German

uniform, who assisted at witness's arrest, wore blue and yellow badges on the lapels of their uniform tunics, also does not correspond with the true facts.

When witness G. was interrogated in person by the public prosecutor's office, he made the impression of exaggerating on purpose. His assertion that three quarters of a group of Jews were left lying for dead in the streets, as an effect of the beatings they received, on their way to prison, can hardly be found credible if it is contrasted with the statements of other Jewish witnesses who were themselves affected by the same events. Witness evaded answering all questions regarding the local circumstances of the crimes, and the request for a description of the uniforms worn by the soldiers taking part in them, by stating that he could not remember them. In addition, only after having been repeatedly admonished that it was his duty to tell the truth, witness was prepared to make statements about the events in Brigidki Prison, and about the killings of prisoners kept there, by Russian guards, before German troops took the town.

The investigation also dealt with the assertions made in the book by David Dallin, *German Rule in Russia, 1941—1945,* where it is said that the Nachtigall *Regiment (sic!* Nachtigall was only a battalion) had shown considerable initiative in carrying out purges and pogroms'. The investigators examined the written sources which Mr. Dallin named as evidence, and their conclusion was [27] : —

The author, Mr. Dallin, answered the enquiry what were the foundations for his interpretation [28] by stating that the only sources were the literature named in his footnote. However, when these sources were read it was found that they do not support Mr. Dallin's allegation.

The pamphlet, *German Soldiers See the Soviet Union (Deutsche Soldaten sehen die Sowjetunion),* published in 1941 by Verlag Wilhelm Limpert, contains a chapter, in its Fifth Part, on atrocities in Lwow. This chapter consists of letters written by German soldiers of all military ranks, which report about the writers' experiences in Lwow. They neither mention the Nachtigall unit nor any units composed of Ukrainian volunteers in German uniforms, nor even Bandera's Ukrainian militia. The situation which was of interest for the investigation is only touched upon by one single letter, sent by Corporal Suffner on conditions in Lwow. Suffner says that the surviving Ukrainians, after having seen what happened in the prison, had collected 2,000 Jews, avenged themselves terribly on them, and forced the Jews to carry all the dead from the prison, and to load them on carts.

The *Einsatzgruppenberichte* (Reports of the Special Action Groups), which are also mentioned by Dallin, are those which were put in as evidence in the Nuremberg Trials under the name, *Ereignismeldungen UdSSR des Chefs der Sicherheitspolizei und des SD* (Reports on Events by the Head of the Security Police and the Security Service), which were classified as *Geheime Reichssache* (Top Secret, only for the Use of Members of the Reich Government). Photostatic Copies of these Reports were taken to the files in the present case. The Reports on Events do not contain the slightest hint that their authors even knew of a Nachtigall

Battalion. An *Ereignismeldung* dated July 17, 1941, contains, among other material, only the following note: —

> In Lwow, the population chased some 1,000 Jews from their houses, herded them together, and placed them into the GPU prison, which had been occupied by the Wehrmacht.

No more. — In the same way, an article quoted as a source by Dallin, which had been published by Yarovy Petrov in the magazine, *Sotsialist-itchesky Viestnik* (Socialist Herald; the paper of the exiled Russian Mensheviks in New York), No. 6—7, June/July, 1951 [29], only contains the general statement that, under the rule of the Ukrainian, Bandera, national minorities were subjected to bloody persecutions. Petrov does not lose a single word about the Nachtigall unit.

Did Wehrmacht Soldiers Take Part in the Maltreatment of Jews in the Prisons?

After having settled this point, the investigators under the Rule of Law turned to another question, which had to be clearly separated and distinguished from the foregoing problem: Did their enquiry lead to the result that members of the Wehrmacht took part in doing violence to the Jews concentrated in the prisons?

In some of the cases, the answer to this question is Yes, and from this result the investigation proceeds to the three separate queries: —

Who were the perpetrators of violence,

(a) members of the Nachtigall unit, or

(b) members of other Wehrmacht units, or

(c) members of both?

The investigators incline to the opinion that question (c) has to be answered by Yes, probably. For this decision, a number of factual statements by witnesses can be adduced.

Witness G. [30], made his statement under oath, and the investigators have analysed and evaluated his report. G. speaks of Ukrainian soldiers in German uniform in the courtyard of the NKVD prison. Before entering Lwow, parts of the Nachtigall Battalion had received orders to march upon the prisons in order to liberate, if possible and necessary, prisoners still alive there. The battalion consisted of three companies. First Company was given the order to occupy the cathedral and the palace of the Metropolitan. They did so during the morning hours of June 30. The company stationed guards in the two buildings, and then marched off into prepared billets. There, the men stayed under 'small service' (fatigues) orders. On July 2, the company moved to new billets, and until it continued its march out of Lwow on July 9, it remained there, again under 'small service', for the company only. Third Company was assigned the occupation of the town hall. After having accomplished that, it went on to billets. Apart from supplying men for sentry service, also this unit carried out 'small company service', and was not called upon to carry out other missions. Soldiers whose home was in Lwow were given leave for the day. Therefore, the investigators think it possible that it was Second Company, or part of Second Company, who had to go to the NKVD prison, as ordered, where witness G. saw soldiers in German uniforms. That these soldiers talked in Ukrainian both among themselves and to witness, supports the suspicion that they were members of the Nachtigall Battalion. Nevertheless, this conclusion is not absolutely watertight because — as will be shown later — there were also Ukrainians in the German Field Police, and also Field Police members were seen in the prisons by some witnesses, according to their statements. As a further element of confirmation for their suspicions, the investigators point to the fact that no members of Second Company came forward, as witness (whereas members of First and Third Companies did make statements), but they did not know then that we have now also very important statements of *Feldwebel* (Master Sergeant) K. of Second Company. Through this, at least one platoon of Second Company has been eliminated from the suspicion.

The enquiry then deals separately with the question, to which military unit belonged the five or six German officers who, as witness G. describes, gave the command, which he heard, to chase the Jews through two rows of people to give them a thorough thrashing. On the assumption that the date given — July 1, 1941 — is correct, which is of material importance for the results of the investigations but would require an exceptionally reliable memory, it could be that they were SS officers of the *SD Einsatzgruppe* Staff. This staff of the Special Action Group of the Security Service had arrived in Lwow at 5 o'clock in the morning of July 1. If, however, the man calling for 'making them run the gauntlet' *(Spießrutenlaufen)* by his order was an officer of the Nachtigall unit — perhaps the company commander of Second Company — as the investigators ponder, 'this order might have been prompted by the discovery on June 30 of the body of Shukhevich's brother, who had been shot in prison, as Shukhevich was considered the speaker for the Ukrainians in the Nachtigall Battalion'. — However, further research into the indentities of the persons having taken part in acts of violence against Jews in the NKVD prison is not promising of success, as the investigators state, since the head of *SD Einsatzgruppe,* Dr. Rasch, has died, whilst the names of SS officers on his staff have never been given, and also the name of the company commander of Second Company, Nachtigall Battalion, has remained unknown [31].

As to the soldiers in Wehrmacht uniforms observed by witness J., nothing, according to the results of the investigation, speaks for their having been members of the Nachtigall unit, except their knowledge of the Ukrainian tongue. But this did not require them to be Nachtigall members, and there is evidence to the contrary: The witness emphasized, and photographs put in as evidence show, that these soldiers wore strips round their sleeves with the printed inscription *'Deutsche Wehrmacht'*. This badge was reserved exclusively to members of the German Field Police and Field Gendarmery. These units, too, had always tried to recruit auxiliary staff who knew the country and the local languages, and who were employed as interpreters, some of them in uniform. The German witness, Sch., specifically stated that Brigidki Prison has been occupied by Field Gendarmes. The investigation carried out under the Rule of Law comes to the conclusion that the perpetrators of violence belonged to one of these units. Brutalities committed in Zamartynowka Military Prison could be charged to Wehrmacht members only according to statements made by witness G. His credibility is highly doubtful, and besides, he was contradicted by witness B., who is Jewish, too.

Summing up their answer to the question whether members of the Nachtigall unit or other Wehrmacht soldiers took part in acts of violence against Lwow Jews in the prisons, the investigators say [32] : —

> In conclusion, we can therefore state that in all probability one Ukrainian platoon of Second Company, Nachtigall Battalion, committed acts of violence against the Jews herded together in the NKVD prison, and thus has caused the death of numerous Jews. Against the suspicion that this behaviour was the effect of orders given by the battalion leader, or by higher quarters, there are not only the above-mentioned reasons but also credible statements of the evangelical parson, M., and the Roman Catholic priest, Dr. H. As M. was a member of the *bekennende Kirche* (confessing Church, i. e. the anti-Nazi wing of the German protestants), he had been persecuted by the Nazi authorities. He had been called up for military service as a private soldier, not as an Army chaplain. Only through the efforts of the *Abwehr* chief, Admiral Canaris, he had been sent to the Training Regiment Brandenburg, where he had been directed to become a Paymaster. M. has affirmed credibly that he would have taken upon himself all the consequences (of refusing orders, or protesting) if the Nachtigall Battalion had been given orders to attack the lives of the civilian population — which could not have been hidden from him. The Catholic priest, Dr. H., too, affirmed with convincing power that such orders for action have never been issued.

In view of additional information, which has come to light during the above-mentioned libel suit that is pending, we believe it to be questionable that the finding of the investigators could be maintained even in about the following hypothetical form: — '. . . a Ukrainian platoon of Second Company might have probably joined in the violent treatment offered to the Jews . . .'. Pronouncing judgment in that form suggests that a sub-unit of the Battalion — meaning a group under orders of a single responsible leader — joined in violent rioting against the Jews. Precisely that is improbable. All information available about the discipline kept, and the supervision maintained by officers, in our view, points to a completely different state of affairs. It is, of course, possible that individuals, against orders, but not a sub-unit of the Battalion, may have taken part in some of the brutalities.

MEASURES TAKEN BY 'SECURITY SERVICE SPECIAL ACTION GROUPS' (EINSATZGRUPPE DES SD)

The field of the investigation has been widened, so as to cover also the activities of the so-called Action Groups *(Einsatzgruppen)* which, on orders given by the Head of Security Police and *SD*, Heinrich Himmler, followed closely upon the steps of the fighting units towards the front. Detailed information about their activities is available, and this evidence has been dealt with by the Nuremberg War Crime Trials. It was the Action Group of Dr. Rasch that was dispatched to Lwow. The time of his staff's arrival at Lwow is known exactly — it was five o'clock in the morning on July 1, 1941. The strength of Dr. Rasch's Action 'commandoes' was about 2,000 men; these reached Lwow during July 1 and in the morning of July 2. Because of the discoveries of the corpses in the prisons, Dr. Rasch, reputedly on Hitler's orders, gave orders for retributory action to be taken *against the Jews guilty of the murders in the prisons.* It is the horrid truth that, to-day, we possess proof for the Soviet authorities' responsibility through having given orders for the liquidation of the imprisoned Ukrainians, whereas thousands of Jews, who were innocent of the murders, had to pay with their lives for their alleged guilt. Rasch, with the assistance of the Ukrainian militia, collected a few communists and several thousand Jewish men, and herded them together at a number of collecting points in the town. There most of them had to wait for two days in a sitting position, closely confined in narrow spaces, and then all men over 60, all youths under 15, and craftsmen and labourers were picked out to be spared. The remainder was taken away in groups to be shot, starting on July 5. The *Ereignismeldung* (Report of Events), dated July 16, 1941, of the Head of the Security Police and the *SD* contains documentary proof for this mass murder. It says: 'The Security Police collected about 7,000 Jews in retribution for the inhuman atrocities, and they were shot.' The *Einsatzkommandos* (Action Commandoes) carried out similar mass executions in other towns, and therefore it is not certain whether the number of 7,000 victims refers to Lwow only. After some time, the Action Staff again followed the fighting Army units into the Eastern Ukraine.

Regarding the allegations against Nachtigall, the investigators operating under the Rule of Law are drawing attention to the fact that their findings have not only used the above-quoted evidence but also the Brief for the Prosecution and Judgement in the so-called *Einsatzgruppen* Trial before the Inter-Allied Military Tribunal in Nuremberg. They are summing up [33] :

> Responsibility for this mass murder has been unambiguously fixed. There remains not the slightest suspicion that the Nachtigall Battalion had any part, in any form, in this shedding of blood.

The Murder of the Polish Professors in Lwow

Among the crimes for which the verdict of the East Berlin court placed responsibility upon Professor Oberländer, there was also the murder of a great number of Polish university professors. It is true that the reasons given for the verdict do not pin guilt for this act directly on the professor, but by inference, Oberländer is purposely named as an accessory to the crime in its whole context. The investigation carried out under the Rule of Law again has taken great trouble to clear up this problem. The result is that the Nachtigall unit had absolutely nothing to do with these atrocities. It is possible to reconstruct the events almost completely.

Particularly revealing evidence was given by a Polish witness. He is the Polish Count of B. [34] , now 71 years old and living in Austria. His full testimonial appears in the Appendix. For our present purpose, the following quotation is sufficient: —

Count B. was living under police surveillance. Until Lwow was captured by German troops, he had been working as a bookbinder.

'I was expecting my arrest any day, and every time I heard Russian armed groups coming I went into hiding. It was known to me that the Russians had already drawn up lists for a large deportation scheme, to take suspected people to Siberia. My name also figured on one of these lists.

During the last few days before German troops occupied Lwow, it became widely known that the Russian NKVD had killed the prisoners in a number of prisons. The prisons referred to were mainly Brigidki Prison in Kazimierzowka Street, and the NKVD jail in the bend of Kopernika Street. I must add that the NKVD, in carrying out arrests, had usually employed as helpers the Jewish citizens of Lwow. Each NKVD agent and each Russian policeman were accompanied by a Jew serving them as an interpreter, and they also assisted through their knowledge of the locality.

Whereas the Poles and, later, the Ukrainians, too, did not show a very friendly attitude towards the Russians, the Jews, in the beginning, developed a highly positive inclination towards them. As far as I know, even those Jews who had been employed by the Russians in their offices and service centres were killed by shots in the back of their necks by the NKVD and the Russian Police before these left Lwow. Part of the Jewish population of Lwow left the town for an easterly direction together with the Russian Army.

I myself inspected the prisons where the Russians had killed their prisoners only after the arrival of the German troops. The occasion came when I met again by chance an old acquaintance and good friend of mine, Count Erwein Th.-H., who at that time served as *Rittmeister* (Cavalry captain) of an armoured company. I accompanied him when he went to view the places in the above-named jails where the prisoners had been done to death. After the German capture of Lwow — during the first week, though I cannot remember the exact date — I witnessed the following scene: One day I was visiting the above-mentioned Professor Groer in his flat, in Romanowicza Street. Towards evening, I saw from Professor Groer's balcony a closed police van stopping in front of the house opposite, where a Polish professor of surgery lived. Several men jumped from the van, ran into the house, brought out under arrest all the people living in that house, pushed them into the van, and drove away. The armed men coming with the police van were not German Wehrmacht soldiers. Their uniforms were not those of the German Wehrmacht but different ones which I later learnt were those of the *SD*, or of the Gestapo. After that event, I quickly cut short my visit to Professor Groer, and returned home. The next day I heard that also Professor Groer had been arrested shortly after the incident which I have described. Again, a few days later, I was informed that during this raid, altogether about thirty Professors of Polish nationality had been arrested.

During these first days after the German capture of Lwow, members of the Ukrainian underground movement had formed a Ukrainian militia. These militiamen, at the beginning, wore civilian clothes with a yellow and blue armband as their badge of office. It was only later that they were given uniforms. The militiamen carried out raids against the Jewish inhabitants of Lwow. Once, two militiamen dragged me from a queue, that had formed in front of a food store, and forced me to go with them. Apparently, they thought I was Jewish because I was better dressed than the others in the queue. By accident, we were passing two German Wehrmacht soldiers, and I called to them for help quickly in German. The two chased the Ukrainian militiamen away and took me to my home.

I can say with certainty that German troops, during these first days, showed an absolutely correct behaviour towards the civilian population.

One could almost speak of open fraternization of the Lwow people with the arriving German troops. This situation underwent a change only later, after the arrest and assassination of the Polish professors, and after the measures carried out against the Jewish part of the Lwow population by the *SD* units.'

The situation procuced by these events is sketched as follows by the investigators operating under the Rule of Law: A small *SD* group arrested the Polish professors in the night between July 3 and 4. For this purpose, they were using lists drawn up in advance. A large number of these professors were shot immediately, whilst some professors were released again. The former Polish Prime Minister, Bartel, was executed on July 22 by special order of Hitler. According to the enquiries made under the Rule of Law, there ist no doubt that the raid was carried out by the *SD*. The group detailed for making the arrests did not wear the uniforms of the Wehrmacht, but of the *SD*. Professor Groer himself has stated that he was arrested by the Gestapo. Also the Polish author, Lewitzki, whom we quoted earlier on, describes these events clearly and unambiguously: —

> Most of the arrested persons were taken to the Abrahamowicz Theological Institute, and groups of them were shot in several places between Kadecka and Walecka Streets. There was no cross-examination of any of the arrested men, but the documents, which are certainly genuine, state that the professors were cruelly maltreated immediately after their arrest. The shootings of Polish professors were also mentioned during the Nuremberg trials. Among the documents about the Nuremberg trial published in the Soviet Union in many volumes, the third volume, pp. 43—45, contains precise and detailed reports.
>
> 'Already before the capture of Lwow, Gestapo units, by order of the German government, had drawn up lists of the names of leading intellectuals, who were to be liquidated. Immediately after the capture of Lwow, mass arrests and executions began. The *Gestapo* arrested ...' — then follow the names of 38 Lwow professors.
>
> This document carries particular weight. for nobody ever asserted during the Nuremberg Trial that Professor Oberländer and the Nachtigall Battalion had been responsible for these crimes.

Though this report does not distinguish very clearly the sub-divisions of *Einsatzgruppe C*, and makes a mistake in naming SS Brigade Führer Schöngart, as the man in command of *Einsatzkommando Galizien*, it is correct in its essentials describing the raids for the arrest of the Polish professors, and places responsibility for the murders committed against these persons where it actually belongs.

This particular document deserves to be treated with the greatest attention, because it is the best proof for our thesis, formulated in the very beginning, that crimes of such weight as Moscow and East Berlin try to charge against Professor Oberländer, and against the Nachtigall and Bergmann units, if they had really taken place, would have been dealt with already by the first trials against war criminals after the war. And so it was — the Nuremberg Tribunal did indeed deal with the murders of Polish professors in Lwow. It was the Soviet prosecutor himself, who, in his brief, defined responsibility for these misdeeds as follows: The group of Professors was arrested, according to lists drawn up beforehand, by order of the German government, i. e. on the highest German authority. The Soviet representative also pointed to the instrument which caused their death violence, viz. the Secret State Police (Gestapo).

The Soviet representative for the prosecution, Smirnov, in the Nuremberg Trial sitting of February 15, 1946, quoted from the report of an *Extraordinary State Commission* on *Crimes of the Germans in the Lwow Area* [35], filed under the reference 'Document USSR-6'. This report states: —

> Already before the capture of Lwow, *departments of the Gestapo* had in their hands lists of leading intellectuals, who were to be annihilated. These lists had been compiled by order of the German government. Mass arrests and shootings started immediately after the Germans had taken Lwow. The Gestapo arrested Professor Tadeusz Boi-Djelenski, member of the Association of Soviet Writers, and author of many literary works; Professor Roman Renzki of the Medical Institute; Wladimierz Seradski, Rector of the university and professor of Forensic Medicine; Roman Longchamps de Berrien, Doctor-at-Law, together with his three sons; Professor Tadeusz Ostrowski; Professor Jan Grek; the Professor of Surgery, Henryk Giljarowicz . . .

The list contains three more names of leading representatives of the Lwow intelligentsia, which I leave out, to pass to the next paragraph: —

> Professor Groer of the Medical Institute at Lwow who, by a lucky chance, escaped death, made the following statement to the Special Commission:
>
> 'I was arrested about midnight on July 3, 1941, and pushed into a motor lorry. In the lorry, I found Professors Grek, Boi-Djelenski, and others. We were taken to the Abrahamowicz Theological Institute. Whilst we were led through the corridors, the *Gestapo men* abused and maltreated us; they hit us with their rifle butts, tore us by the hair, and beat us over the head. Somewhat later, I saw the Germans take away five professors from the Abrahamowicz Theological Institute. Four of them carried the bloodspattered body of the son of the famous surgeon, Ruff. The Germans had killed him during their cross-examination. Young Ruff himself was a medical specialist. All these professors then walked away, under escort, towards Kadetskaya Hill. After fifteen or twenty minutes had passed, I heard shots from the direction in which the professors had been led away.'

There is no ambiguity in the description of the authorites which gave orders for the murders, and which carried them out. The report says: 'This lists had been compiled *by order of the German government.* The *instrument for carrying out the order* is also named, it is the *Gestapo.* The documentation compiled at the time by the Soviet State Commission does not contain the slightest hint referring to the Nachtigall unit, or to the person of Professor Oberländer. But now, the new Moscow Commission, and also the *verdict* passed in the Soviet Zone, assert that the self-same group of Polish professors has been allegedly killed by Professor Oberländer and the *Nachtigall Unit.* It is clear that it became worthwhile to discredit Oberländer and his unit after only he had become a member of the Adenauer government.

The reasons given for the judgment passed in the Soviet Zone state:

> During the stay of the unit commanded over by the defendant (it has, however, been proved that Oberländer never commanded the unit), 36 members of the Lwow intelligentsia were shot in the first days of July, 1941, after terrible tortures.' [36]

This is followed by a lengthy list of the professors' names and their positions. After that, the presiding judge read the statement of a witness, Mrs. Kukhar, who, twenty years after the murders, asserted that she could identify Professor Oberländer as the officer whom she saw from the third floor of her house, when he allegedly supervised the killings.

The investigation carried out under the Rule of Law later then examined accusations against Professor Oberländer contained in a number of Eastern publications. Among them was a 'documentation for the press', issued by the Polish Chief Prosecutor's Office, and a so-called Brown Book, *The Truth About Oberländer,* published by one of the many publishing houses in East Berlin. According to the Press Documentation, the Polish professors were killed by a unit of the Secret Field Gendarmery, which was commanded by Professor Oberländer, and the Nachtigall unit, so it is alleged, took part in the execution. Professor Oberländer also appears in this story as the leader of the activities of a strong *Operational Group,* a unit of the Secret Field Police, and troup of *Abwehr II.* The *Operational Group* is said to have been given the task of provoking a military and political revolt in the Western Ukraine. Professor Oberländer, it is said, called himself the direct representative of Admiral Canaris. The investigators proceeding under the Rule of Law make the following comment: The Polish Chief Prosecutor's Office makes its assertions that the Polish professors were arrested by a unit of the Secret Field Police under Professor Oberländer's command *without producing any scrap of evidence or proof.* Also, the Polish report does not say one word about the '*Einsatzgruppen* Trial, where both documentary evidence and admissions of the persons sentenced in that trial provided proof for the activities of the *Einsatzgruppen,* and the *Einsatzkommandos* subordinate to them, all over the occupied Eastern territories, and especially for mass slaughter perpetrated by them against the Jewish citizens of Lwow during the first days of July, 1941.' The investigators under the Rule of Law draw the conclusion that 'the Polish *Documentation* does not attempt to arrive at objective truth but serves only propaganda purposes.' [37]

In this context, the investigators also give their reasons why they did not issue summonses to the persons named in the Documentation and Brown Book as witnesses, for their interrogation in Bonn: 'Interrogation of these witnesses — as in the cases of the Jewish witnesses who now live in Israel — would have been the task of the individual prosecutor dealing with the case and, if their statements were found to be important, of an examining judge. This is the only procedure available for sifting the truth of the evidence offered as proof. However, summonses sent to witnesses resident in the countries of the Eastern Bloc for the purpose of their interrogation by the Public Prosecutor's Office, or by a court of law, in the Federal Republic of Germany, have never been accepted, according to present experience. For example, the Polish witnesses summoned to appear before the court and jury proceeding here against the former concentration camp guards, Sorge and Schubert, have never turned up, although they had written directly to the Public Prosecutor's Office during the preliminary proceedings. Also, as some of the witnesses have testified in the trial before the court in the Soviet Zone against Professor Oberländer, it was not to be expected that they would have been granted permission to travel to the Federal Republic for a second interrogation, especially as all of them are Polish and Russian citizens.' [38]

However, the investigators examined the written statements made by these witnesses, and arrived at the following result: —

> To a large part, these statements, especially those made by members of the intelligentsia who are used to choosing their words with great caution, only confirm materially the conclusions drawn from our enquiries made up to this time.

For example, the evidence offered by the Polish professor, Sokolnicki, that Professor Bartel was not killed on the spot but ten days after the arrest — his actual day of death was July 22, 1941 — refutes the allegation that Professor Oberländer and the Nachtigall Unit committed these crimes. Sokolnicki's statement, on the contrary, points to the Secret State Police having ordered the arrest. The Nachtigall unit was not mentioned in Sokolnicki's statement.

The allegation of Professor Bartel's widow that Bartel was killed by the Nachtigall unit can be disproved by simply referring to the War Diary of the unit. On the day in question, the battalion stood already in front of Vinnitsa.

The written deposition made by the former Director of the Lwow City Library contains descriptions of some incidents during the pogrom, but it never mentions the Nachtigall unit. Professor Koranyi, who mentions a *fascist Special Commando*, can only be interpreted as speaking of the *SD Einsatzkommandos*.

What Mrs. Szkurpellu-Waiser says materially confirms the result of the investigations made in Bonn. The units described by her were obviously groups of Ukrainian militia. Besides, the investigators under the Rule of Law are justifiably doubtful of her credibility because the full text of her statement, which was read to a press conference held in East Berlin on October 22, 1959, contains the assertion that the Soviets on their leaving Lwow before the German occupation had released all their prisoners — which is evidently untrue.

Also the depositions made by Yakub Dentel, Goldwyn Khaim Yehuda, and Zigmunt Tune agree with the results of the enquiries made under the Rule of Law. One of them makes the remark that German soldiers took photographic snapshots of the pogrom in Zamartynow Prison, without joining in the riots. The others confirm that the pogrom was carried out by Ukrainian civilians and Ukrainian militia. Statements by other witnesses, viz. Sulim Seidel, Gorczak, Syrojed, and Welicker, consist only of general accusations against *the Germans* (whom they also call fascists, Hitler fascists, etc.), without making any definite charges against individual units, or the Nachtigall battalion.

FOOTNOTES

The Nachtigall Unit

[1] *Kurzprotokoll* (Abstract from the Minutes of Court Proceedings), p. 11.
[2] Judgment (Verdict), p. 11.
[3] *l. c.*, p. 11.
[4] *l. c., passim.*
[5] *Kurzprotokoll*, p. 82.
[6] see Appendix, p. 198 passim.
[8] *cf.* H. Rothfels, *Bismarck, der Osten und das Reich;* Stuttgart, 1960; p. 23 *passim*, where the author speaks of the 'Prussian kingly socialism' of Möller van den Bruck. Hans Schwarz, the editor of *Der Nahe Osten*, was Möller van den Bruck's pupil.
[9] See Appendix p. 205.
[10] Decision of Chief Public Prosecutor's Office in Bonn to Quash Proceedings, Sept. 9, 1960 (File No. 8 Js 393/60), Nachtigall Case, Folio 3.
[11] *Kurzprotokoll*, p. 68 *passim.*
[12] *l. c.*, p. 77 *passim.*
[13] *l. c.*, p. 83 *passim.*
[14] *l. c.*, p. 87 *passim.*
[15] *l. c.*, p. 89 *passim.*
[16] *l. c.*, p. 91 *passim.*
[17] *l. c.*, p. 96 *passim.*
[18] *l. c.*, p. 99 *passim.*
[19] *l. c.*, p. 101 *passim.*
[20] Decision to Quash etc., Folio 4.
[21] *l. c.*, F. 7.
[22] *l. c.*, F. 8.
[23] *Reichsgesetzblatt* (Reich Law Gazette), 1940, II, p. 4.
[24] Decision to Quash etc., Folio 9.
[25] *l. c.*, F. 10.
[26] *l. c.*, F. 11.
[27] *l. c.*, F. 11 *passim.*
[28] *l. c.*, F. 13.
[29] *l. c.*, F. 13 *passim.*

Eye Witness Reports

[1] Nachtigall Files, Vol. II, Folio 107 *passim.*
[2] *l. c.*, F. 122 *passim.*
[3] *l. c.*, F. 10 *passim.*
[4] *l. c.*, F. 18 *passim.*
[5] *l. c.*, F. 43 *passim.*
[6] *l. c.*, F. 76 *passim.*
[7] *l. c.*, F. 81 *passim.*
[8] *l. c.*, F. 102 *passim.*
[9] In the Collection of Documents, '*Bolschewistische Bluttaten in Lemberg*' (Bolshevik Atrocities in Lwow), Supplement, p. 239, published by the German Foreign Office *(Auswärtiges Amt)*, 1941.
[10] Nachtigall Files, Vol. III, Folpio 145 *passim.*
[11] *l. c.*, F. 126 *passim.*
[12] *l. c.*, F. 136 *passim.*
[13] Nachtigall Files, Vol. II, Folio 127.

[14] Translated passages from *Kultura;* Nachtigall Files, Vol. I, Folio 147 *passim.*
[15] Decision to Quash, etc., Folio 22 *passim.*
[16] Supplementary Nachtigall Files, Supplement 1, Document No. 112.
[17] *l. c.*, Document No. 88.
[18] Nachtigall Files, Vol. III, Folio 145 *passim.*
[19] Supplementary Nachtigall Files, Supplement 1, Document No. 88.
[20] Nachtigall Files, Vol. II, Folio 1 *passim.*
[21] *l. c.*, F. 38.
[22] Decision to Quash, etc., Folio 45.
[23] Nachtigall Files, Vol. II, F. 176 *passim.*
[24] *l. c.*, Vol. III, F. 163, F 168.
[25] Decision to Quash, etc. F. 45 *passim.*
[26] *l. c.*, F. 46 *passim.*
[27] *l. c.*, F. 48.
[28] Supplementary Nachtigall Files, Supplement 1, Document No. 125.
[29] *l. c.*
[30] Nachtigall Files, Vol. III, Folio 136 *passim.*
[31] Strictly speaking, this information is already out of date: Leader of Second Company was Lieutenant Daimm, in his civilian life a teacher. Former members of the Nachtigall Unit do not think him capable of cruelties and acts of violence. This information became available from the libel suit that is still pending, which was mentioned by us. It is very likely that more relevant evidence will be brought to light during this court case.
[32] Decision to Quash, etc., Folio 53.
[33] *l. c.*, F. 58.
[34] Nachtigall Files, Vol. II, F. 97 *passim,* see also enclosures.
[35] Judgment (verdict), p. 12.
[36] Decision to Quash, etc.
[37] *l. c.*, Folio 63.
[38] *l. c.*, F. 64.
[39] *l. c.*, F. 64 *passim.*

III

THE BERGMANN UNIT

Upon further information having been laid against Professor Oberländer by the *VVN*[1] *(Vereinigung der Verfolgten des Naziregimes,* i. e. Association of Victims of Nazi Persecution), the Chief Public Prosecutor *(Oberstaatsanwalt)* at the Bonn District Court *(Landgericht)* started a second investigation against him. Information laid maintains that the Bergmann Battalion, under Professor Oberländer's command, and under his orders, Oberländer taking part himself in the crimes, committed numerous murders and acts of pillage in the Northern Caucasus betwen September, 1942, and January, 1943. *VVN* made its application for a criminal investigation within twenty-four hours after a Moscow press conference held on April 5, that is, on April 6, 1960.

ASSERTIONS MADE BY THE SOVIETS AND IN THE SOVIET ZONE OF GERMANY

The *VVN* accusations reproduce information issued during a press conference, which was held in Moscow on April 5, 1960, for the purpose of publicizing the *findings* of a *Soviet Special Commission.* On the same day, *Pravda* printed a report, from which the following is a quotation: —

> In the autumn of 1941, Oberländer was appointed commanding officer of a special battalion, which was named Bergmann, and which was recruited from prisoners of war. Oberländer and his close collaborators, in violation of international agreements and principles of warfare, travelled through prisoner-of-war camps and blackmailed people, whose resistance had been broken by hunger and torture, into joining the Bergmann Battalion, and later into taking the oath on Hitler. It was Oberländer who, in his own person, administered the oath. The period between September 1942 and January 1943, when the Bergmann Battalion was stationed in the Northern Caucasus, had as its main features acts of violence against the local population, pilfering, and atrocities. One of the cruellest bandits was Beshtokov, leader of a sub-unit in the Bergmann Battalion, who acted as a veritable robber in the surroundings of Naltchik. Beshtokov's aides, upon Oberländer's instructions, shot people, robbed them, burned down houses, and sent the pilfered valuables to Germany. A large part of the thieves' booty was intended for Oberländer's personal use. During the second half of October, 1942, Oberländer, with his own hand, shot fifteen imprisoned Soviet citizens in the Piatigorsk jail. The

Extraordinary Commission resolved that it has received proof for Oberländer having committed crimes against peace, war crimes, and crimes against humanity.

The Prosecution before the Supreme Court of the Soviet Zone of Germany alleges [3] : —

> To the same purpose Oberländer, under his own political and military responsibility, set up, trained, and used in the field the Bergmann Battalion. In crude violation of all the principles and rules of International Law, Oberländer blackmailed the prisoners of war, who were kept under inhuman conditions in fascist prisoner-of-war camps, into taking up arms against their own troops and compatriots. Having caused, at Mittenwald Training Camp, the execution by shooting of at least seven members of the battalion, and the transfer of another 50 members of that unit to fascist concentration camps, Oberländer carried out with the Bergmann Battalion so-called punitive expeditions in the Caucasus. During the period from August 1942 to the spring of 1943, the Bergmann Battalion, on Oberländer's orders, committed large-scale atrocities, pillaging, acts of violence, and murders against the defenceless Soviet civilian population, and against prisoners of war.

The *Kurzprotokoll* (Abstract of Minutes of Court Proceedings) [4] adds the following details: —

> The Brief for the Prosecution goes on to discuss the violations of International Law, which consisted in blackmailing Soviet prisoners of war, through the threat of letting them die from hunger, into volunteering for the Bergmann unit. The Brief then describes their training, the assassination of the patriotic Tsiklauri group, the killing of 15 prisoners in the Piatigorsk jail under the personal leadership of Oberländer, and the *scorched earth* tactics applied by the Bergmann Special Unit during its retreat form the Northern Caucasus.

Later, in the same Minutes [5] , we read the following allegations: —

> Both the shootings caused by Oberländer among members of the Bergmann Regiment *(sic!)*, who justifiably refused to commit crimes against their compatriots, and the deportations of others, also the *punitive expeditions* against the defenceless Soviet civilian population, represent acts of organised murder.

If these accusations can be proved, they represent several groups of different crimes. Among the first group of alleged crimes, we find the assertion that the Bergmann unit could only be formed by exerting inhuman blackmail on captured Caucasians. In this context, it is also stated that prisoners who were not physically fit were murdered on Oberländer's direct orders, or under his responsibility. If that could be proved, this would indeed have been severe violations of the status of prisoners of war, who are protected by International Law.

During the trial held in the Soviet Zone, a number of witnesses were heard, making statements about the blackmailing allegations of the prosecution (prisoners from the Caucasus having been press-ganged into the Bergmann unit). For example, witness Shagulidse [6] stated: —

Many Caucasians were not willing to serve the Hitler people. However, the situation created was such that we could not get out of that impasse.

Witness Okroporidse [7] followed with: —

Here, in those camps (where, it is alleged, the prisoners were blackmailed), conditions were created artificially, in which people had only one choice — to serve the enemy, or to die from hunger.

Witness Aleskerov [8] gave a detailed description of the procedure, allegedly applied on the instructions of Professor Oberländer, which served to obtain voluntary registrations from prisoners in the camps immediately behind the front in the Caucasus. This description has been quoted extensively in the Judgment, which accepted it as proved. Briefly, this procedure allegedly starved the prisoners for five days by giving them practically nothing to eat. After the five days, they were allegedly given somewhat improved rations, and again after that, blackmail was used in the form of a promise of even better food, which usually resulted in the victims volunteering for service. In the reasons given by the Soviet Zone court for its verdict, we read [9] : —

As established by the Secret Report of *SD III BIP* of November 11, 1943, which has been quoted already, defendant was 'employed, after his Galician activities, for some time by *OKW Abwehr II.* After this he led a battalion composed of foreign nationals (Bergmann Unit)..., which was under the general command of the General of Eastern Troops.'

In carrying out his mission, defendant, together with *Sonderführer* (Special Mission Officer) von Kutzschenbach, visited prisoner-of-war camps in the Soviet Union and press-ganged into military units in violation of all the rules of International Law, members of the Soviet Forces.

In the prisoner-of-war camps, the prisoners were treated inhumanly, in crude violation of all the rules of International Law. Famine was raging in the camps, and hundreds died from hunger and epidemics. Defendant had caused this situation, and he profited from it for his purpose of collecting volunteeres for the Special Bergmann Formation. Generally, selected prisoners of war were transferred to a camp near Sagan, normally used for keeping French prisoners of war, where they were put in French uniforms. In December, 1941, they were then taken to the Neuhammer camp, where the Special Unit Bergmann was set up and trained. The officer commanding this unit, which had Field Post No. 19019, was the defendant, Oberländer. By order of the defendant, witnesses Aleskerov and Okroporidse, among others, were detailed to *collect volunteers* from among the other prisoners of war.

Volunteers whose health made them unfit for service were liquidated, in order to keep secret the existence and national derivation of the special unit, which was carefully camouflaged. It has been established that, in one case, thirty men were caused to be shot by the defendant, and in a second case, seven sick prisoners of war were killed by injections in the Isolation Ward.

Defendant made speeches to the battalion, declaring that the prisoners of war belonged to the effectives of the German Army, and therefore had to fight for the Germans. Those who refused to do so were liable to die from famine.

He forbade them to leave camp, and if anybody asked them about their country of origin, he gave them orders to say that they were Spaniards or Yugoslavs. This was another expedient for camouflaging the character of the unit, which had been constituted in breach of International Law.

This goes on as follows: —

In November, 1942, witness Okroporidse was given direct orders by the defendant to go with Alim Barashvili to the camps of Mosdok, Georgievsk, Prokhladono, Piatigorsk, and Naltchik for selecting men for replacement purposes. It was particularly in these camps that the defendant, Oberländer, intentionally created appalling conditions for the prisoners of war, in order to break their resistance, and to cause them to join the German Army.

Defendant gave instructions to supply only starvation diet to the prisoners of war; they were given nothing but linseed cake and uncooked corn grains for four or five days. Only after that, the appeal for volunteers was made. The first group of prisoners of war was selected and housed in a separate room. Whilst the other, hungry men saw it, they were issued with slightly better rations, and some tobacco. After that had been done, defendant gave orders to stop the selection for some time. When, a few days later, selection was resumed, the prisoners of war had only the alternative to die from hunger or to join the German Army. The state of the prisoners at that time was described by witness Mukhashavari as follows: 'We had lost all human dignity and were prepared to do anything people asked from us for a crust of bread.'

Defendant also issued instructions to beat to death three prisoners whom he believed to be Jewish.

The court never attempted to investigate the questions whether there might not have been also different motivations causing the prisoners of war to decide that they would join the fight against the Soviet Union. But a Communist court is apparently congenitally incapable of conceiving, or even discussing, such a hypothesis, because its principal task is to give legal support to the political programme of the supreme authority of the State.

On the other hand, any impartial investigation will always have to start from the fact that, since the time when modern consciousness of nationality was born, nationally mixed states have invariably experienced the tensions arising from national conflicts within their frontiers, so that larger or smaller national groups will be prepared to fight against their official overlords in cases of war.

Well-known examples for this fact from the First World War were the Polish Legions which, under the leadership of Pilsudski, fought against their sovereign, the Russian Tsar, and his state, and also the Czech Legions who took up arms against their emperor, the ruler of Austria and Hungary. The possibility that similar formations were born during the Second World War, and opposed Soviet Russia, must not even be considered by a court in the Soviet Zone, nor may it be examined by suitable and thorough methods of investigation.

It is only natural that an examination of facts under the Rule of Law has to take as its starting point actual conditions in the Caucasus at the time when the alleged crimes were committed. It has to analyse the nationality problem there, and thus to create the only objective basis available for evaluating the motives that drove Caucasians into the ranks of the fighters against the Soviet Union.

CRIMINAL INVESTIGATIONS UNDER THE RULE OF LAW

Volunteers or Caucasians Pressed into Service?

The verdict produced by the court of the Soviet Zone alleges that Caucasian prisoners of war were shanghaied into the German unit, because the application of a number of inhuman pressures drove them to join up against their will. It is obvious that it was the duty of the investigators under the Rule of Law to examine the problem why Caucasian prisoners of war were willing to fight against the Soviet Union on the basis of an enquiry into the political structure and conditions of the Caucasus. The investigators say [10] : —

> Both the fiercely independent and nationalistic nations of the Northern Caucasus, which were split into many separate tribes, and the larger Transcaucasian peoples — Georgians, Azerbeidjanis, and Armenians — had resisted the advance of the Great Russian Tsarist Empire in a long and tough, but eventually futile, struggle since the eighteenth century. Not before 1864 did the Russians succeed in subduing the last independent area of the Circassians in the Western Caucasus, so that it could be incorparated in the Tsarist Empire. The Caucasian nations' indomitable will to regain their freedom, however, reemerged after Russia's breakdown in the First World War, and many independence movements led to the formation of independent national states both in the North Caucasus and in Transcaucasia. These states received international recognition, but their independence could be defended for a few years only. The Soviet Army subjugated the entire Caucasus again in 1921, and the newly-formed states were incorporated in the Union of Socialist Soviet Republics. But a large part of the Caucasian population remained anti-Russian and hostile to the Soviets in their feelings, and these were reinforced especially by the forced collectivization of agriculture and by the anti-religious attitude of the Soviets. During the decade after 1921, this led to a number of revolts, but they were quickly and cruelly put down by the Soviet Power. Latent hostility against the Soviet was still alive when the German-Soviet war broke out.

This hostile attitude of the Caucasian nations is a result of their earlier and recent history. They are both anti-Soviet and anti-Russian, and this was the factual basis that made it possible to form Caucasian units in the

German Wehrmacht. Without this basis, such attempts would not have made sense, but as these feelings existed, they go far to explain why Caucasian prisoners of war were willing to join in. The investigators under the Rule of Law continue [11] : —

> *OKW Abwehr* and the officer in command of the Special Unit Bergmann based their intentions upon the political situation in the Caucasus, which has been described. Its mere existence was planned to contribute to the advancing German Army being welcomed by the Caucasian nations as their liberator from the Soviet regime, which might enable them to regain their political independence. It was intended to throw airborne troops from the unit behind the enemy lines, to encourage revolts against the Soviet regime among their compatriots, so that the fighting morale of the Soviet troops would be weakened. After completion fo their mission, specially gifted members of the unit were to be selected to form the cadres for setting up autonomous administrations for the individual Caucasian nations.

Professor Oberländer had a different position in the Bergmann unit, as against his mission in Nachtigall, for he was indeed its commanding officer. He had been promoted in the field from First Lieutenant to Captain. The creation of the unit, and the tasks assigned to it, were his own idea. These facts are important for us, if we try to understand the frequent remarks in German witnesses' statements that Oberländer was far from treating Caucasians brutally, or worse than the German members of the unit — as is alleged by the Soviets and by witnesses brought forward by them. On the contrary, he was inclined to excuse the Causasians even some slight violations of discipline.

From the general attitude of the Caucasian prisoners that had been generated by the history and politics of their native lands, it is easy to understand that many of them were inclined to support the German plans outlined above. But this also implies that — quite independently of the highly questionable value of soldiers pressed into service — there was not the slightest reason for forcing people into service by blackmail. The description of the situation given by the investigators under the Rule of Law presents a convincing picture of the propaganda attracting people to the Bergmann unit, which flatly contradicts the statements made by the Soviet Zone court, namely [12] : —

> Recruitment of volunteers was carried out at a large prisoner-of-war camp near Poltava. Persons subjected to recruitment propaganda were North and South Caucasian Red Army deserters and prisoners, who were approached by other Caucasians entrusted with this mission. The response to their approach was so huge that the selection had to be extremely strict.
>
> About 700, relatively young, Caucasians were chosen, who were completely fit for military service. The condition was, of course, that during the interviews given to them they made the impression of being political opponents of the Soviet regime. The Caucasian volunteers who had been picked out were first billetted on kolkhozes round Poltava, to allow them to recuperate from the

rigours of life in the prisoner-of-war camp. After about three weeks, towards the end of October, 1941, they were taken by rail to the military camp at Stranz near Neuhammer, Silesia, for training. At Stranz, they met a small panel of German training staff, most of whom knew one or more Slav languages. The Caucasian soldiers were first issued with captured French uniforms, but after a very short time received German army dress. They underwent infantry fighting drill. Altogether, five companies were formed, and the volunteers were sorted out according to their tribal allegiance and nationality, and sent to separate companies.

In a different context, it is stated [13] : —

It has already been established in Paragraph I that Dr. Oberländer and his collaborator, *Sonderführer* Kutzschenbach, during their propaganda visit to the prisoner-of-war camp near Poltava, produced such a run of volunteers from the ranks of Caucasian nationalities for the planned new unit *that it was necessary to proceed selectively.* Former Caucasian members of the Bergmann Battalion, G., H., Dr. K.-S., G., and B., testified unanimously and convincingly that, in order to obtain volunteers, not the slightest pressure was ever applied. As these witnesses stated, in the absolutely overwhelming number of cases, volunteers came forward because they felt impelled by the above-mentioned, political motive — the will to liberate their homeland from the Soviet regime, and the desire to establish independent national states — whereas in the balance of the cases the hope to be able to leave the prisoner-of-war camp, and thus to improve their personal situation greatly, will also have been a contributory cause for their decision.

All the former German members of the unit, too, testified without exception: That most of them were in close contact with the Caucasian volunteers from 1942 to the end of the war; that, after overcoming the linguistic barriers, they enjoyed extremely good personal relations with them; that in their talks with the Caucasian soldiers, there was never any doubt that the Caucasians had decided without any pressure having been used towards them, entirely out of their own free will, to join in the armed fight on the German side. The former German members of the Bergmann unit credibly pointed out that the German men in the unit represented only a skeleton staff (the ratio in the fighting companies having been about 1:8), so that front service would have been utterly impossible for units consisting of prisoners of war who had been pressed into service by force. Both during the fighting of the companies in the Caucasus, where positional warfare was waged by widely thinned-out covering units, as already described, and especially during the long drawn-out retreat to the Crimea, the Caucasian members of the Bergmann Special Unit could have easily deserted to the Soviet troops, or disappeared and submerged in the countryside, which for many of them was their actual home district. All the survivors of the Bergmann Special Unit agree that only a minimum of Caucasian soldiers got lost as stragglers, whereas the remainder kept faith to the unit up to the moment of capitulation, inspite of the severe military setbacks and defeats of the German armies, which can be accepted as incontrovertible proof that the assertion is untrue about Caucasian prisoners of war having been pressed into service on the German side.

Moreover, it was essential for the military and political morale of that Caucasian unit that its members had taken a military oath of fealty, which definitely *did not contain on oath binding them to the person of Adolf Hitler.* The formula had been worked out and agreed upon with Admiral Canaris; the omission of the passage obliging the soldiers to keep faith with Hitler proves that the Bergmann unit was *politically autonomous.* The investigators specially underline the fact that the unit was equipped with the same arms as any corresponding German unit. That, too, proves that its leaders had confidence in their men. If the men had been pressed into service — under such conditions as Prosecution and Verdict allege — it would have been militarily irresponsible to arm a shanghaied gang too well, and if the unit in fact had been a product of the press-gang, it is very unlikely that it would have ever been armed so well [14] : —

> The Group was armed in the same way as a German infantry battalion, according to the then most up-to-date requirements. One platoon, called „S-Platoon", was additionally trained as pioneers, to be used for special missions of breaking enemy resistance nests. S-Platoon therefore received additional equipment. Parts of Fifth Company has also been trained as parachutists. Caucasian members of the Bergmann unit had the same rights and duties as German soldiers. Caucasians who had been officers or n.c.o.'s in the Soviet forces were later, during fighting activities, used as group and platoon leaders and granted the apposite badges of German n.c.o. rank. A number of Caucasian soldiers, who had been officers before, were sent to a German officer training school and given officers' commissions later during the war. They received these commissions for service with the Bergmann unit.

Such political and psychological conditions make it easy to understand, possibly more than anything else, the later successes in calling for volunteers in the Northern Caucasus. For the simple Caucasian soldier, the presence of the German Army in the North Caucasus, on the gateway to Transcaucasia, must have been a powerful motive for joining up with this apparently victorious military force. The later drives for volunteers in the North Caucasus have been treated by the investigators under the Rule of Law, in the paragraphs dealing with military actions of the Bergmann Unit in the Caucasus, as follows [15] : —

> Captain Dr. Oberländer was freed from front service, and he very soon started to increase the strength of the battalion, with a view to transforming it into a regiment. The reason was, that in the sections of the front held by the companies under his command, an exceptionally large number of Caucasian deserters came over. Most of the deserters declared their readiness on the spot to take fighting service on the German side. In such cases, they were not handed over to the division for channelling them into p.o.w. camps but were kept back as replacements for the Bergmann unit. In addition, Dr. Oberländer initiated a recruiting drive in the p.o.w. camps immediately behind the front, which contained a high number of Caucasian deserters and p.o.w.'s. In this, he was assisted by Caucasian officers from the Bergmann Special Unit. The number of men who volunteered

was so large that, inspite of strict selection, eight more companies were formed until December, 1942, and also two cavalry squadrons. The newly enlisted Caucasians were assembled on a state farm near Ruski, organised in companies, and battle-trained by a small German training staff. The two cavalry squadrons, one of them led by the Georgian exile, Gabliani, were immediately thrown into action in the Kalmyk Steppe, to carry out operations against advancing Soviet raiding parties, but the other eight new companies were not completely ready for action when the retreat began. The Bergmann Special Unit had, at that time, reached a strength of altogether 2,800 men.

Inhuman Treatment of Prisoners of War?

The Prosecution and Judgment charge Professor Oberländer with the extremely grave responsibility for having caused, through his own initiative, the inhuman treatment of prisoners of war, both when setting up his unit, and during the drive for its enlargement in the p.o.w. camps behind the Caucasus front, so that he could be held responsible for it. The Bonn investigators have tried to clear up also charge by examining the entire problem of prisoners of war and p.o.w. camps in the rear areas behind the eastern front. Their method under the Rule of Law endeavours to sift the true from the false [16] : —

It is a historical fact that, during the first year of the war between Germany and the Soviet Union especially, conditions offensive to human dignity prevailed in the large p.o.w. camps in the rear areas of the eastern front, but also on the soil of the Reich, so that a high proportion of the prisoners died through hunger and epidemics raging in the camps. One of the reasons for this state of affairs was that the encircling battles of the first months of the war resulted in immense and unexpected numbers of Soviet soldiers being taken prisoner — over 3,500,000 until December, 1941. Looking after them, and feeding them properly, even if the responsible authorities in the area of operations and the staffs of the individual armies had harboured the best of intentions, would have created almost unmanageable problems of supply. The German armies advancing through the wide spaces of Russia were themselves in great difficulties to secure sufficient supplies for the fighting troops. The inevitable effect was that the army leaders treated the task of supplying prisoners of war as a problem of the second rank only. On the other hand, it cannot be gainsaid that the creed adopted and disseminated by the National Socialist leadership that Soviet men are subhuman, so that Hitler ordered the *OKW* (Wehrmacht High Command) to issue instructions on the treatment of Soviet p.o.w's (so-called 'Commissar orders'), contributed decisively to killing any possible initiative towards an improvement of conditions in the camps, and encouraged bad treatment and shootings, which became the order of the day in case of the slightest offence against camp regulations. Contrary to this attitude of the leaders of the Reich and *OKW* in the question of treatment of Russian prisoners of war, Admiral Canaris, as head of *Abwehr,* who controlled the Bergmann Unit, instructed General Lahusen to point out to a conference of the *Allgemeine Wehrmachtsamt* (General Office of the Forces), which had controlling authority in all p. o. w. questions, that the *OKW* were in breach of International Law. This intercession proved in vain as was Admiral Canaris' personal and impassioned protest against all shootings and maltreatment of prisoners.

Regarding this point, the investigators under the Rule of Law have reached the following, clear result [17] : —

> It has been proved to be untrue that, as has been alleged, Dr. Oberländer caused himself horrible conditions of life in the p.o.w. camps situated in the rear areas of the eastern front, especially in the Caucasus;

and also [18] : —

> In the context of these facts, the assertion that the then First Lieutenant, Dr. Oberländer, of *OKW-Abwehr II, himself created* the conditions, as they existed in the p.o.w. camps, is completely insupportable, especially as Oberländer was never at any time officially in charge of organising and managing p.o.w. camps.

Besides, the good relationship and mutual confidence between the officer in command and all the Caucasians of the Bergmann Unit would have been unthinkable, had Oberländer been really guilty of such behaviour.

The Truth About the Principles of Treating Prisoners and Runaways Who Went Over to the Bergmann Unit

That the reasons given for the *Verdict* are those characteristic of a show trial in this particular point, too, has been made clear beyond all doubt by the factual examination of the case under the Rule of Law. Evidence produced by the Accused, which has been thoroughly examined and evaluated by the investigators under the Rule of Law, has shown convincingly that the position was the exact reverse. The investigation shows that Professor Oberländer, 'on the contrary, not only disapproved strongly of inhuman treatment of the Russian prisoners of war but did everything in his power to improve conditions.' The Report of the investigators quotes passages from letters written by Professor Oberländer from the front to his wife, as follows —

Letter dated September 9, 1942 [19] : —

> There are great difficulties over the treatment of deserters and prisoners, but only well-treated prisoners will make men for us. I let myself in for a lot of trouble by demanding good treatment, but my Superior Authority is behind me in this. Yesterday, a staff officer went for me personally, but in the matter under discussion, I almost made him see reason. Our men will go through

hell for us, because they know that we have a heart for them. This means, of course, that we have to make their cause our own everywhere.

(Footnote: 'Superior Authority' means *OKW-Abwehr Berlin II).*

Letter, dated October 3, 1942 [20] : —

If I consider that hundreds of thousands of Caucasian, whose bodies were physically beaten in German prison camps, have returned to their homeland eager for revenge, we certainly have not made good propaganda. In the Bergmann Battalion, the position is exactly the reverse, but that is like a needle in a haystack. We have to make good many evil things. Unfortunately, new mistakes are made again and again. We must try to live out of our depths against shallowness, which expands more and more to-day and covers a large surface. Actually, the task set me here is attractive, and I enjoy the trust that all nationalities put in me. Without trust, such units cannot be led... My chief worry is the unreasonable treatment meted out to prisoners, and in some cases also to the civilian population. Caucasian deserters are being beaten up and kicked in the camps by Ukrainian auxiliary police. I have now dispatched confidential agents of mine to all camps, one to each camp, in order to make a clean sweep of these conditions.

Letter, dated February 7, 1943 [21] : —

... During the last few days, I have again received proof of some cases of maltreating prisoners by German service men, and I have reported them. These reports are not very welcome but one has to admit that I am right. At some future date, I must show you the notes I have made during these weeks. This fight, which I am waging harms my official record, but the inner man reaps much more profit from it, and in addition to my military achievements, I am sure my methods contribute to eventual success. Two officers have already been compelled to look for assignments elsewhere...

The report of the Bonn investigation has assessed these letters convincingly as follows: '... these letters... have a particularly high value as evidence, because they were written on the spot, under the influence of the contemporary situation, when there was not the slightest reason for the writer to fish for cover against self-incrimination, or to invent alleged facts to paint his rôle in a favourable light. [22]

Additional Charges in Individual Cases

The Prosecutor in the Soviet Zone alleges, and the Verdict of the Soviet Zone court follows him in accepting as proved, that by order of Professor Oberländer all Caucasians who were not fit for military service were killed for reasons of camouflage, among them three Jewish prisoners of war. The result of the investigation under the Rule of Law regarding this charge is: —

For these assertions, as for many other ones, not the slightest reason could be found to accept them as probable.

On the one hand, not a single one of the ex-members of the unit, who were interrogated, was able to give any indication that such a crime was committed. As the investigators point in their comment, such misdeeds could not have remained hidden from them.

On the other hand, medical care for the members of the unit was not the job of a German but of the Caucasian, Dr. K.-S., who was a former staff medical officer in the Soviet Army. It is stated in the investigators' report that the Caucasian medical officer would have, withaut doubt, resisted any order for the liquidation of his own unfit compatriots.

During the examination of the accusations levelled against the Nachtigall unit, it struck the investigators that the Soviets and the authorities in the Soviet Zone frequently used the tactical ruse to charge the Nachtigall unit with crimes which had, in fact, been committed, but by other organizations or authorities (both non-German and German ones). The same method of forging, or distorting evidence has been applied to the Bergmann Unit. The investigators under the Rule of Law suggest that the factual basis for these charges against Bergmann was the so-called *Zeppelin Action,* which formed the subject of evidence and proceedings in the so-called Wilhelmstrasse trial. In the same way as in the case of the Lwow *Einsatzkommando, Zeppelin* was a project designed and carried out by the Reich Chief Security Head Office *(Reichssicherheitshauptamt).* Neither the Bergmann Unit nor Professor Oberländer had anything to do with this project, which was the exclusive domain of the *SD* (Security Service, i. e. the Gestapo). The official Report says [23] : —

> It was the CZ Department of the *Reichssicherheitshauptamt* which planned and carried out the *Zeppelin* Project. This was intended to lead to the selection of Russian civilians and of inmates of p.o.w. camps who might be suitable, through their anti-Communism, and through their personal talents, for training as agents, who were eventually to be sent to the Soviet rear. The Allied Court was supplied with documents (Ref. No.'s NO 4724, 5444, 5446, NG 5220—23, 4720) to show that such agents, if their fitness for service became questionable through serious illness, were transferred for their liquidation to a concentration camp (the annihilation camp of Auschwitz-Oswiecim) by the *SD* officials responsible for the *Zeppelin* Project.
>
> The defendant, Professor Oberländer, however, was at no time employed in carrying out the *Zeppelin* Project, whose execution was the exclusive responsibility of *SD* and SS agencies. This fact has been specially confirmed by the C.I.D. officer, Heimbach, who is now held in a remand prison. Heimbach had been a member of *Einsatzgruppe* (Special Action Group) D and was transferred from there to the *Zeppelin* Project.

Under the Rule of Law, further charges and allegations became the subjects of examination: The Prosecution and Judgment in the Soviet

Zone state that Professor Oberländer was *much-feared* and *brutal*, and that he wielded *great power*. Even German military officers allegedly did not dare to contradict him, and for the slightest infraction of discipline or regulations, Oberländer inflicted harsh punishments. The Report of the investigators under the Rule of Law discusses these allegations under two different and important aspects. The investigators emphasize particularly that the alleged traits of Oberländer's character do not constitute criminal actions, so that allegations of this kind need not be examined. However, they unterline their importance because such qualities, if proved, may assume significance in regard to the probability and credibility of further crimes with which Oberländer was charged, namely the alleged injuries done by him to the health, honour, or lives of Caucasian members of his battalion. The same applies to the alleged, sadistic cruelties with which Professor Oberländer has been charged against Caucasian civilians, in particular against a Soviet woman teacher. This subject receives the following treatment in the Report [24] : —

> ... All the former German and Caucasian soldiers of the Bergmann unit, who could be interrogated, unanimously, and without any exception, stated that this evaluation of Dr. Oberländer's personality is contrary to the facts. According to their statements, Dr. Oberländer, in his work as leader of the Bergmann Unit, did not behave in any different way as other German troop leaders did whose behaviour was good. During training of the unit at Neuhammer and Luttensee, Oberländer hardly ever interfered with service duties, and at the Caucasian front, too, he turned up only occasionally to inspect the five companies who were in action under orders of other Army units. He used his disciplinary powers justly. All available statements repeatedly underline the extremely strong confidence of the Caucasian volunteers in Oberländer. The reason was that he treated them on an absolutely equal footing with the German soldiers of the battalion, and that his excellent knowledge of languages and the land caused him to pay heed to the special characteristics of the various tribes, and to their religious customs (the majority of the Caucasians were Moslems). Through his frequent addresses to German n.c.o.'s and men, he gave the Germans among his subordinates ample information about the geography and the people of the Caucasus, as well as about political conditions there, and he always insisted upon treatment of the volunteers as soldiers with equal rights, not as second-class persons. Some of the German subordinate leaders even testified that among them, there was temporary dissatisfaction, because they felt that Dr. Oberländer showed preference to the Caucasian soldiers in some respects. In some cases of German subordinates of his treating Caucasian volunteers badly, Dr. Oberländer immediately used his disciplinary powers of punishment, or insisted on the transfer of the offenders to other units.

The Tsiklauri Case

The verdict of the Soviet Zone court also accepts the allegations in the so-called *Tsiklauri Case*. This story has the following background:

During the time when the Bergmann Unit was trained in mountain warfare at Mittenwald, the Leader of the Battalion received information that a small communist cell had been formed in the unit and was led by the former Soviet captain, Tsiklauri. During a visit to Berlin for sightseeing purposes, the entire cell was arrested. As all its members had already taken the military oath — not on Hitler's person but as members of the German Wehrmacht — they were dealt with by a German court-martial in the normal way. The proceedings were taken by a Senate of the Reich Court-Martial, which sat at Garmisch-Partenkirchen. The court of the Soviet Zone interprets this as a case of exceptionally cruel persecution of Soviet patriots, during which Professor Oberländer acted as assistant to the prosecution and as a vile calumniator. The Report made by the investigators under the Rule of Law offers the following comment [25] : —

In the Tsiklauri case, we have come to the following conclusions: —

The Georgian, Tsiklauri, formerly a captain in the Soviet Forces, had not signed on as a volunteer in the p.o.w. camp near Poltava, but a subordinate section of *OKW-Abwehr II* had detailed him for service with the Bergmann Unit. After this unit had already been transferred to Luttensee near Mittenwald. Tsiklauri who had perhaps been infiltrated by the Soviets as their agent, or who had always been a convinced communist, organized a small group consisting of some dissatisfied Georgian volunteers. This group planned, when the battalion reached the Caucasus, where it was soon to be used for front duties, to kill the small German skeleton staff, and to use this opportunity for causing the entire unit, if possible, to desert to the Soviet Army. When Tsiklauri tried to enlarge his group, other Georgian volunteers were approached with a view to joining it, and these new recruits to the conspiracy informed on the conspirators to the leaders of the battalion. Dr. Oberländer used the official way to channel his report with his findings to *OKW-Abwehr II* (Counter-Espionage). In order to avoid any sensational incident, a large group of Caucasian soldiers was invited to Berlin for sightseeing at the beginning of June, 1942. The Tsiklauri group was arrested in Berlin on June 6, 1942. Dr. Oberländer had nothing to do with the ensuing investigations and cross-examination by court-martial. Judgment on the accused was passed by a Senate of the Reich Court-Martial, which sat for the purpose in the garrison quarters of the *Gebirgsjäger* Division stationed at Garmisch-Partenkirchen. Of the defendants, seven were sentenced to death, among them the group leader, Tsiklauri, and some others received imprisonment. The court-martial sat for twelve days, and Dr. Oberländer did not act during the proceedings either as prosecutor or as judge. The only part he had to play, according to his diary of 1942, which has been taken to the files as an original document, was that of a witness in court. He testified on June 27, 1942. He did not attend when judgment was passed. The only member of the Bergmann Battalion who was present during the entire court proceedings was the German soldier, H. von T., who had been born in Reval (Tallinn), and who acted as interpreter to the court. This soldier has confirmed that the proceedings were those of a normal court-martial. The Files of the Court-Martial in the Tsiklauri case have not been available. The Federal Archives at Kornelimünster stated that it holds only the Court Martial Files of the Fleet, whereas most

Court Martial Files of the Army were destroyed, and the remainder is not in the Federal Republic.

As Tsiklauri and the other defendants who were sentenced had already taken the oath prescribed for German Wehrmacht soldiers, they were subject to German court-martial jurisdiction. There is therefore no criminal act to be investigated in connection with judgment having been passed by the Reich Court-Martial.

Another, particularly aggravating, accusation made in the Soviet Zone alleges that, following the Tsiklauri affair, Professor Oberländer caused about 60 Caucasian soldiers of his unit to be taken to concentration camps, where many of them died. This is reduced by the investigators under the Rule of Law to the following true facts [26] : —

The additional charge that, after the Tsiklauri group had been sentenced, the defendant, Dr. Oberländer, gave instructions for sending 60 unreliable Caucasian soldiers of the Bergmann Unit to concentration camps, is untrue, according to evidence produced.

Dr. Oberländer has given the following explanation: After sentence had been passed on the Tsiklauri group, the question was raised in Berlin how reliable the remainder of the unit was. Oberländer had a talk on this question with *Sonderführer* Kutzschenbach. The two discussed the possibility of discharging some Caucasian soldiers, because they were suspected to be unreliable, and of transferring them to other tasks. Oberländer, however, cannot remember whether men who were believed not to be absolutely reliable received their discharge, because he left already on July 18, 1942, (according to his diary) for the Eastern front with an advance group.

What actually happened was that during July, 1942, some Caucasian volunteers — about twenty, whilst the exact figure cannot be ascertained — received their discharge from the Bergmann Special Unit. They were transferred to a factory in Hanau as foreign workers. The former member of the unit, then n.c.o. of the reserve, H., stated that he was given orders at the time to take this group of Caucasians to Hanau, where they found good billets. A former member of the unit, the Caucasian G., met one of these foreign workers from Hanau, his fellow-Georgian Valerian Maglakelidse, in the Argentine after the war.

Crimes Against Caucasian Civilians?

A separate chapter in the catalogue of charges made against Professor Oberländer is devoted to alleged crimes against the civilian population of the Caucasus. Up to this point, the investigators under the Rule of Law had to deal with alleged crimes, cruelties, and injustices against Caucasian prisoners of war of the German Wehrmacht. These allegations have been proved to be without any ground. The victims cited in the new chapter are civilian inhabitants of the Caucasus. In this context, the gravest incriminations were raised against Professor Oberländer.

As its point of departure, the enquiry made under the Rule of Law uses the assertion made in the Soviet Zone that

> the period between September 1942 and January 1943, when the Bergmann Battalion was in the Caucasus, had as its main feature acts of violence, pillage, and atrocities, committed against the population. Under instructions of Professor Oberländer, the people were allegedly shot down and robbed, houses were burned down, and the booty of the thieves was allegedly shipped to Germany. A major part of the booty was allegedly reserved for Oberländer himself.

The results of the enquieries made under the Rule of Law require a thorough discussion, because they are of great importance in view of the problem of Oberländer's memoranda, which will be treated separately in this book. The results were summed up by the following dictum: —

> ... this highly generalized but extremely grave accusation against Dr. Oberländer and the Bergmann Unit has been made without any justification, as all the results of our enquiry under this head prove.

On this subject, no less than 25 Caucasian and German witnesses, all of whom are named, were heard, and their statements resulted in the following general picture [28] : —

> In agreement with Dr. Oberländer's own description, *all* the former Caucasian members of the Bergmann Battalion, and also *all* former German members of that unit, who were heard as witnesses, have testified that Dr. Oberländer did not only disagree with the policy of exploitation and oppression against the Soviet nationalities, which had been tolerated, approved, and often even demanded by the Reich Leadership, but that he advocated again and again with all the leading authorities of the Party and the Wehrmacht, a policy of understanding and cooperation with the population, especially with those nationalities who, through their historical development, might be won over as allies against the Soviet regime — namely the Balts, Byelorussians, Ukrainians, and the nationals of the Caucasus. It was especially the creation of the Bergmann Unit, where Caucasian volunteers fought shoulder by shoulder with German soldiers with completely equal rights, that was designed to serve this aim, and to be a model for further developments along this path. During the training period, Dr. Oberländer repeatedly opposed German official teaching about subhuman bolsheviks, and he never tired to elucidate his own idea of trying to win over the Caucasian nations as allies for the Germans. Before the unit was sent to the Caucasus for fighting duties, Oberländer, consequently, implored his men to treat the people in the front areas correctly and in a friendly fashion. He particularly forbade all unauthorized requisitioning, and people who might offend against his admonitions were threatened by him with the strictest use of his disciplinary powers, and/or court-martialling. Every German member of the unit was issued with a pamphlet written by Oberländer on the subject, *What Must We Know About the Caucasus?* This is a quotation from Oberländer's pamphlet: —
>
> 'The success of our occupation but especially our future policies are utterly dependant on the behaviour of the German soldier, and of all who follow him. Their behaviour must be absolutely just, it must be adapted to the peculiarities of the nations met, lest we do harm to Germany's reputation.

Unless we do uphold these principles, we might see the development of partisan activities as we have never experienced them before.

On no account must we make the following mistakes in the Caucasus: Illegal requisitioning, so-called organizing, and usury. Those who intend to buy something must pay for their purchases; they must not simply pocket the things they want and abscond. It is absolutely inadmissible to use your revolver for taking away the last cow, the last seed corn, or anything else. People who have something left over will gladly give to us, but you must know how to deal with them. Your own conscience, allied to common sense, will show you the right way.

I am certain that people will treat us with extreme hospitality and enthusiasm, because we liberate them from the worst slavery of all times! We have been offered a unique historical chance for gaining the allegiance of the Caucasian nations.'

Both in the Caucasus and later, during the retreat to the Crimea, there was always an exceedingly good relationship between the civilian population and the Bergmann Unit. Isolated infractions of discipline, committed by individual members of the unit, through illegal requisitioning of cattle and other food (never anything worse), were always punished by the officer in command of the battalion, Dr. Oberländer, and also by individual company leaders, and in one grave case the guilty soldier was reported to the court-martial sitting in the area. These facts have been described at length by former members of the unit, who reported about individual cases.

Last, but not least, came the success of repeated interventions by Doctor Oberländer — as many statements prove — when the Army issued orders to its units fighting in the Caucasus, demanding correct treatment of North Caucasian civilians. The effect of this attitude was that the entire population of the Northern Caucasus treated all German troops very well, and there were never any reports about partisan activities in this area.

Evidence was also presented by North Caucasians, who were living in the area as civilians during the war, but are now resident in the Federal Republic of Germany. All of them, the witnesses H., M., A., Z., and K., testify to the correct behaviour and friendly relations of the Bergmann unit to the North Caucasian civilian population. These witnesses have given additional evidence

that about 12,000 inhabitants of the Caucasus left their homes when the German Army was forced to retreat, to flew in a westerly direction, *because they wanted to avoid their return under Soviet rule.* That the population took a pro-German and anti-Soviet attitude during the temporary German occupation of the Northern Caucasus, led eventually to *the Soviets uprooting and deporting entire Caucasian tribes, comprising altogether over one million North Caucasians, to other areas of the Soviet empire in 1943/44.* [29]

The Report on the investigations under the Rule of Law underlines the complete contradiction between the results of cross-examining numerous Caucasian and German witnesses, and the accusations made in the Soviet Zone. Further evidence was adduced from the period under review by quotations from Professor Oberländer's political memoranda, which will be discussed in a different context.

Allegations About Murder Committed against Jewish and anti-Hitler Elements of the Caucasian Population

As already mentioned, the verdict of the Soviet Zone court has tried to hold the Nachtigall Unit and/or Professor Oberländer responsible for crimes committed by the *SD Einsatzgruppen* alone, and for which evidence has been produced and evaluated in other courts and trials. This method of distortion continues in the case of the Bergmann Unit, whose commanding officer was this time in fact Professor Oberländer. The investigators under the Rule of Law have divided the charges into two separate groups, and examined them separately [30] : —

(1) Mass Assassination of Jewish and Caucasian civilians (opponents of Hitler) by the Bergmann Unit;

(2) Murder by shooting of a German *(Volksdeutscher)*, who had been appointed Police Chief, and of a Communist from Mineralnoe Vody.

Professor Oberländer himself denies flatly that he ever took part, with the Bergmann Unit, or parts of this unit, in any act of mass extermination against Jews and Communists in Naltchik.

> He never was informed of such activities, and he doubts that they ever happened, because neither in Naltchik nor anywhere in the Northern Caucasus could there be any question of the existence of larger Jewish communities. Oberländer also refers to the entry in his 1942 diary, which shows that he was never in or near Naltchik during October, 1942 [31] .

The Report adds the comment that the investigators never found any factual indications

> that there ever happened any killing of a larger number of Jews or Communists in Naltchik. Activities of this type in the rear areas behind the eastern front were undertaken by the *Einsatzgruppen* (Special Action Groups) of the Security Police and the *SD* [32] .

The investigation carried out under the Rule of Law then extends — as in the Nachtigall case — its enquiries to the activities of the *Einsatzgruppen* in the Caucasus. The report on this subject is introduced by a general review of the Action Groups' organisational structure, in the course of which the fact is underlined that they were led always and exclusively by higher SS officers. What the *Einsatzgruppen* did, especially their larger extermination and kidnapping raids (arrest of masses of people), is all known with very few gaps in our knowledge. The so-called *Ereignismeldungen* (Reports on Events) of the Chief of Security Police and *SD*, wich were kept top secret at the time, are known as well, because they were used as evidence in the Nuremberg Trials. The Central Office of the Land Administration of Justice in Ludwigsburg (which collects and sifts evidence about all war crimes) has examined the activities of *Ein-*

satzgruppe D and published a final report on them. This has been used by the investigators under the Rule of Law. The results are [35] : —

Einsatzgruppe D and its *Einsatzkommandos* had received their marching orders for *immediate execution of security police tasks* immediately upon the start of the attack in the southern section of the eastern front (offensive against the Caucasus). (Dispatch No. 16 of August 14, 1942). Further dispatches sent up to January 8, 1943 (No. 36), report the locations reached by *Einsatzgruppe* Staff and the various *Einsatzkommandos* in the Northern Caucasian Area. According to Dispatch No. 36, *Einsatzkommando* 10 b, led by Persterer, was stationed at Naltchik. In striking contrast to lengthy reports about several large kidnapping (arrest) and liquidation activities against Crimean Jews and Communists, there are *no such reports whatever contained in the Action Dispatches from the Caucasus.* The only subject of the dispatches was the „*security police overhaul*" (screening) of the occupied places, and the arrest of individual communist activists. There are no indications of a larger raid against Jews, especially in Naltchik. This does not completely exclude the possibility that also the Caucasian area may have seen arrests and executions, as the jargon of the *Einsatzgruppen* often used euphuisms like *'seizing' (erfassen)*, *'security police activities'*, etc., when they meant something much worse. But such terms were only used for describing small and isolated cases, or the suppression of small groups, whereas it was their custom to describe larger-scale raids for arresting and killing people in detail, giving also figures, etc.

None of the former members of the unit heard as witness knows anything of the alleged shootings in Naltchik.

For evaluating the credibility of statements made by former German members of the unit, one important factor is that they were not a community of national socialists imbued by the Nazi ideology. The German skeleton staff of all ranks was composed of some professional soldiers, both officers and n.c.o.'s, but they were reinforced by Germans and Austrians who had only be called up for military service *during the war.* Most of them — as can be seen from their statements — were in no way enamoured of war service, and some of them were even opponents of any military and warlike activities.

The Georgian exiles, too, who had joined the Bergmann Unit for nationalist reasons only, were already then quite open about their rejection of the Nazi policies of racial oppression and extermination of entire races. As they have stated, they would have no reason to protect murders and murderers, if killings in fact did take place.

For another reason, it is again unlikely that the Bergmann Unit was detailed for carrying out a mass execution at Naltchik: All its companies were in the fighting front without interruption, till the great retreat began. Only Fourth Company — as mentionend earlier — had been left as a local garrison in the town of Gundelen after its capture. Only during December, 1942, did the Staff of the Unit transfer to Naltchik.

Evidence given by the four former Caucasian members of the Bergmann Battalion — Okroporidse, Aleskerov, Shavgulidse, Mukhashavari — which is the basis also for this grave accusation, must be considered incredible, after our investigation was able to prove that their allegations forming the basis for other accusations, which were disproved earlier on, especially under No. 4, were completely untrue.

Many former members of the Unit, who remember quite well especially Okroporidse and Aleskerov, are of the opinion that these witnesses made their untrue statements either under pressure, or in order to shield their own persons. Both were sub-leaders in the Unit, and later received officers' commissions. They remained with the Unit till the end of the war. They supported Dr. Oberländer's proclaimed aims without any reservations, and they themselves made strong propaganda for them among their compatriots. They enjoyed the special confidence of the Battalion's leaders and of their own subordinates, and were generally very popular. Okroporidse had lived in the Federal Republic of Germany up to 1947, and he occasionally met former members of the Unit in Germany. But he had not been able to find his feet in civilian life and had lived of black market deals.

VVN, which had laid information against the defendant, and the defence have applied for extending summonses to the four named witnesses for the prosecution to hear their evidence, and to confront them with other former members of the Unit. This application could not be met, as there is no agreement on mutual aid between the judicatures of the Federal Republic and of the Soviet Union. Therefore, it was not possible to send an application for such aid to the government of the USSR. Moreover, it is no longer necessary to cross-examine these witnesses after the unambiguous results of our enquiries.

This means that exhausting enquiries made under the Rule of Law have recognized also this particular accusation as completely groundless.

The investigators under the Rule of Law then examined a number of crimes alleged against Professor Oberländer by a witness named Hammerschmidt. H.'s allegations reproach Oberländer with some of the most shameful misdeeds that could be asserted about a soldier, especially an officer. Witness does not tell us — at least, the Abstract from Minutes of the Court Proceedings in the Soviet Zone does not say anything about it — how he came to change from a soldier of the Soviet Army into an apparently German soldier of the Wehrmacht, or possibly a man directed into service, at the headquarters of the First Panzer Army of von Kleist. H. asserts that he stayed in that headquarters from the beginning of September, 1941. In the text of the verdict passed in the Soviet Zone, H. is described as *quartermaster* in Kleist's HQ. — In the Reasons given for its Verdict, the Court of the Soviet Zone, we read that it accepted H.'s deposition which had been read in open court. The judgment calls his statements 'concrete and detailed'. Allegedly, they do not contradict the rest of the evidence but agree with it, at least in part, and they are said to describe *acts of the defendant which correspond completely with his other actions*. The Court *cannot doubt the truth and impartiality* of all witnesses' statements, including those of Hammerschmidt. The Court does not say how it was able to evaluate and assess the reliability of this witness, whom it neither heard nor saw, so that it did not get a personal impression about him. For Hammerschmidt's statements form the contents of a written deposition made on January 1, 1960, at the Public Prosecutor's Office in the District of Moscow. The deposition was merely read during the trial in East Berlin. The Soviet Embassy to the so-called German Democratic Republic informed the court by letter that witness Hammerschmidt was not able to travel. It is worth while to deal with H.'s assertions at length, just because they are such obvious lies.

Hammerschmidt states that he was given orders to proceed to *Abwehr* Group 101 in September, 1942. There he was allegedly told by a former member of Reich Security Head Office *(Reichssicherheitshauptamt)*, named Borchardt, that Oberländer was the head of a special unit consisting of *Headhunters,* which had *much experience in killing people in the most bestial fashion.*

Borchardt allegedly quoted examples to Hammerschmidt, how this *Special Oberländer Commando* tortured and exterminated people in the most refined way.

Hammerschmidt said: —

> As far as I remember, Borchardt told me that this Commando does not waste any bullets on killing children. Usually children were murdered in their parents' presence, by using rifle butts and bayonets, or by bursting the child's head open through hitting his head against a wall, or by tearing the body of the child in two limb from limb, and by other bestial methods [34].

Hammerschmidt then states that he met Dr. Oberländer and his officers personally several times and was in their company about the middle of October. This was in the Caucasus. The published Abstracts from the Minutes do not say anything credible why H. was there, and in which military mission. H. states that he saw Oberländer also at Naltchik in December, 1942. Oberländer himself cannot remember a man named Hammerschmidt *. H. then gives approximate dates for the scenes which allegedly happened during October or early in November, and for which no paraphrasing could supplant the words of the Minutes [35] : —

> The *Abwehr* staff often visited Oberländer at Kislovodsk. At the end of October or early in November, we — that is Borchardt, Lockhardt, I myself, and others — were again with Oberländer.
>
> We started with having supper at Oberländer's in Naltchik. During supper, there was some hard drinking. This drinking bout led to a nocturnal orgy with women present. During the orgy, somebody started a quarrel about the superiority of the soul and strength of the spirit, respectively their steadfastness, of Western nations and members of Eastern peoples, in the presence of certain death.
>
> The opinions of the company were divided. Lockhardt and some other officers affirmed that Western men, especially the Germans, were steadfast and heroic in the frontline, and were therefore indubitably superior souls.
>
> To support his view, Lockhardt added that, during the Russian civil war, he had not seen a single case of communists or commissars, who had been

---

* Personal information of the author through Oberländer.

sentenced to death by the White Guards, not begging for mercy, not whining and wheedling, and not calling to God for help. Oberländer took the opposite view. He stated that the Soviets — meaning the Soviet people — had changed. In his opinion, they met death without fear and regardless of all tortures.

The conclusion drawn by Oberländer was that nobody must show any mercy especially to those people, meaning the Russians. If we show mercy to them — Oberländer stated — they will wring our necks. But History has always granted the victors justification to prevent such intentions. Oberländer discussed the Russians in a biological sense, saying that people are able to bear torture better, and to look death more calmly in the face the nearer to nature, and the more primitive they are.

In order to bring the quarrel to an end, because it went on and on, Oberländer suggested an *excursion by car* to the Piatigorsk prison where Soviet citizens were kept under arrest.

The people who had taken part in the orgy took a number of cars in order to drive to Piatigorsk through the night. There, in the prison building, Oberländer offered coffee that was laced with brandy to all his guests, und then we went to one of the prison cells. I remember that there were one man and one woman kept in the cell.

The first victim of this "examination" was a Soviet woman teacher. Oberländer asked her to take off her clothes. She refused, and Oberländer then ordered the officers of his Special Commando to tear the clothes off the girl's body. It has to be added that Oberländer had a riding crop. He used this riding crop now to beat the girl, demanding that she should tell him about her contacts with the partisans.

The girl remained obdurate and did not talk.

As his beatings were of no avail, Oberländer in his frenzy took his pistol and shot the girl in the right breast.

He did that to avoid killing her on the spot, and to lengthen her sufferings. Yet nobody heard anything from her but the single word, 'You damned person!' Then Oberländer fired a few more shots into the girl's body. His second victim was a Soviet citizen of German descent, who had been made Chief of Police by the occupants. He had been guilty of sympathies with arrested Soviet citizens, and of aiding and abetting attempts to escape. He saw his end coming and begged Oberländer for mercy. Oberländer, quite wild and in a bestial state, shot him through the head.

As a third victim, Oberländer selected a communist, who sat in the cell. This man was from Mineralnoe Vody, and had been left behind for doing underground work. When Oberländer beat him up, this prisoner tried to resist, and to pull Oberländer's riding crop from his hands. When one of the officers of Oberländer's Commando came to his chief's aid, the arrested communist laid him out by a blow with his fist.

Then Oberländer shot this prisoner dead with his pistol.

A large number of former members of the unit do remember the witnesses, Aleskerov and Okroporidse, so that they were able to state, for example, how highly popular they had been in the unit, and suggested that they made their untrue statements either under pressure, or in order to safeguard their lives. But none of them can remember the witness, Hammerschmidt. In addition, the Abstract from the Minutes *(Kurzproto-*

koll) states that the witness, Hammerschmidt, was not present during the public trial, so that his statement had to be read to the court. In spite of this, the Verdict makes no attempt to evaluate the credibility of H.'s monstrous accusations, but states that they have been found to be '*true*' and '*unprejudiced*' [35a].

It is a misfortune that the Minutes do not allow the reader to judge how the court in the Soviet Zone was able to judge the statements of a witness, of whom it did not get a direct impression, whom it neither saw nor heard, to be *true to the facts,* and even *unprejudiced.*

The Report of the investigation under the Rule of Law passes the comment that Professor Oberländer has called the shootings, allegedly carried out by him in person, a figment of the imagination and untrue. The evidence given by former members of the unit is then summarized as follows [36] : —

> Not a single one of the members of the unit, who were heard about the alleged events, has ever seen or heard anything about them. They underline particularly the incredibility of the incidents which are said to have happened in the Piatigorsk prison. All of them declare unanimously that Dr. Oberländer drank very rarely and was highly abstemious of alcohol. Drinking parties were an object of his hatred. He was thought to be *prudish,* and people often smiled at his manners which were the contrary of rough.

Especially illuminating is the statement of a witness, Dr. Sch., who said in this context: —

> The allegation about how the incident is said to have started is in flat contradiction to Oberländer's habits of living. He was not only a puritan but, as we called him, a super-puritan. He hardly ever drank, you could say he was practically abstinent. Drinking parties were a physical horror to him, and for 'parties with ladies', even in the most harmless form, he had not the slightest understanding. His German officers complained and sighed more than once about this puritanical streak in him [37].

Allegations About Shootings of Prisoners of War During the Retreat

In investigating these accusations, the enquiries made under the Rule of Law were based upon the accepted historical fact, which had been confirmed by numerous witnesses heard during the investigations, that the p.o.w. camps in the Operational Area Caucasus were evacuated when the retreat of German troops began early in January, 1943, and that the prisoners were taken westward under guard, marching long distances on foot in inhuman conditions. These huge treks are described in the Bonn Report as follows [38] : —

> Food supplies which, already in the camps, hardly reached the indispensable minimum, deteriorated during the retreat because it became progressively more difficult to obtain supplies from the surrounding countryside, or from Germany. Thus, many prisoners of war dropped behind, unable to march on, as they were weakened by exhaustion, hunger, and epidemics and illnesses caused by famine. It is the truth that many of these stragglers, who could not continue the trek, were shot dead by their escorts. Front troops, who started their march back later, often saw the road ditches filled with dead prisoners of war, who had been shot.

It is, however, quite a different story if it is alleged that the Bergmann Special Unit had been detailed to take back Soviet prisoners of war, and that members of that unit, by Oberländer's orders, or under his responsibility, committed such cruelties. The investigators under the Rule of Law give the following commentary on this point [39] : —

> Enquiries about the reproaches made against defendant have resulted in clear proof being obtained that the Bergmann Special Unit was never, during the entire retreat, assigned to escort back Soviet prisoners of war. Escort duty was the exclusive duty of the camp guards, who were a mixture of German army personnel and Ukrainian auxiliaries. These operated under the Quartermaster of the Army.

The Report goes on to state that the Bergmann Special Unit, too, on its retreat repeatedly saw corpses of prisoners of war, who had been shot. Seeing them had a terribly depressing effect on the Caucasian members of the unit. Among the victims of the shootings, there were many of their own compatriots, in some cases even individually identifiable ones. After this, the following statement is of particular importance [40] : —

> Former Caucasian members of the unit, who were heard as witnesses, strenuously denied the charge that the Bergmann Special Unit took part in shootings of prisoners, either under orders of their commanding officer, or on their own account, and the same strong denial was heard from former German soldiers of the unit. On the contrary, they have made out a credible case — which agrees with statements by the defendant, Dr. Oberländer — that Doctor Oberländer did everything in his power to prevent this inhuman treatment of prisoners of war, especially the killing by shooting of prisoners incapable of marching on.

These general denials made by Caucasian and German ex-members of the unit are given strong support by another, factual statement. Count K., who served as a staff officer on the staff of Colonel-General von Kleist, has testified [41] that

> Dr. Oberländer appealed in person, and by written petitions, to colonel-General von Kleist to take measures against inhuman treatment and shootings of prisoners of war during the retreat. Dr. Oberländer submitted a written report, which contained numerous cases. Witness states that this report had the effect *that Colonel-General von Kleist, who was deeply shocked by these*

> *incidents, immediately dispatched the necessary orders to prevent further cases of the same kind.* Witness's oral statement was confirmed by the following entry in his War Diary: —
> Feb. 20, 1943: —
>
> To-day came a report from Oberländer describing his observations during the march back of prisoners. Those who could not keep in step were shot — often badly, some of them in the centre of the villages, after which the guards turned out the dead prisoners' pockets. And all that after all the things which we saw and experienced since the beginning of the eastern war. This is hairraising.

This behaviour of Professor Oberländer is further proved by other descriptions of events made by Caucasian and German members of Oberländer's unit. Thus, in one case, he suceeded

> in preventing the death by shooting of between 30 and 50 prisoners of war, who could no longer walk. The execution of these unfortunates had already been ordered by the German leader of an escort company, which guarded a column of about 2,000 prisoners. Oberländer negotiated with that escort officer, and obtained mercy for them: The stragglers were handed over to the starosta (headman) of the nearest village with the order to take them to the *Kommandantura* after five days, to feed them well in the meantime, and to supply them with rations for the march. They continued their march with another retreating p.o.w. transport.

The German member of the Bergmann Unit, Dr. Sch. [42],

> witnessed a violent quarrel between Dr. Oberländer and a German captain, in charge of a large column of retreating prisoners of war. That captain had categorically rejected Dr. Oberländer's request to suppress unnecessary cruelties, and to keep the men of his escort unit in better order, not only for reasons of humanity but also because of the effect on Oberländer's own unit, (Bergmann). The captain was of the cynical opinion that much too many prisoners of war had been kept alive. Besides, he called it a '*schnaps idea*' (a harebrained scheme) to form volunteer units from these *subhuman* beings.

Witness continues:

> The quarrel took such forms that I can hardly remember a similar case. We younger men were considering in all seriousness to provoke the captain to such an extent that we would have to shoot him down. During the same night, that officer removed himself to another billet.

A German member of the Bergmann Battalion, R., testified [43] : —

> Dr. Oberländer once took a *Stabsfeldwebel* (Staff sergeant) severely to task, because this man, who led a group of prisoners of war, had beaten several men with a stick for trying to pick up potatoes, which civilians had thrown into the marching column. Dr. Oberländer made a report complaining about this n.c.o.

In concluding this chapter of the accusations, the investigators under the Rule of Law state in their Report: —

In the last instance, this result of our enquiries about Dr. Oberländer's attitude towards prisoners of war, which is the exact reverse of the allegations raised against him, is supported by further documentary evidence. In addition to the letters, which he wrote home from the front, especially the letter February 7, 1943, which have been quoted in part, another letter to his wife, dated April 2, 1943, says among other things: —

'... It is true that I am in difficulties here with one of the authorities, because I have made a report on the shootings of prisoners. But I have protested in the sharpest form, and I will not retreat one single step ...'

Blowing Up the Water Tower at Timoshevskaya

Oberländer himself denies having ordered blowing up the water tower of Timoshevskaya. He states that he did not give a single order of that kind (for blowing up buildings or facilities) during the entire retreat.

The investigators under the Rule of Law acknowledge that all objects of military importance were blown up during the retreat, and the units carrying out such measures were pioneer detachments of the Army, who had the technical equipment for such tasks. They think it possible that water towers were also considered of military importance, because water supplies were difficult in the steppe. The blowing-up under discussion may have occurred, from this point of view. However, there is no indication that it was the Bergmann Unit which carried out the destruction, and there is no trace of an order of this kind by Professor Oberländer. The unit was not equipped with the necessary specialist facilities [44] : —

Members of First Company, who took part in the retreat together with the Army unit under whose general command it had fought, were heard as witnesses, and they know nothing of the alleged blowing-up. They point to the fact that their company had to do infantery duties during the entire retreat, and thus had never time, opportunity, or the necessary explosives for such a task. In addition, the route taken by First Company on its retreat did not lead through Cossack Steppe.

PRINCIPLES OF GERMAN WAR POLICIES IN THE CAUSASUS, ACCORDING TO AN S D REPORT OF 1942

Under the Rule of Law, it has been established by a thorough judicial investigation that the accusations raised against Th. Oberländer in his capacity as officer commanding the Bergmann Special Unit, and against the members of that Unit, did not have the slightest basis in fact. This was the result of numerous statements made by former members of that unit, both of German and of Caucasian nationality. Evidence given by the second of the two groups, most of whose members now live outside Germany, are of particular significance, for they are not subject to German jurisdication, and they have volunteered information out of their own free will. In addition, these statements were supported by former officers of the Wehrmacht, who, through their military service, came into contact with the Unit and/or Professor Oberländer. What they could tell the investigating officials has been, in part, confirmed by contemporary notes and documents (letters written home from the front, war diaries, etc.). Finally, the investigators also used equivalent documents submitted by Professor Oberländer himself (letters written home from the front to Mrs. Oberländer, his wife; his war diary; Memoranda on Eastern Policies). All this evidence without exception — oral statements, depositions, contemporary documents — shows the complete untruth of the accusations made in the Soviet Zone. Furthermore, in contrast to the assumptions made by the Verdict passed in the Soviet Zone, this evidence shows that the principles upheld in Oberländer's memoranda were in complete agreement with the practical work done by the leadership of the Specical Unit Bergmann, and by that Unit itself, in the Caucasus. However, there is an additional document available, which serves to destroy all probability of German soldiers having committed the horrible atrocities alleged against them. This is a Report made by the Chief of Security Police and of the *SD* Commando Staff, Berlin, dated November 6, 1942. The *SD* acted in the Russian areas settled by Slavs as the executive arm of an anti-Slavonic racial policy, as it had been laid down by the racial programme of the Nazi Party and the SS. The memoranda written by Professor Oberländer opposed this programme and these policies on principle. But towards the population of the Caucasus (which, in the *SD* Report, is seen principally as one of the enemies of the Russian nation), the attitude of the *SD* was fundamentally different. That is why this Report is of crucial significance. Under the heading 'Reports from the Occupied Eastern Areas', No. 28, of November 6, 1942, there appears a sub-title, '*Nationalities in the Caucasus Operational Area*' [45], and below it, we read: —

After having crossed the Kuban/Terek river line, we have reached the areas settled by the Caucasian mountain tribes. Up to now, we have penetrated the settlements of the Circassians, Karatchaians, Balkars, and Cabardinians. In this connection, it must be emphasized that the *pro-German feelings of these mountain tribes (positive Einstellung zu Deutschland)* represent a *decisive factor* in our political and military planning (in German, again: *Einstellung)*, and in addition, this would have to be taken account of in trying to answer the question of the future destiny of these areas. *The general propaganda attitude of all the German authorities agrees* in treating these areas, *not as enemy territory,* but as that of *our allies.* Using the necessary instruments of propaganda, this attitude has been fostered both among the people of these mountain tribes and among the German soldiers. According to dispatches available, this practice has been *very successful* up to now, whilst enemy propaganda, for the time being, has made no impression on the mountain tribes. On the other hand, orders issued to the contrary effect by a number of service authorities, especially touching questions of regional home rule, attract strong attention among the local population. It has been pointed out to us that, likewise, imprudent behaviour of German individuals, who have no training in the subject of nationality policies, may harm, or even destroy, relations based upon mutual trust which had been achieved. The antagonism between the local population and Russia, which has *historical* roots, the people's hatred against Bolshevism, their strongly developed urge for *freedom,* and their attachment to Islam, are all *foundations for cooperation (Anknüpfungspunkte)* for a lasting pacification of the Northern Caucasus, which would make use for this purpose of extensive and responsible assistance through the mountain tribes.

The Army Group has issued an order which takes account of these facts. The order specially underlines the following points: —

(1) The Caucasian nationalities are to be treated as friends of the German people;

(2) Nothing must be done to prevent the mountain tribes from destroying the system of collective farms;

(3) Freedom of religious worship is to be guaranteed;

(4) Private property of the mountain population is to be safeguarded;

(5) Supplies may only be taken from them against payment;

(6) All special measures caused by the war and affecting the population, have to be explained, with reasons given for them, to the mountain people;

(7) The honour of Caucasian women has to be protected.

Elucidating these instructions further, the opinion is held that kolkhozes will be dismantled in such a way that each individual farmer is given back the land and cattle which he owned before collectivization was enforced. It is, however, forbidden to divide up land and cattle which may be available over and above this original private property. It is noteworthy that teh Balkars, numbering about 60,000 people, wish to give up their connection with the Cabardinians, and instead to merge with the Karatchaians, who consist of about 120,000 inhabitants of the area.

Already the evidence given by witnesses during the investigation under the Rule of Law has shown how untrue are the charges made in the Soviet Union and in the German Soviet Zone of alleged crimes said to have been committed by Oberländer and the Bergmann Unit against

Caucasian civilians. It appears now that such misdeeds would have also run counter to the friendly attitude which the leadership of Army Group showed to the local population. And in this particular case, such misdeeds would have also challenged the *SD* in the Caucasus to extreme opposition.

Memoranda on Eastern Policies

Policies and actions alleged against Oberländer, however, would also have run completely counter to the contents of his contemporary writings on the principles of German Eastern policies — whose existence has never been denied.

Witnesses' evidence has mentioned several times Oberländer's memoranda, which criticized sharply the principles followed by the occupation authorities in the eastern territories, evolving in their place principles of his own, that stood in complete opposition to instructions issued by the political leadership of the Reich, and to administrative practices used by most of the civilian authorities established in occupied areas. *During the trial in the Soviet Zone, Oberländer's memoranda were specially declared to form part and parcel of the case for the prosecution,* and were included in the Prosecutor's brief. Also, in his oral pleading, the Prosecutor stated that these memoranda do not help Oberländer's *de*fence but range among his *of*fences. The prosecution alleges that they deal exclusively with questions of methods and tactics but do not protest against the policies of oppression and exploitation as such. In other words, they were assessed as a camouflaged form of recommending and justifying the commission of war crimes (illegal treatment of the civilian population in the occupied Eastern territories). Under this heading, they have to be discussed here. The verdict passed in the Soviet Zone accepted the prosecution's case [46] in this question.

During the trial [47] in the Soviet Zone, the documents under review were dealt with by reading passages from three selected memoranda. After that, witness Okroporidse was called and asked whether, in his hearing, Oberländer had ever pleaded for humane treatment of the civilian population. Okroporidse answered 'No', and asseverated on the contrary that Oberländer had, in his hearing, often advocated the opposite. Besides, the true facts were shown by Oberländer's actual (alleged) crimes in the Caucasus. After that, the court called as an '*expert*' a certain Professor Spiru, to hear from him that Oberländer's memoranda did not oppose bad treatment, pilfering, and starving of the population, but advocated a more humane policy only as an expedient serving a purpose. Oberländer's writings, according to the professor, dealt with 'objective values', but it was a fact that 'his practice was atrocious and served the purpose of decisive features of the political solution recommended by Oberländer's memoranda. For an objective overall assessment of Oberländer's policies, it must also be determined whether his theses agreed, or disagreed, with the principles and directives of the then political powers, meaning in the main, the Nazi Party and the SS.

Oberländer's Principles on Eastern Policies, Compared With the Findings of the Nuremberg International Military Tribunal

The best way for comparing these two standpoints is the application of the yardstick offered by the *Judgment of the International Military Tribunal (IMT)* on the basic intentions of the National Socialist leadership and government, regarding Russia, to Oberländer's theses and principles, which — according to innumerable witnesses — also determined his practice, and that of the military unit under his command.

The IMT Verdict says on this subject [49] that the

> outlines for the future political and economic organization of the Eastern territories provided for the destruction and dismemberment of the Soviet Union, which would cease to remain an independent state, also for the formation of independent Reich Commissariates and the *transformation* of Latvia, Esthonia, Byelorussia, and other areas into German colonies.

In another passage of the verdict: —

> In the case of the Soviet Union, pillaging of the areas to be occupied, and the cruel treatment of the civilian population, had been planned down to the last detail before the aggression started.

The impression given by Oberländer's *Twenty Theses* is quite clear: There can be no doubt that he stood for a completely different policy. This policy is based on the insight that all Slavs, including the Eastern Slavs living in the Soviet Union, belong to the family of European nations. In the Memorandum on the Ukraine, which we have quoted, the author fights against the fundamental doctrines of Nazi racial policy towards the Slavs. That memorandum makes an eloquent plea against the fundamentals of *German civilian administration*, which considered the *Ukrainians a people of inferior rank,* seeing in them a natural *object of exploitation.* Oberländer engages in sharp polemics against one of the basic notions cherished by the Party and the SS, who saw the officials of German local government as a *master race* (or *superior caste),* who treated the Ukraine only as a mute object of their policy. Oberländer generally protests against the misapprehension of the Eastern Slavonic peoples; he demands for them, as for the Caucasians, recognition as members of the European family of nations with equal rights.

The same flat contradiction exists between the principles upheld by Professor Oberländer, and those of official Nazi policies, governing the treatment of prisoners of war; moreover, he practised what he preached. *The verdict of IMT, naturally, also dealt with this set of problems.* It is especially in this case that the crude distortion of the truth by the *judgment* passed in East Berlin hits us in the face, and supplies new proof that the political task of the judicature in the Soviet Zone prevents it from doing justice. The IMT Judgment quotes an order signed by General Reinecke, Head of the *Prisoner of War* Department in the Supreme Command of the Wehrmacht. The order states that Red Army soldiers have forfeited any claim to being treated as honourable soldiers under the Geneva Agreement. It goes on to say, among other things, that it is permissible to shoot at fleeing prisoners of war without delay, and without calling 'halt!'. The use of armed force against Soviet prisoners of war is declared to be generally justified. The IMT Judgment then quotes Admiral Canaris' protest against this order, of September 5, 1941 [50] : —

> The Geneva Agreement on Prisoners of War does not apply between Germany and the USSR, so that prisoners of war are only under the protection of the general principles of International Law. These principles have gained a certain firmness since the eighteenth century, and according to them war imprisonment is neither revenge nor punishment but only protective custody for the sole purpose of preventing the prisoner of war from continuing to take part in the fighting. This principle has evolved, in the general context of the views held by all armies, into the belief that it is contrary to the military attitude to kill or injure the defenceless ... Instructions on the treatment of Soviet prisoners of war, submitted as Enclosure No. 1, are based on fundamentally different principles.

The Judgment makes the comment that this protest was disregarded.

Statements of many witnesses prove that Professor Oberländer, in opposing official policy, pleaded with energy for humanity towards Soviet prisoners. Through evidence given by the former A.D.C. to Colonel-General von Kleist, it is even established that a report submitted by Professor Oberländer on atrocities committed against prisoners during the retreat caused the Colonel-General to issue an order against such cruelties.

Admiral Canaris' attempt to plead for human treatment of prisoners of war was recognized by the IMT judgment as an effort to humanize war — though it remained without effect. Oberländer's intercession, which sprang from similar motives, did not only save the lives of many Soviet prisoners of war in the area under his personal command but even caused the issue of instructions in this direction for the entire area of Army Group von Kleist. These acts, therefore, supplement and rectify the general picture painted by IMT.

and the military dangers of dismantling them would forbid this. And then, the weight of such units would ensure the impossibility of continuing the policy of oppression, and that would throw open the gates for a mass transfer of allegiance among the nations oppressed by the bolshevik regime to the German side.

It may be added that this analysis of the situation proved its correctness later: The influx of volunteers grew to gigantic dimensions, and from the same motives which had led to the creation of Bergmann a number of similar units were formed. But there were, in addition, many *Hiwi (Hilfswillige,* i. e. voluntary auxiliaries) units, which had been set up by German commanders everywhere along the front, as wildcat experiments without any political planning, because the shortage of manpower was so pressing. These auxiliary units had the same psychological effect.

This also affected basic German policies towards the East. But because of haughty stupidity in higher quarters, and of the moral cowardice of many who should have known better, the change came about too slowly and too late. The most famous and most well-known example of such a complete about-turn was that of Himmler, who originally persecuted without mercy all those who stood for the idea of recruiting volunteers, but who became the high protector of the project of forming volunteer armies under the former Soviet general, Vlassov, in 1944.

Witness continues,

that basically, it was a highly adventurous and risky undertaking to oppose the proclaimed decision of the political leadership, and the inborn or instilled unintelligence and indifference of the normal Army machinery, to set up a volunteer unit whose members could not be given the slightest political encouragment, only with the support of the *Abwehr* Department and of some farseeing and decent individuals from all ranks of the Wehrmacht, and to ask these volunteers to risk their lives and health and the security of their families, who had been left in their old homes. It was the higher-than-average moral courage and rponsibility of Oberländer which was needed to invent such a venture, and to manage it successfully through a number of years of activity.

Discussing the retreat of the unit, witness says: —

Wherever our unit was stationed during the retreat, the civilian population was never molested. We never forced anybody to accompany us on our retreat, the local people remained in their huts and houses, and we did not kill anybody on our way back. I myself was in charge of leading our companies and cavalry squadrons back. Infantry and cavalry units marched together, without stragglers, and I can assure you that no civilian and no prisoner of war came to any harm during that period.

From the large number of statements made by former members of the unit, we select here some of the most revealing ones.

Witness R., now a businessman in Hamburg, stated [54] : —

Oberländer, whilst visiting Berlin, often criticized the official Eastern policies, which he believed to be wrongheaded, and he was relieved of his post. I do not remember exactly when that happened. I should like to mention in this context that, in the summer of '43, Oberländer was in the Crimea and, at one particular occasion, addressed the German skeleton staff of the unit. To my astonishment, he stated it as his opinion that the war was then already lost. Each month gained in ending the war quickly added to our chances by five per cent — so he said. As I myself had hardly thought deeply about the termination of the war until that moment, I was surprised by his speech. That was also the reason why I remembered it so well.

Feldwebel (Master Sergeant) von Th., serving as an interpreter, stated: —

According to my own experience, the former first lieutenant, Oberländer, repeatedly urged improvement of the conditions in the prisoner of war camps, when he was in the Caucasus in 1942.

This witness was court interpreter during the trial against the Tsiklauri conspirators before the court-martial: —

The conspiracy became known to the authorities with the aid of Okropridse. He reported it to Oberländer, who passed the report on. Okroporidse himself had belonged to the group of conspirators, and he attempted to save himself by laying information, as he feared that the plot would in any case be discovered.

The interlocutor of the witness asked him whether Oberländer was the prosecutor in the subsequent trial. Witness stated he could not even remember having seen Oberländer in court. In conclusion of his statement, witness said he could explain the statements made by the Caucasian witnesses (in East Berlin) only by the situation in which they are to-day, which compels them to paint their former connections with the German Wehrmacht in such a light that they appear to have engaged in them under iressistible compulsion.

However, I would not put it past them that the same men would make quite different statements under different political conditions, and would speak the truth. I am convinced that their statements have the only purpose to protect and rehabilitate themselves.

Statement of the same witness about p.o.w camps: —

I was myself a visitor to a p.o.w. camp at Mosdok and saw there how many of the prisoners volunteered for our service. Their number was so great at the time that we could not accept them all, especially as we restricted our recruitment drive to Caucasians.

I am not competent to judge, in what way that evidence by witnesses (in East Berlin) is intended to serve political purposes. But it struck me as curious that the trial against Oberländer was delayed until he had become Federal Minister in the Federal Republic of Germany.

The statement made by one of the medical officers to the Unit, the Caucasian, Dr. K. S.[56], is of particular interest. Dr. K. S. had been member of the medical staff in a Soviet unit. He was taken prisoner, and was later detailed to look after the health of the Bergmann Unit at Mittenwald. He believes that the reasons impelling prisoners of war to volunteer lay in the hope that the German advance into Russia would

After the troops had left the Northern Caucasus in 1943, about 12,000 North Caucasians followed the Germans and fled with them from Caucasia. I was in constant and close connection with these people. Also they never told me anything bad about our units, and especially about Bergmann. The Bermann Unit was known to me as consisting of excellent and highly disciplined men. All our people told me only the best of them.

How extremely hostile were my compatriots' feelings against the Soviet regime was shown by the fact that in 1943/44 altogether one million North Caucasians, including children, and without being to take any of their possessions with them, were dragged away to Turkestan after the return of the Soviet Army. The reason was that they had helped the German troops.

Witness Barasbi B., born at Terkala, was a member of the North Caucasian National Committee from 1941. He states: —

The feelings of the North Caucasians about the Soviet regime were as unfavourable as possible. The Soviets were always regarded as a foreign and oppressive power in the Northern Caucasus. Through a series of revolts in 1921, 1928, 1931, and 1938, the North Caucasians attempted to throw off the foreign yoke. There was never much hope of success, because Soviet terror was too strong. When the German troops arrived, everybody greeted them as liberators. Therefore, it was not necessary for them to fight for the North Caucasian town of Kislovodsk, because it had already been liberated before the Germans' arrival by North Caucasian partisan units. The population treated the German troops very well.

As a member of the Committee, witness was in constant contact with the Caucasian units. Also he underlines the fact that they consisted of volunteers only, who wanted to fight against the Soviet regime out of their own free will. When the Bergmann Unit entered the Naltchik district, local men reported as volunteers, and the Bergmann Unit could be reinforced by two cavalry squadrons. Volunteers arrived without being called, the Germans needed only to give them uniforms and arms. When the German retreat started, 12,000 North Caucasians went away with them. The number of civilian fugitives would have been much higher if people had known of the retreat beforehand. But the German authorities made a great secret of the impending withdrawal, so that only a small part of the population knew of it.

Witness is of the opinion that all charges raised against the Bergmann Unit are pure communist propaganda.

Witness Mohammed A., too, born in Shali-Grosny, emphasizes [60] that the feelings of the North Caucasian civilian population towards the German troops and the volunteers were very favourable. The German troops were looked at as liberators always and everywhere. Witness knows nothing of any acts of violence.

Witness Fedor Ts., born at Lugovskaya, Caucasus [61], a former member of the North Caucasian National Committee in Berlin too is most emphatic about the bad relations between North Caucasians and the Soviet regime.

During the war, Ts. was in the Northern Caucasus, without having direct relations with the Bergmann Unit. But he knew that the civilian population was enthusiastic about that unit. The fact that thousands of civilians followed the German troops on their withdrawal, interpreted by witness as a sign for the good relations between the local population and the German troops. Everybody said to himself that it is better to go away than to fall again into the hands of the Soviets.

His statement continues verbatim: —

'At any rate, I can give the German troops and the volunteer units in the Caucasus only the best of testimonials. I should like to say that no German need be ashamed of the behaviour of German troops in the Caucasus. They behaved like knights.'

The descriptions given by witness Ali K., born at Sarikamish, Caucasus [62], have the same tenor. He mentions the historical conflicts between the nations of the Caucasus and the Russians. That was the reason why relations with the German troops were so good. Almost all Caucasians saw in the Germans their liberators from the Soviet regime. He has only heard of the Bergmann Unit but emphasizes that all volunteer units had a high reputation with the civilian population. Their behaviour towards the local population was blameless, 'because all of them were people born in the Caucasus.' The local population consisted of relations, acquaintances, friends, and members of their own tribes. Neither did this witness hear of any complaints raised by the civilian population against German troops or volunteer units. He was not able to tell his interlocutors any details about the Bergmann unit.

Field Post Letters as Evidence

The principles of a new German policy for occupied Russia, which were developed by Oberländer in his memoranda, had some practical effect, as has just been shown. That they were taken seriously, and were honestly believed in, by Professor Oberländer, and were not pure window-dressing, as the Soviet Zone court tries to make out, is shown also by a number of contemporary documents, whose value as evidence is justly thought to be high by the Bonn investigators. Letter written by Professor Oberländer to his wife from the war are still available. They contain perfectly frank expressions of his thoughts and worries. A number of passages from these letters that are useful as evidence were added to the files in copies witnessed and certified by a notary public. The following quotations contain a number of typical passages from these letters.

Letter, dated September 27, 1942 [63] : —

Some of the officials here do not love me, but slowly but surely I am getting my way. For the time being, I can do without military decorations. To me, the confidence of my men is more important. My main duty is to save their blood from being shed as much as possible. I am able to take it on my conscience that I have not been brow-beaten over certain questions even by higher officers. A good conscience is still the best property you can have. There is no choice: I have always to fight on two fronts, against the Soviets, and against obtuseness in Caucasian questions.

Letter, dated October 3, 1942 [64] : —

My main worry is the unreasonable treatment shown to prisoners and, sometimes, also to the civilian population. Caucasian deserters in the camps are being beaten up and kicked by Ukrainian auxiliary police. I have now sent to each of the camps a trusted man of mine, in order to suppress such treatment.

Letter, dated October 19, 1942 [65] : —

There are always two fronts on which to fight, the Soviets and our own mistakes in questions on whose solution everything depends. I have been able to win over many, who have become my friends to-day. I have opponents whom I have to fight in all earnest. But to organize the military use of 20,000 Moors * is no child's play, and many of them see in me their man who stands up for them... The trust these men place in me always makes a deep impression on me. King Erich I, however, does just the opposite ** .

Letter, dated December 17, 1942 [66] : —

Unfortunately, all that I have foreseen has become true, and everybody here acknowledges that as a fact. That nothing could be expected in this field from my department was clear to me from the beginning, and this does not trouble me. My ancestors were pastors and lawyers and have always stood for their God and the Law. I shall do the same, no matter what comes.

Letter, dated December 20, 1942 [67] : —

Divine service of the Moslems made a deep impression on me. After it, we proclaimed the dissolution and redistribution of the kolkhoz. At noon, I spoke before the Moslem soldiers about the guarantee of complete religious freedom under German protection. I did not believe before that the Moslems, who are usually so passive, could ever become so active. They clapped their hands in enthusiastic applause, and afterwards emphasized again and again their faithfulness... You need not keep your pistol at the ready here. The people here trust us. If that were the case all over Europe, how different would be the war, and the future peace.

Letter, dated January 25, 1943 [68] : —

That I am no longer under my former department does not cause me any regret. I remain with my unit. Of course, I shall have less freedom of action, but I did not break faith with my convictions, and can prove who showed lack of courage. ... In my inmost self, I feel victorious... When my father under the red land government of Thuringia (in 1923), had to sign a declaration about his party membership, he wrote: *deutsch-national* (German nationalist, i. e. the large, conservative and royalist, right-wing party before the rise of the Nazis), although this frankness could do him only harm. I have not acted differently.

---

* *Moors (Mohren,* in German) was the nickname given by the German skeleton staff to the Caucasians, most of whom had a swarthy skin.

** This refers to the former East Prussian *gauleiter,* Erich Koch.

The Creation of the Bergmann Unit and the Principles of International Law

The Judgment passed in the Soviet Zone states [69] in agreement with the Prosecution [70] that Soviet prisoners of war were treated inhumanly in the p.o.w. camps in flagrant disregard of the rules of International Law. It adds the allegation that Oberländer personally caused this situation and exploited it to press prisoners of war into service for the Bergmann Special Unit.

It would be fruitless to analyse the verdict and the brief for the prosecution in detail, as to whether the allegation about violations of international rules, whose untruth has been proved by the investigation carried out under the Rule of Law, refers only to the assertion that inhuman conditions were created in the camps, or to the creation of a German Wehrmacht unit from prisoners who, at the time, were kept in these camps. Certain passages of the prosecution indicate that the second alternative was meant by the communist prosecutor.

The true situation under International Law has been clarified for this area of international relationships by a document used in one of the trials before the International Military Tribunal [71], which quoted it with approval, and then incorporated its salient passages in its judgment. That document is the written protest by Admiral Canaris against instructions of September 8, 1941, on the treatment of Soviet prisoners of war. Canaris' protest started with the statement that the Geneva Agreement on Prisoners of War did not apply to relations between Germany and the UdSSR, so that only the principles of general International Law on the treatment of war prisoners had to be used: —

> ... These ... have gained a certain firmness since the eighteenth century, and according to them war imprisonment is neither revenge nor punishment but only protective custody for the sole purpose of preventing the prisoners of war from continuing to take part in the fighting. This principle has evolved, in the general context of the views held by all armies, into the belief that it is contrary to the military attitude to kill or injure the defenceless...

The IMT judgment vouchsafes the comment [72] that this protest was in agreement with the true position.

That means: If prisoners of war are under protective custody for the purpose or preventing their renewed participation in the fight against the state that keeps the prisoners imprisoned, that state may also release them from custody at its own discretion. Moreover, it is also within the same state's discretion to permit released prisoners to join its own fighting forces. That judgment was pased on the basis of the London Four Power Agreement of August 8, 1945, and the Statue attached to it. That means that the pronouncements of the IMT on points of law are also binding on the Soviet Union.

INVESTIGATIONS OF THE CASES NACHTIGALL AND BERGMANN AND THEIR RESULTS

The results produced by the two separate investigations carried out under Rule of Law, in the two cases Oberländer/*Nachtigall Unit* and Oberländer/*Bergmann Unit*, have been utterly negative.

In the Nachtigall case, the only possibility left open is that individual members of the unit (disappointed in view of the rejection by the Nazi Reich government of the movement for Ukrainian independence, which was then already foreshadowed, and possibly also by the impression made by the Soviet mass murders) may have taken part in the Lwow pogrom. If that did happen, it happened in breach of the discipline striven for by the leadership of the unit, and against strict orders. No personal participation of Oberländer could be proved, and such would have been practically impossible in view of the principles used for the selection of the Nachtigall unit's leaders. The evidence accepted by the Soviet Zone verdict as proof — allegations made by the witnesses, Kukhar and Hübner, that they were able to recognize an officer whom they had not seen for twenty years, and to identify him with his picture in a newspaper, after having looked at him in the distant past from a considerable distance and allegedly having recognized him already then — is improbable and incredible by every reasonable criterium.

The murder of the Polish professors in Lwow had been made the subject of the prosecution already in one of the main trials at Nuremberg by the Soviet Union. Both German and Polish authorities and witnesses have ascertained that these murders were acts committed by the *Sicherheitsdienst* (Security Service), with which the Nachtigall Unit had nothing to do.

The result of the enquiries made in the Bergmann case was completely negative as well. This has been shown with perfect clarity by the contemporary evidence adduced (field post letters of the defendant, his memoranda, contemporary letters and diaries of third persons). This evidence is fully supported by the completely unanimous statements and deposition made by 150 German and many Caucasian witnesses. In addition, there is the quoted *SD* report, which threw a new and revealing light on the basic attitude of the Party and *SD* towards the Caucasians, whom they considered friendly nations, so that for this additional reason the monstrous crimes alleged against Oberländer and the Bergmann Unit appear completely incredible. Last, but not least, there is no doubt that the creation of the Bergmann Unit did not constitute a breach of International Law.

The entire structure of the allegations made in the Soviet Zone and in the Soviet Union against Oberländer and the units Nachtigall and Bergmann has been blown skyhigh — with the only exception of the slight possibility discussed in the Nachtigall case — but there remains the question *why* the communist authorities had to stage a public show trial on such flimsy grounds. In order to answer this question, it will be necessary to investigate the nature of Soviet and Communist ideas of the State and of Law, and also the general problem of War Crimes in contemporary international law.

Before we proceed to this discussion, however, we have still to deal with the administrative complaint by *VVN* against the decision of the Public Prosecutor to quash the proceedings in the 'Bergmann Unit' case, and the answer to the complaint by the *Generalstaatsanwalt* (general public prosecutor) in Cologne.

THE ADMINISTRATIVE COMPLAINT BY *VVN* (ASSOCIATION OF VICTIMS OF NAZI PERSECUTION) AGAINST THE DECISION OF THE PUBLIC PROSECUTOR NOT TO PROCEED WITH THE 'BERGMANN UNIT' CASE

VVN (Vereinigung der Verfolgten des Naziregimes) had used the allegations of the Special Soviet Commission against Oberländer and the Bergmann Unit as the substance of its information laid against these two defendants with the Public Prosecutor in the Federal Republic of Germany. It was not satisfied with the decision of *Staatsanwaltschaft* (Public Prosecutor's Office) at Bonn to quash the proceedings that had been opened. On June 7, 1961, *VVN* lodged an appeal against the finding that no *prima facie* case had been made out against the defendants, by lodging a complaint under German Administrative Law against the Bonn Chief Public Prosecutor with his official superior, the *Generalstaatsanwalt* (General Public Prosecutor of the *Land* North Rhine-Westphalia, or State Attorney) in Cologne [73].

The appeal stated that the finding handed down from the Bonn prosecutor's office made it clear that the investigations had not been carried out in the proper way, especially by neglecting to extend their purview to a sufficiently large field, which, according to the appeal, would have been possible.

In addition, it was suggested that the suspicion could not be gainsaid that Oberländer's former or present political position had influenced the findings. The complaint contained the following detailed accusations: —

> It is obvious that the Public Prosecutor's Office in Bonn used for its enquiries witnesses who, almost without exception, were former members of the Bergmann Special Unit, and who now reside in the Federal Republic of

Germany. However, this group of persons is likely to have hardly an interest in making the truth known about the activities of the Bergmann Battalion and its commander, Professor Oberländer, because such ex-Bergmann soldiers run the risk of a criminal prosecution. On the other hand, a number of witnesses who had been named to the Bonn Public Prosecutor's Office were not heard. The evidence collected by the Special Soviet Commission, which has made extensive enquiries on the subject of the present investigation, was not used. Furthermore, the Public Prosecutor decided not to summon the witnesses who had testified the prosecution in the trial against Professor Oberländer held by the Supreme Court of the German Democratic Republic.

The appellants then complained about the order in which the witnesses incriminating or supporting Dr. Oberländer and the accused unit had been called, and commented on this sequence as follows: —

If this curious procedure was based on the fact that a number of the witnesses for the prosecution, who have been named, are of Soviet nationality, it must be pointed out that the criminal investigation against Professor Oberländer for suspected murder and for other actions considered criminal all over the world dealt with activities committed on Soviet territory. — The appeal continues: At least the general public will receive the disastrous impression that the Public Prosecuter's Office disregarded a number of factual proofs of guilt but, at the same time, industriously collected masses of alleged evidence for the defendants' innocence. It is difficult to see why the Public Prosecutor prefers to believe in the truth of statements made by former members of the battalion once led by Professor Oberländer, who are to-day resident in the Federal Republic of Germany and are suspect of being accessories to Oberländer's crimes, whilst witnesses for the prosecution, who gave their evidence in the Soviet Union and/or in the German Democratic Republic, have been branded as liars. Such methods are not suitable for establishing true facts, and for finding out whether any crimes have indeed been committed or not, which would be the only way to draw the balance of the National Socialist past.

On December 15, 1961, the *Generalstaatsanwalt* in Cologne issued the following decision to the appellants [74] : —

The complaint has been rejected.

There is no reason for not quashing the criminal investigation.

The investigating *Oberstaatsanwalt* (i. e., the Chief Public Prosecutor in Bonn, against whom the appeal was made) has reached the result of his enquiries for just and true reasons, namely that the accusations made against Professor Oberländer and third persons, who were members of the Bergmann Unit, have been proved groundless. There are no valid grounds for a different assessment of the facts.

In the rejection of the complaint, the superior authority emphasizes the thoroughness and extreme care that went into the clarification of the facts behind the accusations. The *Land* Attorney also completely refutes the allegations that Professor Oberländer's former or present official position influenced the proceedings in any way.

In particular, it is stated about the alleged preference shown to hearing and accepting statements made by former German members of the Bergmann Unit: —

As you have already been told, during extensive enquiries more than 150 former members of the Bergmann unit, and a great number of other witnesses, among them also civilians who, at the time under review, had their normal residence in the Caucasus, have been heard and cross-examined. Part of the Caucasian witnesses heard, who were former members of the Bergmann Special Unit, have moved after the Second World War to France and the United States permanently. This refutes your suggestion that only former members of the Bergmann Battalion now resident in the Federal Republic of Germany were called. All the witnesses without exception, and especially the former Caucasian members of the Bergmann Unit, were unable to confirm the accusations raised against Professor Oberländer in any single point. The unanimous statements submitted by witnesses are also lent decisive support by documentary evidence from the past that is under review. In this context, it was possible and necessary to give particular attention to the four memoranda which Professor Oberländer submitted to the then supreme authorities of the Reich and the Wehrmacht after the beginning of the Caucasus offensive, as well as to a great number of original field post letters written by defendant to his wife. In all these documents, defendant protested and warned clearly and unambiguously against the policy of exploiting and oppressing the peoples of the occupied Eastern territories. Especially these documents, whose genuineness cannot be doubted, have a claim to be considered as genuine evidence, because they were written in the situation then prevailing, when there was no reason whatever for concocting inventions protecting the writer. In addition, the study of documentary material from the files of the former *Reichssicherheitshauptamt* (Reich Security Head Office), which is available among 'Documents of the Nuremberg Trials', did not produce any incriminating indications against the Bergmann Unit and its commanding officer.

The assertions that the Soviet witnesses heard during the trial before the *Supreme Court of the 'German Democratic Republic'* have not been called on purpose are answered as follows: —

Your argument in the written complaint that the investigators of the Public Prosecutor's Office in Bonn did not hear a number of witnesses, of whom it was informed, does not make it clear, which further facts and evidence that might be significant for the decision of the investigators, the enquiry ought to have covered. As far as you specially object to the investiga-
incriminating evidence during the criminal trial held by the *Supreme Court*
ting Chief Public Prosecutor not having heard the witnesses who gave
of the 'German Democratic Republic' against Professor Oberländer, your objection does not establish valid reasons for a resumption of the investigation. Apart from the fact it is impossible to get hold of any witness living in the Soviet Union, because there is no agreement in force between the Federal Republic of Germany and the Soviet Union on mutual aid between the two judicatures, so that such mutual assistance cannot be applied for, it was possible to do without a cross-examination of the witnesses, Okroporidse, Aleskerov, Shavgulidse, and Mukhashavari, whose evidence has supplied the accusations against Professor Oberländer, for reasons of substance. For the

examining Chief Prosecutor had already pointed out that those witnesses' evidence is incompatible with the results of his own enquiries, since such evidence has been refuted both by testimonial given by more than 150 witnesses and by the contents of voluminous documentary material.

Thus the administrative appeal lodged by *VVN* caused a reexamination of the investigation proceedings, which led to the finding that the decision to quash these proceedings by the Bonn Public Prosecutor's Office was based in true and just ground in all points.

FOOTNOTES

[1] *Einstellungsverfügung Verfahren Bergmann* (Decision to Quash the Bergmann Proceedings), dated March 30, 1961 (Ref. No. 8 Js 359/60).
[2] German Text according to the Translation taken to the Bergmann Files.
[3] *Kurzprotokoll* (Abstract of the Minuted of Proceedings of the Soviet Zone Court), p 12.
[4] *l. c.*, p. 17.
[5] *l. c.*, p. 18.
[6] *l. c.*, p. 127.
[7] *l. c.*, p. 133.
[8] *l. c.*, p. 118 *passim.*
[9] Verdict of the Soviet Zone Court, p. 13.
[10] Decision to Quash etc., Folio 7.
[11] *l. c.*, F. 8.
[12] *l. c.*, F. 4 *passim.*
[13] *l. c.*, F. 16 *passim.*
[14] *l. c.*, F. 6.
[15] *l. c.*, F. 10.
[16] *l. c.*, F. 13.
[17] *l. c.*, F. 13.
[18] *l. c.*, F. 14.
[19] *l. c.*, F. 14.
[20] *l. c.*, F. 15.
[21] *l. c.*, F. 15.
[22] *l. c.*, F. 15.
[23] *l. c.*, F. 18.
[24] *l. c.*, F. 19 *passim.*
[25] *l. c.*, F. 21 *passim.*
[26] *l. c.*, F. 22 *passim.*
[27] *l. c.*, F. 23.
[28] *l. c.*, F. 23 *passim.*
[29] *l. c.*, F. 26.
[30] *l. c.*, F. 32 *passim.*

[31] *l. c.*, F. 33 *passim.*
[32] *l. c.*, F. 33 *passim.*
[33] *l. c.*, F. 35 *passim.*
[34] Abstract of Minutes etc., p. 147.
[35] *l. c.*, p. 148 *passim.*
[35a] There is no doubt about the truth and lack of prejudice in all witnesses' statements; Verdict, V, p. 16.
[36] Decision to Quash etc., Folio 38.
[37] Bergmann Files, Vol. VII, 229.
[38] Decision to Quash etc., Folio 39.
[39] *l. c.*, F. 39.
[40] *l. c.*, F. 39 *passim.*
[41] Bergmann Files, Vol. I, 198.
[42] *l. c.*, VII, 229.
[43] *l. c.*, VII, 83.
[44] Decision to Quash etc., Folio 52.
[45] Quoted from a photostatic copy of 'Dispatches from the Occupied Eastern Areas', No. 28, in the Bergmann Files.
[46] Abstract of the Minutes etc., p. 228.
[47] *l. c.*, p. 152 *passim.*
[48] Oberländer's Memoranda on Eastern and Caucasian Policies were circulated in typescript at the time. Their photostatic copies form part of the volume containing Documentary Evidence, attached to the Bergmann Files.
[49] Judgment of the International Military Tribunal (Trial against the Chief War Criminals before the IMT at Nuremberg), Vol. I, p. 189 *passim.*
[50] *l. c.*, Vol. I, p. 259.
[51] Bergmann Files, Vol. I, 76.
[52] Professor Schiller put at Professor Oberländer's disposal this statement when the political campaign against Oberländer started.
[53] Bergmann Files, Vol. VII, 83 *passim.*
[54] Bergmann Files, Vol. VIII, 140.
[55] *l. c.*, VIII, 144.
[56] *l. c.*, IV, 199.
[57] *l. c.*, IX, 155.
[58] *l. c.*, IX, 183.
[59] *l. c.*, IX, 185.
[60] *l. c.*, IX, 186.
[61] *l. c.*, IX, 187.
[62] *l. c.*, IX, 189.
[63] *l. c.*, I, 114.
[64] *l. c.*, I, 114.
[65] *l. c.*, I, 115.
[66] *l. c.*, I, 115.
[67] *l. c.*, I, 115/116.
[68] *l. c.*, 116.
[69] Abstract of Minutes etc., p. 220.
[70] *l. c.*, p. 12.
[71] International Military Tribunal, Vol. I, p. 259.
[72] *l. c.*, I, 260.
[73] Bergmann Files.
[74] *Der Generalstaatsanwalt bei dem Oberlandesgericht Köln* (The General Public Prosecutor at the Higher Land Court in Cologne), Ref. No. Zs. 376/6.

IV

THE JUDGMENT OF THE SOVIET ZONE COURT VIEWED UNDER THE PRINCIPLES OF THE RULE OF LAW — REASONS GIVEN FOR THE COURT'S FINDINGS

Article Ten of the Declaration of the United Nations on Human Rights, proclaimed by the General Assembly on December 10, 1948, runs as follows: —

Everyone is entitled in full equality to a fair, and public hearing by an independent and impartial tribunal, in the determination of his rights and obligations and of any criminal charge against him [1].

In our context, there is also Article Six of the Convention for the Protection of Human Rights and Basic Freedoms which appears to be relevant, because this Article, too, confirms the claim of all and everybody to have their causes heard in reasonable fashion before an independent and impartial court of law, which has to decide about the truth and justice of the criminal accusations raised against them.

The two basic rules proclaim the inalienable claim of the human person to be subjected to just proceedings before courts of law only which merit that name through vouchsafing the independence and impartiality of the judicature. Under Article Ten of the Declaration on Human Rights, it is obvious that a judicial body can be called a *court* only on condition that this body has the two qualities of independence and impartiality. Also, the right established through that pronouncement that every accused person must be given a *fair hearing* of his case has to be interpreted in such a way that the body sitting in judgment must be the court competent to judge the accused under valid rules of law. When, therefore, the Supreme Court of the Soviet Zone tries to prove its competence in the case under review, this attempt must fail from the point of view of the Rule of Law. The tasks set to the judicature in the states of the Soviet and communist type preclude us from accepting the judgments passed by such courts as products of an independent and impartial application of law under the Declaration on Human Rights. It is necessary to discuss these two grave objections against the validity of the judgment passed in the Soviet Zone somewhat more thoroughly. The alleged facts which were accepted as proved by both the Prosecution and the Verdict against Oberländer in the Soviet Zone trial have been extensively examined when we described the problems arising out of the Nachtigall and Bergmann cases.

At first, we shall cast a glance at the standpoints of both the Defence and the Prosecution, which they took up during the trial hearing, and will later examine the Reasons given for the Verdict. The *Defence* accepted as proved the following alleged facts: —

> Regarding the problems of Preparing for War . . .
> Defendant took part in preparations for war through his cooperation in Eastern research *(Ostforschung)*, in the organisations of Germans abroad, as well as in the *BDO (Bund Deutscher Osten*, i. e. Rally for the German East), the *VDA (Verein für das Deutschtum im Ausland*, i. e. Association of Germans Abroad), and the *NSDAP* (the Nazi Party) [2] :

also through his work with *Abwehr II* (Counter-Espionage). In the Nachtigall case, the Defence accepted as proved 'that the German members of this battalion have committed crimes, and that also so-called OUN members (of the Organisation of Ukrainian Nationalists) with yellow and blue armbands as badges, as well as civilians without badges, committed crimes' [3] . Charges going beyond these allegations were not accepted as proved by the Defence. In the Bergmann case, the Defence voiced the opinion 'that the allegations of fact made by the *Generalstaatsanwalt* (Chief Public Prosecutor) were proved by the evidence produced' [4] . In other words, the Defence took the point of view 'that the guilt of defendant, in the Nachtigall and Bergmann cases, has been essentially proved (with the exception of the limitations pointed out)'. Summing up, the Defence argued 'that defendant is guilty in the Nachtigall and Bergmann cases in the sense of the Prosecution, with the exception of small limitations concerning alleged facts, but not guilty of the crime of preparing for war' [5] .

The Defence further submitted that defendant was not the '*central key figure*' in Eastern research but 'took part, jointly with other research workers into Eastern problems *(Ostforscher)* in committing *fascist* war crimes, and was therefore an accessory to them' [6] .

In detail, the Defence stated that defendant 'was concerned in the guilt of Nazi preparations and waging of war but not as one of the principal war criminals', referring in support of this statement to the Nuremberg Judgment of October 1, 1946, against the Chief War Criminals. In this respect, the Defence opposed the opinion submitted by Professor Reintanz who had apparently been called as an expert on International Law. The *Kurzprotokoll* (Abstract of Minutes of Proceedings), where it reproduces the professor's statements does not publish his actual conclusions [7] . But from arguments submitted by the Defence, it appears [8] that Reintanz obviously considered defendant to be one of the Chief War Criminals under the Nuremberg Trial and Judgment. The Defence rejected the allegations about Oberländer having taken part, in a criminal way, in the preparations for war. All this goes to show that the Defence never tried to discuss the credibility of the witnesses for the prosecution — neither in the Nachtigall case (testimonial given by Kukhar and Hübner) nor in the Bergmann case (especially Hammerschmidt's depositions that were read out in court).

The *Prosecution (Staatsanwaltschaft)* immediately rose in open court to counter this limited defence, although the Defence had accepted most of the material allegations against defendant. The Prosecutor maintained that Oberländer had committed Crimes against Peace under Article 2, Paragraph A, of Control Council Law No. 10 [9]. (However — as will be shown later — the Prosecutor left out of account the limitations which this law places even upon non-signatories of the London Agreement, through its Article 1, last sentence, which are of decisive importance for the legal position of the so-called German Democratic Republic.) Against the argument of the Defence that Oberländer was not a member of the group of persons who were able to cooperate in preparation for war, the Prosecution takes the standpoint 'that the totality of criminal acts committed by defendant form a dialectical whole which cannot be pulled to pieces'. The Prosecutor, once again, repeats his earlier reasoning that Oberländer's research activities were to be interpreted as 'reconnoitring of Eastern states, of their territory, and their peoples', and had to be considered as espionage, at the latest from 1936/37 onwards; that his Eastern research included 'disruptive and deviationist activities', and that, finally, his work for *Abwehr* was 'in the way of immediate preparation for Hitler's planned aggression against Eastern states'. All this was going to show that his criminal activities could not be divided up into definite and separate periods. 'Defendant was a prominent representative of a mechanism which worked for aggression from the very beginning.'

The Judgment, which covers 19 large printed pages, again consists of an inseparable mixture of political declamations, new accusations, and lawyers' arguments, but on the whole, the latter are almost submerged by the former [10].

After having found Oberländer guilty of 'extremely grave intentional crimes against a large number of human beings, of murder, of a criminal plot to commit murder, of calling for, and inveigling others to, murder', it goes on to give its Reasons for the Verdict, as follows: —

> Through his crimes, the defendant, in continued action since the advent to power of Hitler Fascism, took part actively and prominently both in preparing for, and in unleashing and carrying out, imperialist aggression by Germany in the Second World War. The crimes committed by defendant are the fruit and also part and parcel of the aggressive policies of German imperialism and militarism which, in the course of barely three decades, have

overrun the world with the bloodshed, the horrors, and the destruction of two predatory wars, and which now again, with the prominent assistance of defendant, are preparing for a third world war [10a].

Then follows a first summary of reasons given for the competence of the Supreme Court in the Soviet Zone for sitting in judgment on these alleged crimes. The reasons are based on the following Main Theses (giving a striking example of the hotchpotch made up from political declamations and lawyers' arguments, which are typical for the form in which the case is being argued in the Judgment): —

(1) Since, through the Great Socialist October Revolution in Russia, the first Workers' and Peasants' State entered World History, it has, however, been possible for the powerful peoples' masses of all nations — under the leadership of the Soviet Union's unflinching policy for peace — to place aggressive war, the annexation of alien countries, and the oppression of other peoples as a means for carrying out economic, political, and military interests, outside the law, and to blackball them as the biggest crime against humanity and against International Law [11].
(2) The principal powers of the Anti-Hitler Coalition had underwritten these principles in the Atlantic Charter, and also through the declarations of Teheran and Yalta, and these principles received their final wording in the Charter of the United Nations, especially in its Article Two, paragraphs three and four.
(3) In order to safeguard the protection of peace and of human rights, there were also created as 'the basic principle of the new democratic international law' [12] the new rights and duties to prosecute and punish all those who commit crimes against peace and humanity by responsibly taking part in preparing, leading, and organizing aggressive wars and terroristic measures against the attacked peoples. Especially in the London Four Power Agreement on the punishment of the chief war criminals and in the Statute of the Nuremberg Military Court had this protection found expression, and it had been confirmed by the decision of the United Nations General Assembly of December 11, 1948.
(4) Article Five of the Constitution of the so-called German Democratic Republic made this *duty under International Law* binding upon the so-called G.D.R.

After this, the Judgment proceeds to describe Oberländer's activities after 1945. It charges him with renewed *aggressive, anti-peace* activities within the *Abendländische Aktion* (Action Group for the Occident, a post-war conservative movement in Western Germany), as well as through rallying and reconstructing *imperialist,* so-called *Eastern research (Ostforschung).* As the central organizations and leading bodies of this research, the Judgment names the *Göttinger Arbeitskreis* (Göttingen Working Group, a research panel of former professors and lecturers of Königsberg university, now based on Göttingen), the *Deutsche Gesellschaft für Osteuropakunde* (German Society for Research into East European Questions), the *Johann-Gottfried-Herder-Forschungsrat* (Herder Research Council, named after Herder, the eighteenth century philosopher-poet, collector of East European and German folksongs, and friend of Goethe), the *Ostdeutsche Kulturrat* (Council for East German Culture), and the *Ostkolleg der Bundeszentrale für Heimatdienst* (Eastern College of the Federal Centre for Homeland Services, the 'Centre' being a government-subsidized adult education organization). In his position as Federal Minister for Expellees and Refugees, Oberländer is alleged to have held 'ideological, political, and financial sway over these institutions and organizations, also over the 29 *Landsmannschaften* (Compatriots' Rallies, i. e. associations of expellees and refugees from the East, divided into groups according to the geographical location of their original homes), and their Central Association. From this, the Judgment draws the following inferences: —

> This shows that, to-day again, defendant is the representative of a policy from which emanates a serious danger to peace in Europe and in the whole world. He proves that he is not willing to reject the crimes which he committed in the service of Hitler Fascism. Therefore, he is to this day fully responsible for those crimes, and there are neither legal nor moral grounds for releasing him from this responsibility [13].

The story is continued by a description of Oberländer's entire career, which paints his scientific and political work, on the lines set out by the Prosecution, as continued activities for preparing of German expansion towards the East. Especially the fact that he was called up for service with *Abwehr II*, and the work he did there, are described as playing 'a dominating part in preparing for aggressive war' [14]. The Judgment takes it for granted, and as proved, that Oberländer contributed directly to causing the war against Poland [15]. What the judges had to say in their judgment about the Nachtigall and Bergmann case has already been examined here. Oberländer's memoranda are not acknowledged by the court as signs of his struggle against ‚fascist methods of violence' but — again accepting the case of the prosecution — as confirmation for criminal intent and acts.

Finally, the Judgment again deals with the question fo the court's competence, protesting against the objection that the alleged crimes could not be adjudicated under the criminal code of the Soviet Zone, and that the Supreme Court in that zone was not competent under Paragraph Three of the German Criminal Code *(Strafgesetzbuch)* and under Paragraphs 13 and 14 of German Criminal Trial Rules *(Strafprozessordnung)* — arguing its case as follows: —

> Under Paragraph Three of the Criminal Code, all criminal acts that have been committed on the state territory of the German Democratic Republic, are subject to adjudication under criminal statute law of the G.D.R. The crimes alleged against defendant are to be assessed as a direct contribution to preparing for, and carrying out, the Second World War — which was waged on

the German side as a fascist-imperialist, predatory war in violation of International Law — and this was directed and organized from the entire territory of the former *German Reich,* and especially by this Reich's central leadership in Berlin. Part of the former territory of the Reich, including Berlin, is now the state territory of the German Democratic Republic. Over this territory — apart from the special and abnormal situation in West Berlin — the G.D.R. in conformity with the principles of democratic international law, holds full sovereign power as one of the two successor states to the *German Reich,* which has disappeared in 1945 when the Nazi regime was broken up [16].

It is particularly interesting in which way the Judgment tries to surmount the legal barrier of Oberländer's parliamentary immunity. The objection raised by the defence that the defendant, as a member of the Federal Parliament in the Federal Republic of Germany, was immune to criminal prosecution is rejected by the court by stating that it was not necessary for the West German Federal Parliament to waive immunity under Article 46, Paragraph 2, of the West German Basic Law, i. e. the Federal constitution. In the first instance, the judgment contends that the so-called German Democratic Republic was not legally obliged to take notice of Oberländer's position as a member of parliament. However, the Soviet Zone court appears to be in favour of normally subjecting its proceedings to the provisions of an M.P.'s immunity for reasons of international courtesy. But in the case under review, it argues that International Law supersedes and thus cancels out the protection granted by Article 46, Paragraph 2 of the Basic Law. Instead, the court produces an interpretation of Articles 1, 2 *passim,* 24, 26, 139, and especially Article 25 of the West German Basic Law, as follows: —

> ... Especially Article 25 of the West German Basic Law establishes the rule that the general principles of International Law have legal power in the Federal Republic and supersede all other statutes. Among these rules of International Law are, in the first instance, the basic principles and prescriptions contained in the Charter of the United Nations, including the prohibition of any aggression and the maintenance of peace, the duty to observe equal rights and self-determination of all nations, human dignity, human rights, and the basic freedoms for all without discrimination on the grounds of nationality, race, sex, and religion. In particular, this international law also includes the rules specially sanctioned by Article 107 of the Charter of the United Nations on the complete and final extermination of German Nazism and militarism [17].

The court also engages in a polemic against the Defence on the subject of the statute of limitations, but this is of no importance for our investigation [18]. The verdict gives its reasons for the decision about the kind of punishment to which defendant was sentenced, by referring to the practice of the International Military Tribunal at Nuremberg. The I.M.T., so the verdict says, permitted exceptions from the rule that criminals of this type should be sentenced to death, and has substituted imprisonment for life.

In the verdict, Oberländer has been found guilty of multiple murder: —

> Defendant is guilty of the most grave intentional crimes against the lives of a large number of human beings, including murder, conspiracy to murder, calling upon others to murder, and inveigling others to murder [20].

Through these crimes, he is alleged to

> have contributed, in continuous action, actively and prominently, to both preparing and unleashing, and carrying out imperialist aggression by Germany during the Second World War [21].

These alleged murders are said to have been committed in and near Lwow and in the Northern Caucasus.

The investigation carried out under the Rule of Law has been able to disprove all these allegations as utterly groundless. But assuming that these calumnious accusations were just, the courts of law of which State would be competent or adjudicate on them? For the purpose of answering this question, it will be necessary to draw a distinction between the alleged crimes of murder and/or incitement to murder, on the one hand, and the second legal notion used by the Judgment, that of *Crimes against Peace,* which will have to be discussed separately.

The alleged crimes are no private deeds, committed for private reasons. Prosecution and Verdict state that they have been allegedly committed during a state of war, when the accused held the rank of officer, and was said to have abused, in breach of the rules of International Law, his military authority of command.

Armies which operate on foreign territories during war suspend the territorial sovereignty of the state where they operate. Jurisdiction over crimes committed by members of the occupying military forces belongs to the occupying state, which adjudicates on them by its own courts-martial. In the case under review, it is the Federal Republic of Germany which has jurisdiction over the alleged crimes, both as the legal successor to the German Reich and under the territorial principle. Professor Oberländer was serving as an officer in the German Wehrmacht, he is now a citizen of the Federal Republic, and he also has his residence there.

However, the traditional legal position in respect of war crimes has been modified by inter-Allied agreements made during the Second World War. These agreements handed over jurisdiction, through the London Statute and the principles enunciated by the Moscow Declaration, to the state on whose territory war crimes were committed. In the cases alleged against Oberländer, this state is the Soviet Union, unless the assumption is preferred that Lwow, and the crimes allegedly committed there, belonged to Polish jurisdiction at the time under discussion, because the German-

Soviet agreements on the division of Poland were not recognized as valid by the Western Powers.

In neither of these two cases is it possible to construe jurisdictional competence for a court in the Soviet Zone.

In order to explain away this legal difficulty, the court in the Soviet Zone uses the expedient to classify the alleged murders, etc., as part and parcel of continued criminal activities which were based on, and grouped round, a so-called *Crime Against Peace*. By finding that Oberländer took part 'actively and prominently' both in 'preparing for' and in 'unleashing and carrying out', the Second World War, the murders, etc., cease to be independent and isolated acts but become dependent parts of the main crime allegedly committed against the peace, and this main crime is said to have been localized in, and centred upon, Berlin. By this expedient, the court in the Zone gatecrashes a limited area of jurisdiction, which has been created by international agreement, but in which it does not possess *locus standi*.

Jurisdiction is claimed for the Soviet Zone court by making two separate assertions. One of them is the following: —

> The crimes charged against defendant are to be seen as . . . a direct contribution to preparing and carrying out the Second World War, which was directed and organized from the entire territory of former *German Reich*, and especially by this Reich's central leadership in Berlin [22].

That means that Oberländer has been found guilty of planning and execution of an aggressive war. The second assertion states: —

> Part of the former territory of the Reich, including Berlin, is now the state territory of the German Democratic Republic. Over this territory — apart from the special and abnormal situation in West Berlin — the G.D.R. exerts full sovereign powers in accordance with the principles of democratic international law, as one of the two successor states to the *German Reich*, which has disappeared in 1945 when the Nazi regime was destroyed [23].

This continues as follows: —

> The acts alleged against Oberländer 'were committed, to a considerable extent on former *German Reich* territory which now forms the state territory of the G.D.R.' [24].

The crimes charged against Oberländer, which he allegedly committed in the Soviet Union and in Poland, under the comprehensive charge construed by the court of the Soviet Zone, are said to have formed a single and indivisible action together with the first-named crime against peace, and this leads to the conclusion that the court in the Soviet Zone has jurisdiction also for the crimes committed on Soviet (and perhaps, on Polish) territory.

Against this, it has first to be pointed out that the notion of a *Crime Against Peace* is a new and strongly contested notion in International Law. Even under the principles forming the basis for the Inter-Allied Military Judicature in Nuremberg, crimes against peace have been charged only against a relatively small group of persons, whose characteristic feature was that they were in possession of a large measure of knowledge of, and took part decisively, in affairs of State, or belonged to the political leadership. Oberländer's subordinate authority excludes his belonging to this group of persons. Furthermore, for the crimes alleged against him in Lwow and in the Caucasus, it is impossible to construe unity of commission of continued activities, and thus punishment cannot be meted out for these alleged acts jointly. Regarding such localized crimes, the jurisdiction of the U.S.S.R. would be competent. Finally, contrary to the assertions made in the Judgment of the Soviet Zone court, Berlin is not part of the so-called G.D.R., even if we accept, for a moment, this questionable satellite province of the Soviets as a state whose sovereignty has been internationally recognized. The Reasons given for the Soviet Zone Judgment contain long arguments trying to prove Oberländer's participation in the planning and execution of aggressive war, and these arguments form a crucial part of these Reasons. We have to examine this alleged participation with regard to the problem of war crimes committed during and after the Second World War.

THE COURT IN THE GERMAN SOVIET ZONE HAS NO *LOCUS STANDI* ACCORDING TO THE INTER-ALLIED AGREEMENTS ON WAR CRIMES

War crimes under the agreements made by the victorious powers take in a much wider group of criminal acts than had been considered to be war crimes under traditional law. But also the traditional notion of war crimes developed gradually during the period of modern international law in which war by itself was still a permissible method of national self-defence.

It is revealing to look up the two headings, *War Crimes,* and *War Criminals,* in the Dictionary of International Law, and to read what this compendium has to say under them in its two editions published in 1924 and 1961.

The first edition [25] defines *War Crimes as acts causing torts contrary to the Laws of War.* A distinction is then made between acts of combat, and ordinary crimes not committed during combat action.

In the normal way, jurisdiction over, and punishment of, such acts is in the hands of the state under whose sovereignty the persons committing these acts stand. The question whether the injured state, too, may punish the criminal is answered in the affirmative under international legal customs (a sort of international Common Law).

It is significant that the problem whether aggressive war ranges under war crimes was not discussed at all in 1924. That question did not exist then.

The new edition of the same Dictionary defines War Crimes as *grave violations of International War Law, committed by the organs of a Power at war against persons or material goods of an enemy state, a vanquished state, or of a neutral territory that has been occupied by force* [26].

A sharp distinction is then made between *Crimes Against Peace* and *War Crimes.*

The doctrine of jurisprudence underlines the vast difference between these two ideas. For example, Professor Dahm [27] says: —

> In punishing War Crimes, the basis upon which the judicature acts is relatively secure. For a long time already, a number of legal customs have formed an international Common Law, according to which infringements of the rules of the Laws of War, committed by members of the Armed Forces or by other persons, may be punished by the courts-martial of the state against which the tort was committed, or by the state whose citizens the offenders are, without regard to the place in which the crime was committed. And on principle, there is also no obstacle to having such crimes prosecuted and punished in international courts of law.
>
> However, the legal nature of so-called *Crimes Against Peace* is totally different. Only during the proceedings taken in Nuremberg have such crimes been defined with some legal precision. But further developments in International Law make it very doubtful whether this can be considered the beginning of a continuous evolution of new international law. Up to the Second World War, the question was answered almost unanimously in the negative. — 'It was only through the London Agreement of 1945, and through the Rules for the International Military Tribunals convened after the war (Nuremberg, Article 6a; Tokyo, Article 5a), that aggressive war has been declared to be punishable retroactively. *But even as these Tribunals were exceptional courts, punishment for waging aggressive war has remained a special and exceptional law affecting a limited group of persons up to now*' [28].

In a similar way, Professor Wilhelm Grewe, former German ambassador to the United States, has analysed and explored more throughly this state of affairs in International Law. He states that it was the Kellogg Pact under which the Prosecution in the Main Trial at Nuremberg inferred direct criminal responsibility of individuals who caused a breach of this pact, and the Tribunal followed the Prosecution in this case. But this interpretation could not be accepted as universally binding mainly for the following double reason: —

None of the contracting partners signing the Kellogg Pact in 1928 ever anticipated the possibility that persons responsible for breaking this pact could be criminally prosecuted. They based their signatures on the conviction that violations of their committment accepted would lead to moral disqualification of the offending state [29].

That the legal position has been correctly described by Professor Grewe can be proved by the international reactions to a number of grave violations of the Kellogg Pact between 1928 and 1939: —

Neither in 1931, during the Japanese occupation of Manchuria, nor in 1934, during the war in the Gran Chaco, nor either in 1935/36, during the war between Italy and Ethiopia, nor in 1937, during the conflict between China and Japan, nor, finally, in 1939/40, during the winter war between Finland and the Soviet Union, did anybody ever seriously suggest that the persons responsible for the outbreak of these wars should be internationally prosecuted as criminals. In most of these cases, public opinion in the world had not doubts whatever which of the two sides engaged in these wars had violated the treaty. It is possible that in most cases there was no power available to prosecute and punish the guilty ones, but it must be underlined that there was never the slightest attempt to claim criminal jurisdiction, even only theoretically and in principle, against persons responsible for the outbreak of these wars. On the contrary, in most of these cases, diplomatic negotiations were carried on with the states that had broken the pact, and with their responsible statesmen, leading to diplomatic arrangements with them, and the conquests made by those states in breach of the treaty were, in some cases, even recognized *de iure* [30].

But not only German authors have contested both the binding character of the notion of Crimes Against Peace in positive international law and its capacity for determining legal policies. Lord Hankey has fought this new definition, in particular because "there is usually some provocation for an aggression and it is often impossible to judge the point at which a provocation becomes itself an aggression. That difficulty is particularly liable to arise in connection with the maltreatment of minorities of different nationality and/or religion from that of the majority of a population." [31] Lord Hankey too, is of opinion that the Kellogg Pact never visualized the alleged personal responsibility. Also the Indian member of the Inter-Allied Tribunal in Tokyo fought the claims made by the London Statute that victors can draw up a definition of War Crimes. "To say that the victor can define a crime at his will... and then punish... would be to revert back to those days when he was allowed to devastate the occupied country, ... appropriate all public and private property therein, and kill the inhabitants or take them away into captivity..." [32].

Since then, the list of violations of the prohibition of war has lengthened. The most striking examples were the Korean War, the Suez intervention, and the warlike intervention in Hungary by the Red Army.

Not a single one of these cases has led to criminal proceedings being taken against the men responsible. The practice of Nuremberg has remained an exceptional procedure restricted to Germans. It has not established a new beginning in making new and binding laws. That the court in the Soviet Zone bases its decision on a legal construction which has never been accepted, either before or after Nuremberg, and especially the 'Reasons' adduced for its verdict in Chapter I of the Judgment, show that this is only badly camouflaged political rancour.

War Crimes and 'Crimes Against Peace'

Inter-Allied agreements on localizing jurisdiction for the war crimes committed during the Second World War in the narrower sense of their definition have been envisaged for the first time in an Inter-Allied Three Power Declaration (the Moscow Declaration of October 30, 1943 [33]). Paragraph 3 of this declaration says: —

> As soon as any government has been formed in Germany, and has been accorded an armistice, those German officers, soldiers, and Nazi Party members who were responsible for the above-cited cruelties, massacres, and executions, or took part in them consentingly, *will be sent back to the countries* where their appalling deeds were committed, in order to be put into court and punished according to the laws of these liberated countries and the free governments formed in them. All these countries will draw up lists showing all the obtainable details. In this, particular regard will be paid to the occupied areas of the Soviet Union, of Poland and Czechoslovakia, Yugoslavia, and Greece, including Crete and other islands, Norway, Denmark, the Netherlands, Belgium and Luxembourg, France and Italy.'

Later on, the declaration says: —

> Thus Germans who take part, or have taken part in mass shootings of Polish officers or in the execution of French, Dutch, Belgian, or Norwegian hostages or Cretan peasants, in the bloodbaths among the Polish people or in the areas of the Soviet Union which have now been cleansed of the enemy, have to expect that they will be *returned to the places where they committed their crimes,* and will be judged *in situ* by the peoples whom they treated with violence.

In our case, it is precisely this example of allied war legislation that is of significance, because the Prosecution alleges the commission of localized crimes by the Nachtigall and Bergmann units in Poland and in the Caucasus. But this declaration is interesting also for three more reasons:

(1) It limits the prosecution to members of the German Wehrmacht and Nazi Party. The declaration does not fix the prosecution of

war crimes by the state on whose territory these crimes were committed as a general rule, not even for all the forces of the Allies' enemies (the Axis powers, e. g. members of the Italian armed forces, members of the Italian Fascist Party, citizens of the smaller Axis satellites, etc.), but exclusively for German citizens of the named groups.

(2) Up to the First World War, there existed competing competences for adjudicating war crimes (both the state whose citizens had committed the crimes, and the offended state, had jurisdiction), but the new Allied rules give the claim to jurisdication exclusively to the offended state. They say that the states *offended* by the crimes named are to have *exclusive* adjudicatory competence.

(3) In view of the practical problems under review, also this is essential: The declaration shows that the countries named started the investigation of the alleged facts (by drawing up *lists showing all the obtainable facts)* already in 1943. This leads to incontrovertible conclusion that crimes of such immense scope as were alleged against Professor Oberländer and the Nachtigall and Bergmann units after the lapse of so many years must have been investigated and known, at least in their outlines, already in 1945, so that this knowledge would have been sufficient for opening a prosecution.

The London Four Power Agreement of August 8, 1945 [34], also refers to the declaration made already during the war. In Article 4, it is stated: —

> The rules laid down by the Moscow Declaration about the return of war criminals to those countries where they committed their crimes will not be affected by the present Agreement.

The agreement made in Moscow was published as a *Declaration* of three powers, whilst the Four Power *Agreement* was a treaty signed by four partners. These were the same four powers which defined the war crimes by the Statute establishing their military court [35] (Article 6), which they called an *International Military Court.* However, a more appropriate designation is, *Inter-Allied Military Court.* International judicature can only exist if the state that is tried by it assents to its competence — by a separate act, or through acceding to its institutionalization. This is, for example, the case with the International Court of Law in the Hague, whose statute provides for the appointment of temporary judges (Judges *ad hoc,* following Article 31 of the Statutes of the International Court of Law). It is in the nature of international law that jurisdiction and competence claimed by the signatory powers of the London Statute, as they are based on a treaty, are limited to the signatories. Accession of additional powers to the Statute is only possible in accordance with Article 5 of the London Agreement, and membership of the United Nations is one of the formal conditions for the accession of new states.

War Crimes were described by Article 6 of the Statute, as follows: Paragraph (b) enumerates the traditional war crimes (through violation of the laws and customs of war). The paragraph adds that such violations, without being limited by this list, also include: —

> Murder, maltreatment, or deportation, for slave labour or for any other purpose of members of the civilian population of, or in, occupied areas; murder or maltreatment of prisoners of war, or of persons at sea, killing of hostages, plundering of public or private property, wanton destruction of cities, market towns, or villages, and any kind of devastation not justified by military needs.

Newly added categories of crimes are defined as Crimes Against Peace and Crimes Against Humanity.

Under Crimes Against Peace are listed: —

> The planning, preparations for, initiation or execution of aggressive war, or of a war in breach of international treaties, agreements, or promises to take part, or participation in the joint planning, or in plotting to carry out one of the afore-mentioned actions;

and Crimes Against Humanities consist of: —

> The murder, extermination, enslavement, deportation, or other inhuman actions, committed against any civilian population before or during a war, the persecution on political, racial, or religious grounds, committed in the execution of a crime, or in connection with a crime for which the Court has jurisdiction, independently of whether this action violates the laws of the country where it was committed, or not.
>
> The leaders, organizers, inveiglers, or accessories, who have taken part in drawing up, or carrying out, joint plans or a conspiracy for the commission of any of the afore-mentioned crimes, are responsible for all actions committed by any persons in the execution of such plans.

Limitation and Definition of the Groups of Persons Against Whom Proceedings were Opened for 'Crimes Against Peace'

The problem how to define and limit the group of persons against whom a prosecution may be opened for committing Crimes Against Peace has been dealt with by a number of statements made in carrying out the London Statute.

During the Nuremberg trials before the International Military Tribunal (Judgment passed on October 1, 1946), 12 defendants were found guilty of *Crimes Against Peace* (Göring, Hess, Ribbentrop, Keitel, Rosenberg, Funk, Dönitz, Raeder, Jodl, Seiss-Inquart, Neurath, and Frick). All the accused organizations, too, viz. the Corps of Political Leaders, Gestapo, *SD*, SA, SS, the Reich government, the General Staff, and *OKW* (Supreme

Command of the Wehrmacht), were charged with *Crimes Against Peace* by the Brief for the Prosecution. Of these, the SA, the Reich government, the General Staff, and *OKW* were eventually not included among the criminal organizations. That part of the Judgment concerning the OKW and which is relevant for us states: —

> ... According to the evidence submitted, their planning activities in the staff units, continuous conferences between staff officers and commanders in the field, their operational technique in the field and in their staff quarters were about the same as those in the armies, navies, and air forces of all other countries. The all-embracing acitivities of *OKW*, which aimed at coordination and direction, are comparable with similar, though not identical, forms of organization in other armies, for example with the Anglo-American Joint Chiefs of Staff.
>
> The inference drawn from this pattern of their activities that there existed an association or group is not conclusive in the view of court. According to such a theory, the supreme commanders of any nation would also represent such an association, instead of a collection of military personnel, which they actually are, a number of persons who, at a given time, accidentally fill the upper military echelons.
>
> If somebody, for example, became an SS member, he did so out of his own free will, or in another way, but certainly in the knowledge of joining something definite. In the cases of the General Staff and of Supreme Commands, he could, however, not know that he joined a group or association; since there was no such association, except in the charges contained in the Brief for the Prosecution. He knew only that he had attained a definite high rank in one of the three branches of the Wehrmacht but could not be conscious of the alleged fact that he thereby became a member of something as definite as a *group* in the usual sense of the term. His relations with his comrades of his own arm, and his connections to those of the two other arms, generally resembled service conditions as they are customary all over the world.
>
> Therefore the Court declares that the General Staff and the Supreme Command were not criminal organizations.

The Court then took the view that, although the number of accused individuals from these groups was larger than in the case of the Reich government, *it was nevertheless so small that individual proceedings against each defendant could be taken.* A trial of this type was the so-called *OKW* trial. The number of defendants in this case was thirteen. All of them were high-ranking senior officers (field marshals, colonel-generals, generals). In a book written by Taylor, one of the American chief prosecutors, the position was described as follows [35a] : —

> All the defendants were accused of having planned and conducted aggressive wars. The evidence consequently showed that many of them had attended the main conferences during which Hitler had revealed his intentions, to make war on Poland, the Netherlands, Russia, and other countries. The IMT based its verdict against von Keitel, Raeder, and von Neurath decisively upon their having taken part in these conferences. Some of the defendants who had not

themselves attended conferences with Hitler collaborated in making drafts for invasion plans.

Inspite of these circumstances, the Court refused to make use of the evidence in question. In the view of the Court, knowledge of Hitler's aggressive designs, and taking part in planning and initiating aggressive wars

was not sufficient for transforming participation in war itself into a crime even with the military leaders of senior rank.

For this, it would have been necessary

that those who were in possession of such knowledge had been, after obtaining such information, in positions suitable for determing or influencing policy, in a way that they could have either fostered or prevented or counteracted it beforehand.

Without entering upon a discussion of the functions and actions of individual defendants, the Court concluded that

the defendants did not find themselves in the positions of leading politicians, and are therefore not guilty in this point of accusations.

The Supreme Court in the Soviet Zone is neither an independent organ of jurisdiction nor does it possess competence under the inter-Allied agreements on war crimes.

As shown above, inter-Allied regulations made during and after the Second World War, which provide for the extradition of persons accused of war crimes to the governments of states where the alleged criminal acts took place, broke with the rules that had been accepted previously under common law customs, which left jurisdiction to the courts-martial of the armies operating on foreign state territory, or to the states whose subjects the offending persons were. The new rule was the guiding principle proclaimed in the Moscow Declaration and agreed upon in the London Agreement. Control Council Law No. 10 also refers to the two agreements, declaring that the Moscow Declaration, the London Agreement, and also the Statute of the Inter-Allied Military Court are part and parcel of that Law itself.

Clear prescriptive international law — meaning, clearly outlined acts that are described as criminal activities — existed for the Inter-Allied Military Court of Nuremberg only through the definition given by the London Statute, especially in its Article 6 [36]. This is not the place to discuss the legal problem as such, which is presented by the fact that the victorious powers created, in part, completely new definitions of crimes in international law by agreement among themselves, whose effects in criminal law were not even extended over the entire vanquished camp but applied only to selected enemy powers, namely Germany and Japan.

Not only German but especially British critics have protested against this procedure. The Soviet prosecutor in Nuremberg, General Rudenko, believed to be able to state that, by having been created on the basis of the London Agreement, the International Military Court sprang from 'an unassailable and adequate legislative act', so that it was based on sufficient foundations in international law. The basic legal fact that agreements create new law only for the partners to the agreement was not touched upon by Rudenko [37]. The statement that the four Powers had acted in the interest of all the freedom-loving nations is an *ex parte* assertion, which does not replace the requirement that new international common law customs can only be created by agreement and common conviction among the powers taking part in the creation of an international rule of law [38]. (The question whether the *affirmation* of the *Nuremberg Principles* by a resolution of the United Nations General Assembly may serve as the expression, or as a substitute, for such a universally agreed conviction of the justice of new international rules will have to be discussed later). In view of the interpretation of the new legal notions, which had played their part for the first time in Nuremberg, during the trial before the Supreme Court of the Soviet Zone, we have first to point to a fundamental procedural rule contained in the London Statute, and incorporated and interpreted in Control Council Law No. 10. According to Article 5 of the Statute, member governments of the United Nations may accede to the agreement. According to the preamble of Control Council Law No. 10, it was the purpose of this law to carry out the rules set out in the London Agreement and in the Moscow Declaration, and to create a unified legal basis in Germany for the criminal prosecution of war criminals, except those who were tried in the Inter-Allied Military Court at Nuremberg. According to Article 1, the Moscow Declaration of October, 30, 1943, 'regarding the responsibility of the adherents of Hitler for atrocities committed', and the London Agreement, 'regarding the prosecution and punishment of the chief war criminals of the European Axis' are forming inseparable parts of that Law. But the last sentence of Article 1 determines: —

> The fact that one of the United Nations accedes to the London Agreement, as provided for in its Article 5, does not entitle that nation to take part in the application of the present Law in the area of sovereignty under the Control Council in Germany, or to interfere in its execution.

The principles laid down by the London Agreement and Statute, and by Control Council Law No. 10, are obviously fixing the basic rules for the procedure against the selected number of war criminals of the Second World War, who were to be prosecuted. The signatory powers to the London Agreement assumed competence for their prosecution and judging.

For the chief war criminals, the signatories passed on their competence to the Inter-Allied Military Court in Nuremberg, or to national military courts. Localized crimes were referred to the state where they have been committed. Even those member states of the United Nations which had acceded to the London Agreement were expressly excluded by Control Council Law No. 10 both from applying and from executing that Law. Article 4 of that Law accepts the general rule that localized crimes have to be referred to the state where they were committed, for judgment. The article regularizes the procedure for this: The governments of such states (or the supreme commander of the relevant occupation zone) have to apply to the occupation authorities in Germany for the criminal's extradition.

Another rule laid down by the Statute is also important for our case. According to Article 14 b, the Committee of the four Attorneys-General (or Prosecutors-General) has the duty to make the final decisions who will be considered a chief war criminal and handed over as such to the Court for prosecution.

Only if new evidence is unearthed which, in the opinion of the Control Council, may form the basis for a new prosecution, the Committee of the Attorneys-General can be asked to act under Article 29, and its procedure is again regulated by Article 14.

These various rules outline the legal character of the inter-Allied settlement on the prosecution of war crimes committed during the Second World War. The basis of these rules is an agreement concluded between individual parties, the Four Power Agreement of August 8, 1945, which was signed by France, the United Kingdom, the Soviet Union, and the United States. Under this Agreement, those four powers defined the crimes to be prosecuted by the Inter-Allied Military Court, which was also set up by them, or according to the subsidiary rules contained in Control Council Law No. 10. Judicial office is devolving upon the judges appointed under Article 2 of the Statute, or upon their substitutes. These judges were appointed by the signatory powers only. Members of the United Nations are permitted to accede to the Agreement but they thereby do not acquire a seat on the judges' bench, nor do they participate in applying and executing Control Council Law No. 10 in the area of sovereignty under the Control Council for Germany — on the contrary, they have been specially excluded from this. Who will be prosecuted as chief war criminal is determined by the Committee of Attorneys-General under Article 14 of the Statute; their decision is final. Subsequent, new prosecutions are dependent on the submission of new evidence, and are only possible under Article 29, Paragraph 2.

The Supreme Court of the Soviet Zone bases its claim to competence on the alleged existence of a continued single crime. Oberländer's alleged crimes against peace are supposed to provide the basis and the inner connection between otherwise isolated and localized, alleged crimes in Lwow and in the Caucasus.

However, the Reasons given for the Verdict on the alleged crime against peace cannot convince anybody. The Judgment passed by the Supreme Court in the Soviet Zone carefully avoids any discussion of the above-mentioned IMT judgment, which rightly confined the group of persons able to commit crimes against peace to a very narrow circle, whose members might have been able, through their senior positions, to contribute to forming, and influencing, Hitler's policies. The sweeping statements about *Ostpolitik* (Eastern policies) and eastern research, which show their character as political polemics clearly, are not a valid substitute for such a reference. The Soviet Zone judgment then passes over in silence the fact that the *OKW*, under which Oberländer did his military service, was not considered a criminal organization. As if it could not care less, the communist court considers his activities in and for the *OKW* — all in subordinate positions as a lieutenant, and later first-lieutenant, of the reserve — and the fact that they fell in about the same periods as the occupation of the Sudeten area and the start of the Polish campaign, sufficient proof for his guilt. The court neither touches with a single word the inexplicable fact that, inspite of the alleged uncommon gravity and scope of the crimes charged against the Nachtigall and Bergmann units, the Soviet government, which had been collecting incriminating material from the date of the Moscow Declaration (1943), onwards did not start proceedings against these units and against Oberländer already in 1945, whether as chief war criminals (which the Prosecutor-General in East Berlin trial attempted to do against the rules of Control Council Law No. 10), or as local war criminals. The judgment also took no account of the fact that the murder of the Polish professors had already formed the substance of a prosecution started by the Soviet Union in 1945, without then mentioning Oberländer or the Nachtigall Unit. In the light of the judgment passed on all these crimes, the allegation that Oberländer committed crimes against peace is evidently groundless. The only motive for making this allegation appears to be the attempt to exclude the state from jurisdiction where these crimes are alleged to have been committed.

Apart from this, the actual subdivision of jurisdictions made by the Four Powers in the field of war crimes excludes any competence of a court in the Soviet Zone. The London Agreement broke down the criminal jurisdictions between the Inter-Allied Military Court, on the one hand, the courts instituted by the Supreme Commanders in the Occupation Zones under Control Council Law No. 10, and the local courts adjudging localized crimes, on the other hand. Control Council Law No. 10 excludes any other state from participation in carrying out these agreements.

This applies even more to the so-called German Democratic Republic, which is not a member of the United Nations — and only such may accede to the agreements. (And even if she were a U.N. member, she could not take part in applying and executing the law.) The court in the Soviet Zone has gate-crashed the exclusive legal circle, which had been specially drawn, as a court which has no jurisdiction under inter-Allied agreements. That means that it lacks all jurisdiction even in the purely formal sense.

The 'Nuremberg Principles'

Another argument is being marshalled by the Supreme Court of the Soviet Zone for proving that it possesses judicial competence. This is the assertion that the *Principles of Nuremberg* have become generally valid International Law, so that the constitution of the so-called German Democratic Republic requires their application.

It is true that the United Nations General Assembly gave approval to a resolution on December 11, 1946, which took cognizance of the establishment of the Inter-Allied Military Court and its Statute, also that similar principles had been proclaimed by the Statute of the Inter-Allied Military Court for the Far East. The Assembly instructed the Committee for the Codification of International Law to give priority to the formulation of the principles recognized by those Statutes and by the Courts' Judgments. The Committee passed on this task, 'because it requires careful and lengthy studies', to the International Law Commission [39].

The International Law Commission, in one of its meetings, appointed *rapporteur*. In the beginning, the view prevailed that the Commission had only to find an adequate wording for the said principles, as the General Assembly had affirmed them by its resolution of December 11, 1946 [40]. The *rapporteur* then produced a report, which outlined seven principles, and this led to an extensive discussion in the Commission, during which material objections were raised against the substantive contents of these principles, e. g. by both the Dutch and the Yugoslav delegates [41]. On December 12, 1950, the Sixth U.N. Committe received the report on the work done by the International Law Commission, and the U.N. member states were asked to make their comments known. These opinions were used for writing a second report by the International Law Commission. This Commission now held the opinion that it was not bound 'to take over the Nuremberg Principles in their entirety into its codification.' *On the contrary, it considered itself entitled to propose modifications of those principles, and to embody these in its codification.* It decided to deal with criminal responsibility only as far as it was borne by individuals [42]. And from 1952 onwards, the heading, *Nuremberg Principles,* did not make any more a single appearance in the General Index of the United Nations Yearbook. The question, as can be seen from the description of the work done by the Commission 1951, has changed materially, and has been swallowed up by the mainstream of a far more general problem, that of codifying all International Law.

That means that the *Principles of Nuremberg* have never become general principles of law, and thus also not a source of positive law under Article 38, Paragraph 3, of the Statute for the International Court of Law. They were definitions of restricted effects in one practical case. Looked at from the standpoint of International Common Law, they represent material for a history of the law, and it remains to be seen whether, in due course, and through more general agreements, they may become, with possible modifications, generally binding rules.

Merely the consideration that the crimes defined by the Nuremberg Principles would have become binding upon future signatories of an agreement to be hammered out by the International Law Commission, and that no such agreement has ever been signed, goes to show that the so-called Nuremberg Principles, at present, do not possess binding and regulatory power, as the judgment of the Soviet Zone court assumes.

Further developments in International Law also confirm this statement. Neither after the war between Israel and the Arab states, nor after the Korean War, nor after the attack upon Suez against Egypt, nor, of course, after the Red Army's intervention in Hungary, was there any hint that somebody might start criminal proceedings against some defendants according to the general principles used for the Nuremberg trials. The trials held in Nuremberg and Tokyo, in this context, can be shown to have been exceptions from the general rule, and never had the effect of legal precedents.

In this legal situation, the arguments used by the Soviet Zone judgment to show that, 'according to modern, democratic', international law, the obstacle of parliamentary immunity (Article 46 of the West German Basic Law) which would have made criminal proceedings against the then member of the Federal Diet, Oberländer, dependent on the assent of that Federal Diet, need not be taken seriously, and require only the briefest of rebuttals. As the Supreme Court of the Soviet Zone states, the so-called G.D.R. is not bound in law to follow such a constitutional rule but, on principle, observes it as a matter of international courtesy. But in the case under review, the Court asserts that the general rules of International Law, especially according to Article 25 of the West German Basic Law, supersede this rule, and thus do away with the legal obstacle of immunity. It is, of course, to be admitted that parliamentary immunity does not grant absolute and perpetual protection against a criminal prosecution, but only a temporary and relative one. (Also the Bonn Public Prosecutor's Office conducted its investigation with a view to eventually applying for the waiving of parliamentary immunity, dependent on the result of its enquiries.) The assertion that the gravity of crimes to be prosecuted under International Law automatically breaks down the obstacle in the way of a prosecution is untenable as an internationally valid general rule. Even in cases of proved or highly probable crimes under International Law, it is formally necessary under the Constitution that immunity be waived. The results of the investigation under the Rule of Law have shown to sufficiency that the assertions made in the Soviet Zone about Oberländer's alleged criminal activities are untrue in every single point. This is the very reason why the prosecuting authorities in the Federal Republic of Germany never applied for the waiving of Oberländer's immunity under Article 46 of the Basic Law.

The additional assertion of the Judgment that the Supreme Court in the Soviet Zone has local jurisdiction for a criminal prosecution under the rules applying to successor states, regarding criminal acts alleged to have been committed in Berlin as the former capital city of the Reich need not be discussed any more, in view of the legal situation in substance.

Adjudicatory Powers of the Soviet Zone Court

This court, therefore, has no jurisdiction, for various reasons, namely: —

(a) The so-called G.D.R. is not one of the offended states under the Moscow Declaration of 1943, or under the London Statute of the International Military Tribunal. On the assumption that the alleged crimes have, in fact, been committed, the offended state(s) might be the Soviet Union, and/or Poland.

(b) The London Statute, and also Control Council Law No. 10, do not even grant states which make use of their right to accede to these statutes a share in the judicature and jurisdication.

(c) The so-called G.D.R. is not generally recognized as a state under International Law. In addition, she is not a member state of the United Nations, and only such member states can claim accession to the agreements in question.

(d) Professor Oberländer was not one of the persons, or groups, who were capable of committing a Crime Against Peace under the London Statute. After we have quoted the rules delimiting the groups of persons who would have been so capable, it is superfluous further to discuss the assertion made both by the Brief for the Prosecution and the Judgment passed in the Soviet zone and to prove that neither the then lieutenant and first-lieutenant of the reserve, nor his work in *OKW*, nor the former national chairman of the *Bund Deutscher Osten* and provincial chairman of the East Prussian *VDA*, who already in 1937 had been deprived of all his offices, belonged to the extremely limited circle of persons who, possessing the necessary secret knowledge, would have been able to influence Adolf Hitler's policies. Even if membership in this circle should be confirmed, it is still open to question whether the claim for jurisdiction by the offended state, under the Moscow Declaration and the London Statute, does not claim precedence. But as Oberländer did not belong to this narrow circle of persons, because of his subordinate position, the alleged continuity and connection between a series of alleged crimes did not exist.

(e) Finally — as will have to be discussed further — the courts in the Zone, in any case in political cases, are not independent courts of law, as defined by Article 10 of the Declaration of the United Nations on Human Rights, and by Article 6 of the European Convention on Human Rights, but merely executive instruments of a political leadership, which uses these instruments for obtaining quasi-legal confirmation for its preordained decisions.

THE LAW OF THE GERMAN SOVIET ZONE AND LEGAL CHARACTERISTICS OF THE JUDGMENT IN THE OBERLÄNDER CASE

In the beginning of our investigation, we emphasized that the key to understanding of the Oberländer Case can only be found in Soviet views on the nature and functions of law. The Law and the judicature of the Soviet Occupation Zone have been closely modelled on the lines of the Soviet pattern. It is sufficient for our purpose to study its most important characteristics, and we cannot go deeply into the highly significant changes that occurred only in the Stalin era, in part through Stalin's own intervention, and which led to the creation of the idea of a *socialist state,* which had been unknown before his time. But these changes, perhaps, lead to a clearer understanding of the functional rôle that Law plays in the Soviet system, for the idea of a 'socialist state', which forms the focus, to-day, of the State theory in the entire Eastern Bloc, had no existence in the theories either of Marx or of Lenin [43]. Lenin followed early Marxism in declaring that the State as such was destined on principle, after the seizure of power by the proletariat, to *wither away.* Following Marx again, he stated that the *Dictatorship of the Proletariat* was only to be a brief, transitory, stage on the way to Classless, and thus Stateless, Society. But later: he opened the gates himself to developing the new idea of a *Socialist State,* which would not only persist for a short period of transition but, as Stalin subsequently taught his disciples in all seriousness, *actually should remain in being for a lengthy stage.* Lenin taught that the Class of the Proletarians must use the instruments, means, and methods of State power against the *exploiters* temporarily, and he described the Soviet dictatorship as a *semi-state,* but he emphasized at the same time that he would on no account deviate from the anarchists' final objective, namely that he aimed at the eventual abolition of the State. The marxist definition of the State as the organized rule of one class could be applied to the real power situation after the foundation of Soviet rule. But it was soon to be seen that this *State of the Soviets* did not enter upon a period of withering away — on the contrary it continued to go from strength to strength. And it was Lenin's successor, Stalin, who laid the theoretical foundations of the *socialist state.* He stated that the tasks of the State had not disappeared during the socialist stage of development in the Soviet state but had, on the contrary, grown, for the function of the State was now to *protect socialist property against thieves and pilferers, and to afford military protection to the country against foreign aggressors,* and remained. This uses the basis for the need to maintain an army, an apparatus of criminal jurisdiction and prosecution, as well as a penal system, and an intelligence service [45]. In the end, the *economic and organizational, and cultural and educational, tasks of the State organs remained in being and continued to evolve further.* This further development of the State and of political conditions, and their forms, naturally also reflected upon the Soviet Theory of Law, and on the Soviet Theory of the State. *After a theory of the socialist state had been born, this inevitably also led to a new concept of Socialist Law — as a system of binding and prescriptive rules, which served to give expression to the imperious and coercive will of the State* [46].

An author who played a particularly prominent part in the creation of this theoretical system, so that his book on Soviet Law has acquired lasting significance to this day, was Andrey Vishinsky, who became notorious, first, as the prosecutor in the great purge trials, later, as a diplomat of a particularly aggressive cast, and especially as the head of the Soviet delegation to the United Nations. He saw Law as *one of the weapons in the fight for Socialism,* an instrument *serving the reconstruction of Human Society on a socialist basis. Socialist Law* thus, on the one hand, resumes law's general character as a set of permanently valid, practical legal rules. On the other hand, it serves the central task of fulfilling a political mission in the interest of a class.

The function of Law in the *socialist State,* which is to mature, as a product of historical transition, towards the utopian and final objective of a fully communist society [47], is defined by the saying of Lenin 'that the dictatorship of the proletariat is but the form of the class struggle conducted by the victorious proletariat, which has taken possession of power and uses this power against the bourgeoisie which, though vanquished, has not been annihilated, since it has neither disappeared nor ceased to resist — on the contrary, it has increased its resistance' [48]. Related to this type of state, Vishinsky defines Law as the totality of the rules of conduct laid down through a legal order, which expresses the will of the ruling class, as well as the totality of the customs and rules of a community life, on so far as they are affirmed by State authority [49]. The efficacy of all these rules is guaranteed by the total coercive power of the Soviet state. These rules serve to deepen relationships and institutions benificial to the worker, to secure and develop them further, and finally to exterminate capitalism and its remnants in the economy, in all forms of life, and in human consciousness, so as to build eventually a communist society [50]. This leads the author to infer from his premises the specific functions of Law and of the courts under this dictatorship of the proletariat. The dictatorship cannot conduct its struggle against the class antagonist, which is continued by different means, with the instrument of extraordinary administrative measures. *The dictatorship of the proletariat acts with the aid of legal means through the courts and the rules of procedure* [51], which are the guiding principles of the political order of the Soviets. Concentration of the political powers (which necessarily leads to the rejection of the principle of division of powers) is of fundamental importance especially for the Soviet system of justice. The Soviet system essentially rests upon the programme: '*All Power belongs to the Soviets*' [52], including the power of jurisdiction and of judicature.

Inspite of all the changes and vacillations in the official acceptance of scientific, and thus also legal, theories, which are typical of all totalitarian regimes, the description given by A. Vishinsky of the legal system of the Soviets has remained a classic to this day. We are also interested in his discussion of the tasks of the courts, and their relationship with the prosecuting authorities. Vishinsky describes the court and the prosecutor's office as *powerful and important levers of power for the dictatorship of the proletariat,* which the dictatorship uses *to secure the fulfilment of its historical tasks* [53]. A court in the Soviet Union is an instrument *for safeguarding the interests of the State and the Soviet citizens;* by protecting the interests of the State, it also safeguards the interests of the citizens [54]; *the court must destroy all enemies of the people without mercy* [55]. As an illustration of this mission, Vishinsky chose *an example that had been contemporary at the time of writing, namely the task set to the courts to carry out the final extermination of the Trotsky-Bukharin gang.* Under the Soviet system, Court and Prosecution must be in the *closest possible contact,* and work hand in hand. They are acting jointly through insoluble and organic ties existing between them [56]. *Vishinsky emphasizes that they have identical tasks, though their methods of fulfilling them are different.* It is clear that the opinion that courts have to act in the interest of the entire social community, and to follow the rules of what is right, and of justice, are a *purely bourgeois theory and fallacy.*

Soviet courts radically reject such views. In another context, Vishinsky uses Lenin's words in order to describe the chief tasks of the courts as:

(1) waging the struggle against the former ruling class, and

(2) securing the maintenance of the strictest discipline and self-discipline among the workers [57].

Naturally, these principles apply also, and especially, to Criminal Law as it is practised in the Soviet Zone of Germany, since it is continually underlined that it is *socialist criminal law* that is practised there, which is intentionally different from traditional criminal law *(bourgeois* criminal law). Hilde Benjamin, the much feared woman who is the Minister of Justice in the Soviet Zone, expressed this point of view as follows: 'We do not only proclaim that the Law and the Courts of the Socialist State are instruments of Socialist Democracy, *we also prove it through our jurisdiction*' (we may add: particularly through the judgment against Oberländer). It is one of the essential features of this type of criminal law that it rejects expressly the principle of the division of powers; and this means that there is no independence of the courts. Thus, Michael Benjamin [59], in his essay, 'Lenin on Socialist Courts', for example wrote about *the invaluable legacy left by Lenin* regarding the theoretical foundations of the character and tasks of the courts. Fundamentally Lenin's theory is described as *emphasizing the identity of the activities of the judicial authorities, the local administration, and the general power of the State.* In addition, the courts' task is to use the criminal law for *enforcing discipline and self-discipline among the working masses.* Benjamin follows Vishinsky in quoting Lenin's phrases which give the courts the *even more important* task to secure the strictest observation of discipline and self-discipline among the toilers. Thus, Criminal Law becomes an instrument for re-educating and *guiding* especially the working class *on its socialist way.*

This feature of criminal law is untiringly underlinded and re-emphasized, e. g. in a report called, 'The Class Struggle and the Criminal Law' [60]. Following this basic teaching of Lenin's, communist legal theory declares that the lawyers' profession has become superfluous, on principle, and will not be tolerated.

The criminal law of the Soviet-occupied Zone of Germany accepts Lenin's concept down to the last detail. Paragraph Two of the Law on the Constitution of Courts in the so-called German Democratic Republic lays down [61] : —

> Jurisdiction as practised by the courts of the G.D.R. serves the building of Socialism, the unity of Germany, and Peace. Their tasks are: —
>
> (a) to protect the social and State order based on the Constitution of the G.D.R., and its legal system;

(b) to protect and to foster the foundations of Socialist Economy, in particular Socialist Property and the National Economic Plans;
(c) to protect all constitutional interests, and the political, economic, and cultural organizations;
(d) to protect the legal rights and interests of the citizens.

As Criminal Law has been made an instrument serving the class struggle exclusively, the definition of criminal acts is filled with a specific content. There is an official 'Textbook *(Lehrbuch)* of Criminal Law in the G.D.R.' [62], which has been written by a number of learned lawyers in the Soviet Zone. It makes the following statement on this subject: —

> Only such acts are subject to prosecution under the criminal laws of the Workers' and Peasants' State which directly endanger the People's Democratic order in State and Society, and the carrying out of its Laws of Development, and must therefore be prevented under any condition by the use of coercion by the State, which takes the form of punishment.

Built on such foundations, the criminal law in the Soviet Zone could not but discard the notion of guilt as used by classical Criminal Law. The effect is also that such criminal law has no ethical or moral content in the traditional sense. According to communist criminology, the main feature of any judgment is *political disapproval* of certain acts [63]. Thus, the habit of legal theorists in the Soviet Zone to describe their own form of justice proudly as '*political justice*', whilst at the same time using that expression as a term of abuse intended to put, for example, the West German judicature in disgrace, is not as absurd as it appears.

The division of Germany enforced and maintained by the Soviet Union, and the existence of a Soviet-occupied Zone, have caused jurisprudence in the Federal Republic of Germany to study and discuss more carefully than others the problems of communist notions and ideas of the State, and of Law. We shall only refer briefly to some of the results of these investigations, in so far as they touch directly on our subject.

Professor Richard Lange has examined the relationship between the notions of Law and the prevailing legal ideology [64], in view of the changes in Soviet doctrine of the State, which have been sketched by us in their fundamentals. Most will agree with him when he sees the root cause for the contrasts between the legal theories of East and West, not in the dispute about the influence of social conditions, but in the fundamentally different, basic, views of the State, and its character and tasks, which have their immediate effect upon all law. Whilst we believe the State to be the servant and protector of the Law, which existed before the State, and which limits its powers, *official doctrine both in the Soviet Zone and in the Soviet Union maintains that the State was always there before and above the Law, and that Law exists only for the State, as its artifact, expressing the will of the State to power*[65]. In support of his findings, Lange quotes from the Great Soviet Encyclopedia, using the German translation published in 1956, a definition of Law: —

> Law * is the will of the ruling class raised to the form of statutes. This will is determined by the material conditions under which that class lives. Law * is the totality of rules of behaviour (norms) which have been fixed through the power of the State, or sanctioned by it, and the implementation of which is being safeguarded by state measures of coercion having the aim to protect, to strengthen, and to develop those social conditions which are convenient and of advantage to the ruling class (and, under the conditions of Socialist Society, represent the vital interests of the entire people).[66]

Another quotation from the Encyclopedia defines Law * in the following terms: —

> The Law * reveals the policy of the class ruling in the individual State, and this can be seen, not only when legal norms (statutes) are created, but also in their application[67].

On the other hand, Professor Lange observes that we, in the West, have discarded legal positivism and are returning to a true notion of Law. In the course of this change, human freedom — so Lange argues — proved to be real, also, and especially, as a result of viewing Man from the standpoint of natural science. And freedom is the source of all law, so that the notion of Law has become possible again, not only as a product of speculative thinking but based on human reality. As the State and the Law are fundamentally different on the two sides of the Iron Curtain, Lange thinks it impossible to address the Soviet-occupied Zone as the 'German Democratic Republic', 'G.D.R.' for short, as if there were two German states in the same legal sense. Accepting the official communist denomination of the Occupation Zone would also mean the acceptance of the communist theory of power, which is the fulcrum of all the communist theories of the State and on Law. Everybody, however, who accepts our convictions about the functions of Law must see that there are no judges, in our sense of the term, officiating under the communist system, because

---

* Both in the German and Russian language, 'Law', as an abstract and collective noun, is expressed by a different word from 'the law', or 'the laws', meaning statutes, acts of parliament, or government decrees. The abstract, collective noun is expressed by '*Recht*' in German, so that the Rule of Law can only be translated by, '*der Rechtsstaat*' (the State under the Rule of Law); but *Recht* means also, 'right', both in the sense of a legal or moral claim and of something that embodies justice. The same ambiguity is contained in the Russian word, '*pravo*'. — Laws, meaning statute laws, laws of nature, etc., however, are, *Gesetze,* in German, and *zakony,* in Russian. In the sentences quoted above, 'Law' = *Recht, pravo,* is meant; where the first sentence uses, 'statutes', the German and Russian texts have, '*Gesetze*', '*zakony*', respectively. — Note of Translator.

that system defines the basic task of the judge as having '*partynost*' *(Parteilichkeit)* ** .

Basic problems of Soviet legal and State theory (and also those of the Soviet Zone) were discussed by the First Judges' Congress in Berlin, convened by the Berlin Association of Judges. At this conference, main speakers on the fundamental and structural questions of this subject were, among others, the then Federal Attorney-General, Dr. Güde, and Senate President (Chairman of High Court Judges), Professor Heinitz. Analysing conditions in the Soviet Zone, Dr. Güde gave a historical review, comparing the Nazi system with that of the Communists. What National Socialism tried to achieve but never managed to complete — namely the availability of a mass of judicial officials, who can be guided and directed arbitrarily, *because they call Law only what they believe to be a socially correct form of action, being unable to see no other form of justice* [69] — has been completed in the Soviet Zone. The regime in the Soviet Zone, according to Güde, has managed to create a system of, and to elaborate on, the last and latest 'achievements' of the Third Reich [70]. Güde, too, saw the fundamental contrast between the Rule of Law and Soviet legal conceptions in the completely contrary definitions of what Law really is. These definitions establish a *difference of principle between the decisions of a judge, who creates new law by his findings, and those of any other state agency:* —

> The power of the State, and the welfare of the Community find their expression in claims to authority, or in measures of social care, which are justified by their purpose, respectively by serving a purpose. But the decision of a judge, which has to serve the claims and values of Law is not a pronouncement based on power and must not be a pronouncement of that type — it has to be a finding of truth. Judges' findings are not justified by their utility, but by their truth, by their agreement with the Law. A judge can only find a true bill by obeying Law in all responsible conscience, but not by being obedient to a powerful will. Where this distinction is lost by forgetting it, or by denying it wilfully, as happened under the totalitarian regimes of yesterday and to-day, there can be neither justice nor jurisdiction [71].

Going on from there, Dr. Güde underlined the difficulty arising from the authoritarian *(obrigkeitsstaatlich)* legacy in all the German states,

---

** *Partynost, Parteilichkeit;* another untranslatable term common to both Russian and German. It means that the person having, or showing, *partynost* will always be biassed, and subject every thought and judgment to the interests of the party he takes. The opposite of *partynost* is 'objectivism', the hankering after objectivity and impartiality, which is one of the major sins in the Communist (and Nazi) moral code; cf. the attempts to create *German* physics, *German* (racial) biology, and *progressive* (Soviet) genetics, which liquidated (killed) the representatives of objective, desinterested science. — Note of Translator.

which leads, also in the Federal Republic of Germany, to *the preservation and continued drilling, in the judicature, of a certain type of servants of the State, full of servility* (obrigkeitsfromm), who — *I make no bones about this — we would much prefer not to see in the offices of judges and public prosecutors* [72]. Güde underlined the specially important problem of the judges' independence, which ought not only to be laid down by the laws but to have social reality, particularly in view of the marxist attacks on '*bourgeois concealment*'. But though he emphasized that this problem is a crucial question for the Federal Republic of Germany, too, Dr. Güde flatly rejected the interpretation of our judicial system as nothing but a product, and the servitor, of the 'capitalist class', and its interests by the Communists. He also stated that actual Law, and the legal conscience, are based upon moral freedom, and must never become a subordinate function of politics, by confronting the marxist scheme with contemporary reality of our society: —

> However, it can hardly be doubted that this schematic attempt to interpret our society as one of two antagonistic classes is insufficient, out-of-date, and, in a way, reactionary, as it has not kept abreast of real developments. By its nature, modern, industrialized, and bureaucratized society is of plural character, provided it is not pressed into the procrustean bed of a monolithic system. That means that it contains a more or less orderly plurality of large organizations, groups of interested parties, and of authorities. Sociologists state that, in such a plural society, the traditional idea of the State changes over to a new concept, that of an umpire and guarantor of the common interest between and above parties and groups, and this makes it evident that the judicial system, together with the idea of justice, grows into a new rôle in a situation where the State has assumed the position of a neutral power arbitrating on conflicts, and deciding on quarrels [73].

Güde's final result is the confrontation of two contrasting legal theories — that of accepting the possibility of administering justice on ethical grounds, against that of complete political functionalization.

The paper read at the Congress by Professor Heinitz arrives at similar conclusions. As it dealt with the details of criminal trial practice, they are of special weight for our case. Professor Heinitz drew particular attention to the fact that especially in criminal trials, the profession of judge in the Soviet Zone has no longer anything with that in the West but the name. In addition, there is no true defence left in the Soviet Zone. And then, with regard to the *most sensitive criteria* of any system of criminal justice, Professor Heinitz registered that significant changes have taken place, both in the laws to be applied, and in practice. These affect, in particular, the Rules of Evidence in respect to the submission of evidence and through the abolition of the duty of the court to accept only direct evidence brought before it. The author stated that it was *clear beyond all doubt that, under such conditions, criminal trials no longer afford any guarantee that justice will, and can, materially be done*[75]. This observation, too, was confirmed by the procedure followed in the Soviet Zone against Oberländer. It may be recalled here that one witness for the prosecution, perhaps the most important one for the Soviet Zone trial (in the *Bergmann* case), viz. the mysterious man called Hammerschmidt, never made an appearance in court. He was excused by a letter of the diplomatic mission of the Soviets in East Berlin. His evidence, as it had been deposed before a political body in Moscow, was simply read in court. Notwithstanding this, the court believed the alleged evidence of a witness whom it had never seen, and even certified his impartiality.

There are a number of other observations made by Heinitz, which impinge materially on our case, including the statement that the gap between our ideas of the Law, and those obtaining in the Soviet Zone, are of salient influence especially in political cases, so that the question must be raised whether, and to what extent, verdicts passed in the Soviet Zone have legal power in the Federal Republic of Germany. On principle, the Soviet Zone is not treated as a foreign country. That means that the principles of International Criminal Law do not apply here. Therefore, Professor Heinitz refers to the reasons given for the passing of the Law on Inner German Cooperation between Judicatures and Public Authorities *(Innerdeutsche Rechts- und Amtshilfe)*, where it is stated: —

> The idea of One Country Under One Law makes it desirable to continue cooperation in legal questions over as wide a field as possible. Moreover, the feelings of the population in all parts of Germany for justice would be deeply offended if criminal acts that have, in fact, been committed, could not be punished only because Germany is, at present, split into several parts. On the other hand, it must never come to it naturally, that cooperation in legal questions, and between public authorities, would lead to a violation of the Rule of Law. The duty to assist other judicial and public authorities must therefore find its limits where it does not appear certain that the Rule of Law is safeguarded in the course of proceedings taken, or where, in connection with proceedings taken, or outside these proceedings, the defendant is threatened by grave disadvantages which are incompatible with the principles of the Rule of Law recognized on the territory of the Basic Law (of the Federal Republic).
>
> That means that the statute in question, in general, accepts the validity of judgments made in the Soviet Zone, but limits that acceptance by stating that violation of the Rule of Law makes such judgments unacceptable[76].

This, naturally, also applies to the "judgment" passed against Oberländer in the Soviet Zone: its legality is determined by the extent to which it conforms, or does not conform, to the Rule of Law. In order to arrive at this determination, one of the main points of departure must be the results of the investigations made by the Bonn Public Prosecutor's Office. The result of the enquiries made by the competent judicial authority, viz. the *Oberstaatsanwaltschaft* (Chief Public Prosecutor's Office) at the *Landgericht* (District Court) of Bonn, are the findings which outline the legal position bindingly for the Federal Republic of Germany, because for the legal system of any state it must be decisive, in the first instance, what its own criminal investigation authorities have found. All accusations that are of material importance under the Rule of Law have been scrutinized thoroughly and extensively by the enquiries made in the *Nachtigall* and *Bergmann* cases, as we have been able to show. Only in the *Nachtigall* case, it had to be left open by the investigators whether Ukrainian members of that unit had absented themselves without leave, and had taken part, against orders received, by their own decision, in the Lwow atrocities. Even if proof should still be forthcoming that this did in fact happen, Oberländer would not have been responsible under Service regulations, as he was not in command of the Unit, or of parts of it. In the *Bergmann* case, the investigations were no less thorough and extensive, and they resulted in convincing proof that all the accusations made against members of the unit, and against Professor Oberländer, who had indeed been its commanding officer, were completely groundless. The investigation made under the Rule of Law has also drawn in its purview a great number of possibly incriminating circumstances (*Zeppelin* Project; possible relations of the Unit with *SD* Special Action Groups, etc.), and also these enquiries did not produce any incriminating evidence. On the contrary, contemporary documents have shown that Oberländer had nothing to be ashamed of, because he dissented in principle from the policies of the Nazis in occupied Russia, and made propaganda for his conviction to the contrary at great and intentionally incurred personal risk. The order issued by Field Marshal von Kleist has shown that Oberländer even caused practical measures to be taken in opposition to official Party policies.

On the other hand, the investigation and trial conducted in the Soviet Zone can in no way be accepted as judicial acts under the Rule of Law. Even under the London Agreement, which defined new war crimes under International Law, the court in the Soviet Zone had no jurisdiction. Furthermore, Oberländer, in his subordinate position, could never be considered to have been a member of the group that was capable of committing Crimes Against Peace. And finally, there was the insufficiency of the trial itself, held in a court without jurisdiction, which obviously did not intend to find the truth and to do justice but, following the Soviet-communist theory of law, endeavoured to smear an opponent in quasi-legal terminology, and to destroy him morally and politically by a verdict that could not, by any stretch of the imagination, be called a true judgment.

For example, the court never attempted to evaluate evidence by discussing the essential question whether the main witnesses for the prosecution were credible. This can be said both of the Soviet witnesses, former members of the *Bergmann* unit, who testified in the *Bergmann Trial,* and also of the witness, Mrs. Kukhar, in the *Nachtigall Trial* who, after more than twenty years, confidently asserted that she was able to identify a man from newspaper photographs whom she allegedly saw only once in her life at dawn from the third floor of her house. The mystery of the Soviet witnesses for the prosecution *in re* Bergmann consists in that the motivation of their recent statements was the exact opposite of their former attitude, which had been described by many of their comrades from the Unit. On the one hand, by testifying against Oberländer and the unit to which they themselves once belonged, they incriminated themselves equally gravely; on the other hand, the court never attempted to find out whether punishment they may already have suffered, or the possibility of a totalitarian power blackmailing them by threats in case their evidence proved to be undesirable, did not cause them to bear witness in the way as was expected of them. Even the defence accepted most of the gravest accusations as true and proved, and never called them into question or discussed them. These are the reasons why the '*judgment*' passed in the Soviet Zone cannot be accepted as a result of finding a just and true bill, and of doing justice, but must be described as the act of a judicature that has been transformed into a functional instrument of politics. Its prescribed task was to find the quasi-legal form in which an opponent thought to be dangerous could be politically and morally killed by smearing him beyond remedy. All this goes to prove that the proceedings in the Soviet Zone were a political show trial. A quick glance at the show trials of the Stalin era will convince us of the close similarity in their motivation.

That such trials are the daily bread of real Soviet jurisdiction, and have their allotted place in Soviet law, has been proved for the Soviet Union by a man of no lower standing than Nikita Khrushchev, the present Prime Minister of the Soviet Union. He made his statement during the XXth Party Congress, *raising devastating charges against Soviet justice.* In his paper read in Berlin, Dr. Max Güde [77] quoted the following passages from Khrushchev's accusations: —

> As a rule, the only proof of guilt, sufficient for a verdict, in violation of all rules of jurisprudence, was the admission by the defendant. As was established later, these admissions were obtained by placing the defendants under physical pressure... The formula "enemy of the people" was introduced specially in order to destroy persons, who had come into conflict with the Party Line. When the cases of some of these so-called spies and saboteurs were investigated, it was found that the charges had been the products of pure invention. If Stalin gave the order that this or that man had to be arrested, people had to accept it in good faith that the victim was indeed an enemy of the people. And what sort of evidence was produced? The admissions of the arrested persons, and the examining judges accepted them; and how was it possible that a person admitted to crimes which he never committed? Only in one way, namely on the basis of applying physical violence, by torturing him until he lost consciousness, and by robbing him of his capacity for judgment, and of his human dignity.

About the examining magistrate, Rodos, who conducted the investigations against Kosior, Khrushchev said: —

> He is a mean and hare-brained creature, completely corrupted in his morals. The question arises whether a man with an intellect of this type was able to conduct the investigation in this way, on his own initiative, that the guilt of men like Kosior and others could be sufficiently proved. During the meeting of the Presidium of the Central Committee where we cross-examined him, he, Rodos, told us: 'I had been told that Kosior and Djubar were enemies of the people, and that I, as an examining judge, had to get the admission out of them that they were enemies of the people.' He was only able to do so by means of protracted torture, for which he received detailed instructions from Beria. We have to report that, during the meeting of the Presidium of the Central Committee, he stated cynically: 'I was of the opinion that I was carrying out the orders of the Party' [78].

Assuming that such methods have been used against the former Caucasian members of the Bergmann unit, but on that assumption only, their admissions can be fully understood by us.

THE MOSCOW SHOW TRIALS OF THE STALIN PERIOD AND THE SHOW TRIAL AGAINST OBERLÄNDER

In a thorough American investigation, the motivations behind the Moscow show trials under Stalin have been exhaustively analysed [79]. According to the results of this study, these motives are to be found largely in Stalin's decision to liquidate the leaders of certain opposition trends in the Party, in order to restore its 'monolithic' character. As there is a complete lack of authentic evidence in the legal sense, this is not judicial proof, naturally, but there are strong inferences for it to be drawn from Stalin's salient theoretical propositions [80]. The authors define the Stalinist variety of Bolshevism by stating that, in Stalin's view, any differences of opinion permitted within the Party on the direction which its policies should take must endanger the substance and existence of the Party [81]. In order to safeguard the required stability, a small, tightly-knit group of leaders was indispensable. Stalin did not like to talk about this in public. But before the Twelfth Party Congress, in 1923, he still defended debates and quarrels within the governing bodies of the State as healthy signs of life, provided that they would lead to the creation of a *hard nucleus of the leadership*. And this appears to be the principle of Stalin's political line that was later put into practice during the trials. He did away with the old bolsheviks because their personal picture of the dictatorship of the proletariat was incompatible with the new reality of Stalinist socialism. The authors agree with the opinion expressed in another study that these trials served a preventive purpose [82]. *The defendants were sentenced for possible crimes which they might commit.* The analysis goes on to show that Stalin especially believed it to be inevitable that political opponents, whose destruction had been pre-determined, must be calumniated.

Leites and Bernaut also deem it likely that Stalin expected the extermination of the old cadres to instil such fear in the Party that he would then be able to preserve its monolithic character with a lesser degree of violence. To support this suggestion, they quote one of Stalin's letters which says that the Party's leaders must be both honoured and feared to the same extent [83]. They also refer to his speech before the Executive Committee of the Communist International *(EKKI)* of January 21, 1926, which, in view of the fight against the group Ruth Fischer/Maslov in the German Communist Party, contained the statement that even *during a fight within the Pary it could not be avoided to discredit certain leaders* [84]. That was because the bolsheviks do not believe, on principle, in the possibility of an attitude of reconciliation, because this makes no sense to them. To prove this, another quotation is given from a typical saying of Stalin's before the same body, which he made to the German Communist, Hansen, who had pleaded for a conciliatory attitude to be taken against the Fischer/Maslov group. Stalin countered Hansen's plea as follows: 'It seems to me that Hansen stands for a sort of clerical morality, which ought to dominate the struggle between ideas within the Party — a morality completely unsuitable for the Communist Party. It seems that he does not oppose the fight for ideas but he would like to conduct it in such a way that the chiefs of the opposition do not lose their reputations. But I must say that he who permits a struggle only on condition that the leaders are not covered with shame actually denies the possibility of any struggle for ideas within the Party [85]'. — The study sums up these considerations as stating that only exaggerated charges make an impression upon the average person, meaning, man in the mass [86]. If this interpretation of the motivation for Stalin's show trials is correct — and almost everything speaks for it — it will also be capable of yielding indications for the motives behind the show trial against Oberländer.

This interpretation would explain especially the monstrosity of the personal accusations — in particular the allegations that Oberländer, personally, almost in his private capacity, committed unbelievably crude crimes in the Caucasus, in the Piatigorsk prison, and during the retreat. It may be recalled that all the members of the Unit, both Germans and Caucasians, unanimously denied the possibility of such crimes, because they were completely contrary to Oberländer's nature and character, so that most witnesses thought the accusations to be ridiculous. But also the extent of the other alleged crimes can be explained in this way, which

Oberländer was said to have committed in his official capacity, when serving in the Caucasus and in Lwow. These accusations, in contrast to the afore-mentioned ones, have the semblance of the credible for the uninformed because they know that, during the war in the East, both warring parties have indeed committed extraordinary brutalities and crimes.

If, therefore, the Moscow show trials were designed to spread terror among the old Party members, the motivation to browbeat and terrorize personally and politically honest and decent ex-members of the Nazi Party into desisting from political activities in the Federal Republic of Germany seems to be completely understandable, in analogy.

The intention to destroy Oberländer morally, and thus also politically, as the main design behind the trial and judgment against him in the Soviet Zone seems to have been confirmed by later attempts to smear him in connection with the assassination of the Ukrainian nationalist leader, Bandera. This attempt has been foiled.

DOES THE 'JUDGMENT' CREATE NEW LAW AND HAS IT LEGAL CONSEQUENCES?

As there is now a judgment of the Supreme Court of the Soviet Occupation Zone, its existence is unavoidably tied up with the question of the legal force it may have on the territory of the Federal Republic of Germany. On principle, court decisions made in the Soviet Zone are not treated as the judgments of foreign courts. The legal position in which the Federal Republic finds itself, as it affirms the continued existence of the German Reich after 1945, includes the effect of the Law on Mutual Cooperation and Assistance Among Courts and Public Authorities Within Germany *(Innerdeutsche Rechts- und Amtshilfe)* in criminal cases — which will be discussed below. Under this law, provided the material and procedural conditions named in that statute are met, any criminal judgment and penal verdict passed in the Soviet Zone is valid within the legal order prevailing in the Federal Republic. As a problem of legal form, the judgment against Oberländer poses a special question under the rule that criminal verdicts passed in the Soviet Zone are capable of execution in the Federal Republic. However, as the trial was obviously a 'cooked' one, serving a preordained, politically determined objective, this special case assumes the features of a test case impinging of fundamentals. The political jiggery-pokery involved transforms the so-called *judgment* into a quasi-legal façade, placed as the final, face-saving ornament in front of a decreed political decision to discredit a political opponent, whom the communist State deems dangerous, to exclude him from the political arena and, if possible, also to destroy him physically. The parallels between this trial and the show trials of the Stalin period are unmistakeable, but whilst Stalin's show trials served the purpose of settling conflicts in internal Soviet politics by using totalitarian, Soviet communist legal policies for disarming and destroying internal adversaries, the campaign waged by the Soviets against Oberländer aimed at the destruction of a member of a foreign government. This makes the campaign, in so far as the Soviet Union contributed to it, akin to intervention, i. e. illegal meddling, in the internal affairs of a sovereign state. With regard to the Soviet Zone, the trial staged before its Supreme Court glaringly highlights the servitude of the judicature in the Zone under the command of political demands and objectives of its communist leadership. Viewed under this aspect, the findings of that judicature cannot even be criticized as stretching, or falsifying the Law, as they correspond, by and large, to the principles established by communist legal theory and State doctrine about *Socialist Justice*. This so-called *socialist justice* enables the totalitarian leadership to discredit any political opponent by slandering him, and it also creates the formal conditions in law for destroying him physically — in our case by sentencing him to life imprisonment. The judgment against Oberländer reveals clearly to what high degree *the subjection of the courts to the political power (theory on the activities of the organs of power*[87]) has already become political reality in the Soviet Zone. Confronted with the results of the investigations carried out under the Rule of Law, the judgment against Oberländer, especially, clearly reveals the immensely complex problems of relations between the two antagonistic legal and judicial systems existing on the territory of the German Reich. It would go beyond the bounds of our task to use this final summing up our case for discussing the general problem of the legal effect and efficacy of criminal judgments passed in the Soviet Zone on the territory of the Federal Republic. We can only outline briefly those aspects of that problem that apply to our special case.

The question has frequently been raised whether the courts in the Federal Republic of Germany appreciate the nature of the problem, meaning whether they have adequate knowledge of the political task set the courts of the Soviet Zone and their judgments by the legal doctrine of the Soviets and the Communists[88]. With regard to the judgment against Oberländer pronounced by the Supreme Court of the Soviet Zone, which terminated a political show trial that had obviously emulated Soviet practice, the question of the legal force and efficacy of such a judgment assumes new dimensions. In this context, however, it must not be forgotten that the subjection of the judicature and jurisdiction to government policy in the Soviet Zone, as it was examplified by the Oberländer trial, has been achieved only through a gradual change extending over years, and has reached an advanced stage only fairly recently. This change was already noted in a case tried before the Federal Constitutional Court, when the highest judicial authority in the Federal Republic had to consider these problems for the first time. In a decision made on June 13, 1952, this Court declared the execution of criminal verdicts made in the Soviet Zone generally admissible, but it stated at the same time that this rule *(Leitsatz* No. 1) excluded the execution of such verdicts if 'the judgment of a criminal court in the Soviet Zone jeopardizes the purpose of any Federal law, or violates basic principles of the Rule of Law, or offends one of the Basic Rights guaranteed by the Basic Law' (i. e. the Federal German Constitution) [89]. When this case was tried, representatives of the Federal Ministry of Justice and of the Federal Ministry for All-German Questions, respectively, had been given the opportunity to make statements in court. The Federal Ministry of Justice agreed with the Court that, as a rule, judgments made in the Soviet Zone could be carried out, whilst execution must be refused if 'the criminal trial preceding the judgment did not safeguard the principles of the Rule of Law, or if in connection with the trial or apart from it the defendant would suffer considerable disadvantages offending the Rule of Law, or if assistance claimed for the execution of the judgment violates the purpose of any Federal law'. The representative of the Ministry for All-German Questions, at the time, drew the attention of the court to a development which, after 1952 has made rapid progress, and for which the judgment against Oberländer probably is a new landmark. This official stated that, at the time of speaking (in 1952) purely criminal offences were still being adjudged in regular trials in the Soviet Zone, and that requests for assistance in carrying out judgments were generally submitted only in such cases, but that in the foreseeable future, the principle of One Law for One Country would probably be jettisoned for good. Already in 1952, this representative of the Ministery for All-German Questions emphasized that 'rapid progress can be observed in the transformation of the judicature and jurisdiction in the Soviet Zone into an *executive organ of a political machine*'. This development has since been pushed forward a great deal, perhaps not yet to its final conclusion, but to a point not far from it.

The above-mentioned West German statute on cooperation and mutual assistance, etc. (German abbreviation: *RAH)*, passed into law in 1953, but it is questionable whether this statute takes full acount of this change to-day. Whether a judgment made in the Soviet Zone may be carried out in West Germany depends on a number of conditions still to be examined. Under *RAH*, a defendant who has been sentenced has the right to apply independently for a declaration of inadmissibility of execution. The statute is based on the opinion given by the Federal Constitutional Court by its decision of June 13, 1952. It is obvious that the statute bases its rules on the recognition of decisions made by courts in the Soviet Zone as judgments in the full sense of the term. It does not answer the question whether certain judicial findings, which appear in the form of judgments, may be a legal nullity [90]. Cooperation and assistance between courts and public authorities must be offered, according to the Act, if their granting does not violate the purpose of a Federal law, can be granted in agreement with the Rules of Law, and if the sentenced defendant is not deprived of basic rights under the Rule of Law. Penalties flowing from judgments made in courts of the Soviet Zone can only be executed if they in their form and the punishment are justifiable under the Rule of Law and do not contravene the purpose of any Federal law [91]. West German jurisdiction has rejected the objection that the *RAH* statute violates Article 6, Paragraph 1, of the European Convention on the Protection of Human Rights and Basic Freedoms, which has become locally accepted international law through a special Act of Agreement [92]. According to a judgment of the Supreme Federal Court of May 9, 1956, however, decisions made by courts in one part of Germany have effect as acts of sovereign State power in the other part of Germany only if they are *recognized* in the other territory. The conditions of such recognition are fixed by 'inter-local' rules of trial procedure, and in cases of criminal verdicts made by Soviet Zone courts, these rules have been laid down by the *RAH* statute in detail [93].

The Federal Constitutional Court has dealt with these questions again in two of its newer decisions. Its ruling of May 31, 1960, says: —

> The Soviet Zone is part of Germany, and cannot be treated as a foreign country in relation to the Federal Republic of Germany. The *RAH* statute assumes that judgments made by criminal courts in the Soviet Zone may have effect as decisions of German courts of law also in the Federal Republic, but that the protection granted to the individual by the Basic Rights, and the constitutional order of the Basic Law, against the public power determines also the admissibility of execution for such judgments. *RAH* takes account of the fact that both the legislation and the jurisdication of the Soviet Zone, in part, have moved along different paths from the Federal Republic, and are founded upon political, social, and general *(weltanschauliche)* principles which are contrary to the constitutional order under the Basic Law. These differences that have developed between the Federal Republic of Germany and the Soviet Zone impose certain restrictions upon inner-German legal cooperation and assistance, especially in criminal cases. These result from the fact that such cooperation and assistance must not lead to the carrying-out of measures in Federal territory that violate Basic Rights and the Rule of Law. Therefore, the *RAH* statute permits carrying-out of a judgment passed by a criminal court in the Soviet Zone on Federal German soil only after some authority in the Federal Republic of Germany which is pledged to observe the Basic Law has examined that judgment as to its compatibility with the above-mentioned rules [94].

It is permitted to carry out judgments made by criminal courts in the Soviet Zone if the sentence is compatible with the claims made by the Basic Law upon the State under the Rule of Law. The ruling concludes with the following sentences: —

> The Basic Law presupposes German unity, and the Act on Mutual Assistance in Legal Matters is based on that assumption, so that the constitutional limits for internal German mutual assistance in legal matters are drawn as follows: Assistance cannot be granted in any case where the criminal law upon which a judgment is based manifests the contrasting incompatibilities between the free and democratic constitutional order in the Federal Republic of Germany and the political system ruling in the Soviet Zone. That means: Legal assistance for judgments which punish the violation of Soviet Zone laws that protect the *de facto* political authority in the Soviet Zone, or the economic system obtaining in that Zone, is inadmissible, because such assistance would but mean that the Federal and *Länder* authorities have to support and aid that system of power. And this is forbidden by the *Ordre public* (French in the original text) of the Federal Republic of Germany.

In another decision of January 17, 1961, the Federal Constitutional Court deals with the question whether any verdict passed in the Soviet Occupation Zone makes the sentenced defendant immune against further prosecution for the same offence. This gave the Court the opportunity for making the following observations: —

> Though it is true that the courts of the Soviet Zone are German courts, their judicial authority is not based on the constitutional order obtaining in the Federal Republic of Germany. These courts, therefore, do not sit under a foreign authority but their power is not subject to the principles of the Rule of Law. Both the constitution and the procedure of these courts are largely contrary to the requirements of our Basic Law [95].

The superior courts of the Federal Republic of Germany, as can be seen from this, make the efficacy of criminal judgments pronounced in the Soviet Zone dependent, under the *RAH* (Act on Assistance, etc.), on the *recognition* of the *RAH*. Whether such a judgment does recognize the rules of the *RAH* has to be determined on its merits — in other words, which relationship can be established between the contents of an individual judgment and the essential principles of the Rule of Law (under the West German Basic Law). It is these principles which are the centre of all relevant considerations; they are the yardstick, by which to measure the effect of any judgment under the Rule of Law, and thereby its quality as judge-made law, as a true judgment. For the rule of law in the Federal Republic of Germany, the question will therefore be: Which are the basic assumptions about a State of Lawfulness underlying our Basic Law? (That the Basic Law does not only speak theoretically about this, but puts the actual, practical Rule of Law into the focus of its prescriptions, can be seen, in our view, from the wording of Article 28, Paragraph One, first sentence, of the Basic Law.) Professor Richard Lange has discussed this question especially with regard to the legal effects of criminal judgments made in the Soviet Zone. He approaches this subject by stating that the idea of a State under the Rule of Law has been defined in different ways during past history. During the nineteenth century, such a state was very simply considered to be a 'State in which every conflict was settled within the Law' (also called a 'State bound to legal procedures'). But he justly emphasizes that the idea of a state under the rule of law is determined materially — and not only procedurally — by the Basic Law: —

> The idea of the law, or of legality, as used by the Basic Law, is much wider. It encompasses the material legality of all Law, which means that a State under the Rule of Law will not only guarantee security for the citizen under the Law, but also strive towards true Justice. It is not only the guarantee that the application of the Law will follow orderly procedures but, in addition, material justice, as practised, which meets the requirements of a State under the Rule of Law, and thus subordinates the State to a true Rule of Law.

He therefore opposes the idea of the State under the Rule of Law which expresses itself by ordering the life of its citizens according to the principles of material justice — as the West German Basic Law requires — to two different notions, which are of importance for the practice of the courts in the Federal Republic of Germany: the positivist, and the socioligical view of the State under the Law. 'Sociological Positivism' is illustrated by him through the definitions presented, for example, by F. Bauer, *Generalstaatsanwalt* (general prosecutor) in Frankfurt, in his book, 'On Crime and Society' [96] *(Über das Verbrechen und die Gesellschaft)*. Dr. Bauer calls a crime, 'a form of behaviour considered to be particularly harmful by a group that has sufficient power to enforce its opinions'. However, those who accept this definition are unable to ascertain the material contents of justice embodied in a given judgment produced in the Soviet Zone, under the Rule of Law as incorporated in the *RAH*. Professor Lange then demonstrates how a given decision made by the *Oberlandesgericht* (Land High Court) at Frankfurt was imbued by sociological positivism, which Lange opposes, as it 'leads to misconstruing and undermining our legal values, on which our legal thought and legal intentions are based' [97]. The court in question had found valid a judgment passed by a Soviet Zone court which had a defendant sentenced to seven years of hard labour and confiscation of his property, because he had imported a large number of perfume flacons from West Berlin to the Soviet Zone, and had exported a typewriter, both without the 'permit accompanying trade goods' prescribed by East German Law, and against a crossed cheque. The only change in the verdict thought necessary by the Frankfurt court was a reduction of the sentence of imprisonment to five years, and the annulment of the property confiscation. In the reasons given for the Frankfurt decision it was stated that no objections could be raised against the East German 'Law for the Protection of Inner-German Trade' under the Rule of Law, as the Federal Republic of Germany operated similar protective devices. Professor Lange, in contrast, quotes, and accepts, a decision made by the *Oberlandesgericht* at Cologne[98], which finds that the said Law for the Protection, etc., enacted in the Soviet Zone, stands in opposition to the Rule of Law, since official pronouncements in the Zone have made it clear that its purpose is neither the protection of supplies for the civilian population nor the furtherance of inner-German trade but that it serves political objects, in particular 'the liquidation of capitalist elements in trade and commerce, and the strengthening of economic controls that serve the establishment of a planned economy, which aims the total subjection of the people in the Soviet Zone'[99]. It is obvious that Dr. Bauer's definition of crime leads to neutrality and precludes any evaluation. On this basis, it is also impossible to criticize judges in the Federal Republic of Germany who, in the past, lent themselves to prosecuting deeds that were considered as socially harmful by the Nazi group in power then — for this group did hold sufficient power to enforce its opinions[100]. Professor Lange then mentions the verdict of the Federal Constitutional Court against the German Communist Party, which thoroughly discussed the communist theories on the State and on Law, and from this inferred the incompatibility of the so-called dictatorship of the proletariat with the free and democratic order, as established under the West German Basic Law. The Court then found that the two views of the State have nothing in common, and exclude each other. In conclusion, it said: —

> The result of the incompatibility between the two State systems is: If rules and institutions, that have been taken over from a free democracy, continue to exist formally in the Communist State, their meaning undergoes a total change (p. 203). The subjection of State agencies to the laws, and the independence of the courts, in view of the newly-created idea of 'Socialist Legality' that serves the requirements of the centralized State administration, and of an omnipotent 'executive', is only of formal importance there.

As already mentioned, in 1952, the representative of the Federal Ministry for All-German Questions had shown, before the Federal Constitutional Court, that the judicature in the Soviet Zone underwent a gradual transformation into an executive organ of the political power. A Law enacted in the Soviet Zone on May 23, 1952, on the Public Prosecutor's Office *(Staatsanwaltschaft)* represented an important stage in this development. Since then, this change has continued apace, as was highlighted by a new *conception of the work to be done in future by the judicial authorities* hammered out at a special school held in the Soviet Zone for judges and public prosecutors[101].

'Guiding principles' *(Richtlinien)* No. 1, 5, and 7 are of particular significance for our case. No. 1 says: —

> The work of the judicial authorities is part and parcel of the activities of the one and indivisible state and its agencies, and therefore subordinate to the work of the public powers. The judicial authorities, by their work (prosecution, jurisdiction, and general supervision), have to carry out the tasks set to, and by, the instruments of public power . . .

No. 5 adds to this: —

> The basis for the work of the judicial authorities, the guarantee for stability and security of Socialist Law, is democractic Socialism . . .

And No. 7 concludes: —

> The separation between the jurisdiction and the political work among the masses is hammful and must therefore be overcome. True jurisdiction is not based on deciding a mere case but on the effect of a judicial decision upon strengthening the discipline, and upon the development of a high socialist morality.

Professor Lange explains how this *basic concept* affects the traditional notions of law and legality, which inevitably have been retained by the laws and decrees enacted in the Soviet Zone, so that the same rules and ideas are filled with a totally different inner meaning. In this context, Lange emphasizes that 'our courts in the West unfortunately are frequently blind to this transformation, believing that the old words and formulae, which are still in use beyond the zonal frontiers, cover the old and traditional values and notions' [102]. He then quotes the Journal of the Moscow University of November, 1950, whose interpretation of the Soviet Constitution may well be used as evidence for what this document really means: —

> 'Judges are independent and subject only to the Law', according to Article 12 of the Stalin Constitution. This formula supplies particularly striking proof for the fact that the same words carry a totally different meaning in Soviet legislation and in the bourgeois world, and in their practical application, they may even have diametrically opposed significance . . .
>
> The courts, in our Soviet state, have always been considered to be part and parcel of the machinery of political leadership, and suitable measures must be taken so that the courts are, in fact, instruments of the Communist Party and of the Soviet Government.

In opposition to this, the Rule of Law in the State, as defined by the West German Basic Law, contains also a material definition of the Court [103]. Through a decision of November 9, 1955 [104], the Federal Constitutional Court expressed its views on this point. Following that decision all the members of a court must be independent and subject only to the Law. It allows for certain differences between the constitution of the Weimar

Republic and the Basic Law in respect of the rule that judges are appointed to their judicial office for life, and says: —

> In view of the traditional situation prevailing in properly constituted courts, the law-giver of the Basic Law — with the exceptions mentioned — has accepted them as models, and has established it as a matter of course that all professional judges in the courts have to be, on principle, full-time and irrevocably appointed, fully established, judges, so that the employment of judges on probation, or for a trial period, may only be practised within limits that are drawn by the reasonable discretion of the appointing authorities, when they fill the need for training junior judges, or for other imperative reasons. — No quasi-judicial bench may therefore be called, or treated as, a court if, according to the rules of any law, one or more of its members are State servants, or — with the exception of the above-mentioned cases — personally dependent employees, who may be transferred or demoted during their period of service at any time, and without due process of law in a properly constituted court.

The independence of the judges is indeed one of the indispensable criteria of a court under the Rule of Law. Two special studies have discussed this requirement recently. Bettermann [105] breaks down the independence of the judges into three separate forms of independence, according to the sources of a possible dependence: The judge must be *independent of the parties to any lawsuit* (independence in the context of the lawsuit, procedural independence); he must be *independent of the State* (political or legal independence); and he must be *socially independent* of non-public powers, pressure groups, etc. (social independence). Eichenberger [106], too, makes the attempt to subdivide the problem under review according to the influences that may affect the judges' independence, by endangering or destroying it. He directs his enquiry to the particular sources of power which may make a judge legally or practically dependent, or against which his independence must be carefully protected. This leads him to breaking down judicial independence into five components: —

> Independence from persons or bodies taking part in the judicial process as parties: this is the refusal of the judge to take any party's particular view. He is not influenced.
>
> Independence from non-judicial forces: this is the political freedom of the judge.
>
> Independence from other judicial authorities: this is the judge's freedom of developing his own informed opinion.
>
> Independence from sociological influences: this is the judge's social freedom.
>
> Independence from motives that have nothing to do with the matter of the case but may be present in the *forum internum* of the judicial bench: this is the judge's freedom to follow his own inner voice, his own counsel and conscience.

Specific problems of the judges' independence in International Law have already been investigated by Reut-Nicolussi [107] a long time ago.

Professor Lange, in his study, examines the question whether *recognition* of judgments passed in the Soviet Zone means that the judicial decision made in the Zone should be accorded the full qualities of new judge-made law, or whether it ought to mean only that they will have the legal effects desired also on the territory of the Federal Republic, and if they ought to have these effects, whether fully or only in part. Lange here tries to make a similar distinction as is made in International law between *efficacité des lois étrangères de droit public*, and *efficacité des actes de droit public*[108]. (Efficacy of foreign general laws, and efficacy of acts [or decision] of public order).

If we now hold against all these definitions the basic traits of the judicature and jurisdiction in any totalitarian state, whose tasks are bindingly established by the political powers, especially in the case of the criminal courts, and their constitution and the principles of appointing their judges, it becomes clear that the subjection of the Soviet Zone courts to politics, which was already seen by the Federal Constitutional Court in 1952, has now reached about the following stage: —

> The judges are officials subject to superior direction. Their former independence has completely disappeared.
>
> Their subordination to the political power has been openly proclaimed, and has been accomplished.

The statement that courts in the Soviet State have always been part and parcel of the political machine of leadership, and that suitable measures have in fact transformed them into tools of the Communist Party and of the Soviet Government, applies also to the constitution and tasks of the courts in the Soviet Zone of to-day[109].

Such conditions must surely be assumed to prevail completely in cases of political trials and judgments of political importance. If the totalitarian leadership takes the decision to slander a political opponent as a *diversionist*, a *Trotskyite*, or a *warmonger*, and to make this slander stick, in order to force him out of political life, and to destroy him morally, the prosecution generated by such a decision makes it utterly impossible to examine such allegations properly, even if these assertions are to the highest degree improbable and flimsy, because the court sitting in judgment over them is a subordinate tool of the political leadership, as has been proclaimed and proudly confirmed. If we accepted, for argument's sake, the possibility that such courts might be given true freedom to decide on such cases, we should assume that totalitarian courts might be suddenly granted the power to reverse decisions made by the totalitarian leadership — which would make us guilty of an absurd belief in a known impossibility, especially in states of the Soviet communist type.

Therefore, if we admit that the reality of the law in communist states is that the courts there are subject to the decisions of the political authorities, we cannot acknowledge their activities in politically important trials to be law-making activities under the Rule of Law. Their *judgments*, in particular, are only quasi-legal confirmations of a politically desirable decision, by which the court follows political instructions that have been passed to it by the prosecution. What the court does is merely participation in a political act of the political power ruling a totalitarian state [110]. The court, by passing judgment, does not creat a new, judge-made law, but cooperates in destroying a political opponent, as has been preordained by the totalitarian state of the Soviet communist type, which is capable of such acts. Under the Rule of Law, it follows that such pronouncements are not judgments; they are non-judgments. They belong to the same group of totalitarian communist judicial acts as the so-called *Waldheim Judgments* *. These are completely illegal and outside the ken of law, as has also been confirmed by the *Kammergericht* (Berlin High Court): —

> The Waldheim judgments 'lack all legal efficacy'. Those affected by them 'cannot suffer any legal disadvantages from them; they are to be treated as if no court proceedings had ever been taken against them, which means, they are to be treated as non-defendants, and as persons against whom no sentence has ever been passed.' [111]

We need not discuss here the possibility of invalid or ineffective judgments under the German rules of procedure for criminal trials *(Strafprozessordnung)*. The *Kammergericht*, following the *Reichsgericht* (the Supreme Court of the Reich from 1871 onwards), and quoting literature, has argued — as we believe, convincingly — that a decision made in a criminal trial may be absolutely and irremediably invalid, so that this non-invalidity must be accepted independently of any appeal, and will rob such decisions of any of their effects. The judgment against *Oberländer* is a conspicuous example of an invalid judgment,

> whose recognition would be unbearable for the community of citizens under the Law . . ., where recognition of a judgment would do more harm to the authority of the law and the jurisdiction than a decision that it is invalid [112].

Also under the rules, and in the spirit, of the *Strafprozessordnung* (rules of procedure for criminal trials), the Oberländer *judgment* can never be recognized. To sum up the reasons for this again: The court had no jurisdiction under the special and particular agreements made on the prosecution of war crimes committed during the Second World War;

---

* Waldheim is the name of an old hard-labour prison near the Saxon town of Bautzen, which is being used by the East German Communists as a concentration camp for political prisoners. The ferocious 'Waldheim verdicts' were passed by a special court in 1953/54 against political prisoners arrested during and after the German revolt in the Soviet Zone on 17th June, 1953.

Oberländer did not belong to the exclusive circle of persons who had the chance to form and influence Hitler's foreign policy; therefore Oberländer was not even in a position to commit the (questionable) crimes against peace under the London Agreement; the fact that the crimes alleged against the Nachtigall and Bergmann units were localized outside the German frontiers; the incredibility of the witnesses for the prosecution in the trial against Bergmann (former members of that unit); the absence of the, completely mysterious, main witness for Soviet prosecution, Hammerschmidt — all that establishes in the case of the Oberländer trial 'a totality of the gravest violations of the rules of procedure, which plays havoc with all properly constituted and practised jurisdiction'[113].

In view of the non-validity of the Waldheim judgments, the *Kammergericht* has found that such judgments are not capable of being legally effective, which means that the verdicts cannot be executed. This, as the court meant, has obviated the main dangers threatening the defendants from the mere existence of non-valid pronouncements.

Regarding the judgment against Oberländer, this is certainly true within the jurisdiction of the Federal Republic of Germany. But the court in the Soviet Zone tries to place the case against Oberländer within the special and particular orbit of international law created for the prosecution of war crimes committed during the Second World War. It is therefore almost certain that the Soviet Union and its satellite states recognize the validity of this decision, and endow it with legal power. This creates the problem of effective legal protection against the danger of third-party states attempting to carry such a non-judgment into effect. To notify the states in question through diplomatic channels of the legal position, according to the results of the investigation made under the Rule of Law, appears to be commensurate with the political reputation of the Federal Republic of Germany, and indispensable, in view of the political importance of the Oberländer case.

FOOTNOTES

[1] Yearbook of the United Nations 1948—49, p. 535.
[2] *Kurzprotokoll* (Abstract of the Minutes of the Trial in the Soviet Zone Court), p. 188.
[3] *l. c.*, p. 188.
[4] *l. c.*, p. 190.
[5] *l. c.*, p. 190.
[6] *l. c.*, p. 191.
[7] *l. c.*, p. 174.
[8] *l. c.*, p. 191.
[9] (a) Article 2 says: (1) Each of the following acts will be treated as a crime: —
(a) *Crimes Against Peace*
To have undertaken aggression by military occupation of other countries, aggressive war in violation of International Law and of international treaties, including the following examples which, however, do not exhaust the acts named above: Planning, preparation for, beginning, or carrying out of, aggressive war, or of war in violation of international treaties, agreements, or promises; participation in a joint plan, or a conspiracy, for the purpose of carrying out one of the afore-mentioned crimes.
[10] The 'judgment' was published as a supplement to the magazine, *Neue Justiz*, 1960, No. 10.
[10a] Judgment, p. 3.
[11] *l. c.*, p. 3.
[12] *l. c.*, p. 3.
[13] *l. c.*, p. 4.
[14] *l. c.*, p. 10.
[15] *l. c.*, p. 11.
[16] *l. c.*, p. 18.
[17] *l. c.*, p. 19.
[18] *l. c.*, p. 19.
[19] *l. c.*, p. 19.
[20] *l. c.*, p. 1.
[21] *l. c.*, p. 1.
[22] *l. c.*, p. 18.
[23] *l. c.*, p. 18.
[24] *l. c.*, p. 18.
[25] *Wörterbuch des Völkerrechts* (Dictionary of International Law); Berlin, 1st edition, 1924, Vol. 1, p. 775.
[26] *Wörterbuch des Völkerrechts,* 2nd edition, Vol. 2, p. 373.
[27] Dahm, *Völkerrecht,* Vol. III; Stuttgart 1962, p. 296.
[28] *l. c.*, p. 303 *passim.*
[29] W. Grewe, *Nürnberg als Rechtsfrage* (The Legal Problem of Nuremberg); Stuttgart 1947, p. 42.
[30] *l. c.*, p. 43 *passim.*
[31] Lord Hankey; Politics, Trials and Errors; Oxford 1950, p. 23.
[32] Dissenting Opinion of the Indian Member of the Allied Military Court at Tokyo, Judge of the Supreme Court at Calcutta, Radhabinode Pal, quoted from Lord Hankey, *l. c.*, p. 26.
[33] Published by Heinze-Schilling, *Die Rechtsprechung der Nürnberger Militärtribunale* (The Jurisdiction of the Nuremberg Military Tribunals); Bonn,

p. 313. — It deserves emphasis that the Moscow Declaration speaks of the 'free governments', whose courts would sit in judgment over war criminals. This rule is also of importance for the legal qualities of the 'judgment' passed in the Soviet Zone.

34 *l. c.*, p. 315 *passim.*

35 *l. c.*, p. 315 *passim.*

35a Taylor, *Die Nürnberger Prozesse* (The Nuremberg Trials); Zurich 1951, p. 106.

36 Grewe, *Nürnberg als Rechtsfrage*, p. 11.

37 *l. c.*, p. 13.

38 *l. c.*, p. 13.

39 United Nations Yearbook, 1946/47, p. 254.

40 United Nations Yearbook, 1948/49, p. 949.

41 United Nations Yearbook, 1950, p. 852.

42 United Nations Yearbook, 1951, p. 841.

43 Alexander Jurcenko, *Die sowjetische Staats- und Rechtstheorie und ihre vierzigjährige Entwicklung* (Soviet Theories on the State and on Law, and their Development during Forty Years); Soviet Studies, published by the Institute for Research into the Problems of the USSR, Munich 1958, No. 5, p. 67 *passim.*

44 *l. c.*, p. 72.

45 *l. c.*, p. 74.

46 *l. c.*, p. 77.

47 'The Soviet State is the historical form for the integration of the state during the period of transition between Capitalism and Socialism.' From: Vishinsky, The Law of the Soviet State, Introduction by John N. Hazard; New York 1954, p. 42.

48 The quotation from Lenin has been taken from Vishinsky, *l. c.*, p. 39, footnote 4.

49 *l. c.*, p. 50.

50 *l. c.*, p. 50.

51 *l. c.*, p. 50.

52 *l. c.*, p. 167.

53 *l. c.*, p. 497.

54 *l. c.*, p. 497 *passim.*

55 *l. c.*, p. 498.

56 *l. c.*, p. 498.

57 *l. c.*, p. 503.

58 *Neue Justiz*, 19 Nov., 1957.

59 *Neue Justiz*, 1960, p. 261.

60 Minutes of a Meeting of the Criminal Law Department in the German Institute for Jurisprudence, held at Berlin on Nov. 16, 1956; Berlin 1956.

61 Law on the Constitution of the Courts of the G.D.R., of Oct. 2, 1952; *Gesetzblatt* (Law Gazette), 1952, p. 983.

62 *Lehrbuch des Strafrechtes der DDR* (Textbook of Criminal Law in the G.D.R.), General Part; Berlin, 1959, p. 215.

63 *Neue Justiz*, 1958, p. 78.

64 Lange, *Rechtsidee und Rechtsideologie in West und Ost* (The Idea of the Law and Legal Ideologies in East and West); Proceedings of the 42nd Congress of German Lawyers, Vol. II, Col. 8.

65 *l. c.*, Col. 9.

[66] Great Soviet Encyclopedia, quoted from Lange, *l. c.*, Col. 11.

[67] Great Soviet Encyclopedia, *l. c.*, Col. 11.

[68] Lange, *l. c.*, Col. 21.

[69] M. Güde, in: *Richter, Staatsanwalt und Rechtsanwalt im geteilten Deutschland* (Judges, Public Prosecutors, and Attorneys in a Divided Germany); 3 Lectures, published by *Berliner Richterverein e. V.* (Association of Judges in Berlin), Berlin 1959, p. 8.

[70] *l. c.*, p. 18.

[71] *l. c.*, p. 9.

[72] *l. c.*, p. 14.

[73] *l. c.*, p. 11.

[74] Heinitz; in the same collection of papers read in Berlin.

[75] *l. c.*, p. 50.

[76] *l. c.*, p. 55.

[77] Güde, *l. c.*, p. 9.

[78] *l. c.*, p. 10. — The passages quoted are taken from an American publication. In 1957, N. Khrushchev denied, in a talk with the American journalist, Cutladge, to have ever made this speech, but much can be said for the truthfulness of the text published by the State Department. It is clear that an expert in this field, like Güde, thinks it authentical. The fundamental problem dealt with in these passages has also been discussed by Milovan Djilas in his book, 'Conversations with Stalin', as follows: 'As long as Stalin's successors are mourning, on the one hand, individual victims of arbitrary rule between 1937 and 1955 but do not talk on the other hand, about the millions of victims of bolshevik persecution among the peasants, the middle classes, and the Russian intelligentsia, we cannot believe them that they have turned away honestly and sincerely from the methods of violent oppression and of terror...' (Wolfgang Wagner, *Die Gespräche mit Djilas*, i. e.: Talks with Djilas, in the magazine, *Die politische Meinung* (Political Opinion), Vol. VII, 1962, No. 75, p. 88.

[79] Nathan Leites and Elsa Bernaut, Ritual of Liquidation, Chicago 1954. This study deals with the trials before the Supreme Court of the Soviet Union between August 19 and 24, 1936, in the 'Trotsky Case', between January 23 and 30, 1937, in the 'Case of the anti-Soviet Trotsky Centre', and between March 2 and 13, 1938, in the 'Case of the anti-Soviet Bloc of the Right Wing and Trotskyites'.

[80] *l. c.*, *passim.*

[81] *l. c.*, p. 13.

[82] 'All the Soviet trials between 1929 and 1937 (this was written before the third trial) had a preventive character... The accused were guilty of potential crimes'; from Anton Cilaga, The Russian Enigma, quoted in Leites & Bernaut, *l. c.*, p. 14.

[83] Leites & Bernaut, *l. c.*, p. 15.

[84] *l. c.*, p. 17.

[85] *l. c.*, p. 17.

[86] *l. c.*, p. 17.

[87] Point 1 of '*Konzeption über die zukünftige Arbeit der Justizorgane*' (Conception on Future Work of the Judicial Authorities).

[88] Richard Lange, *Zur Frage der Anerkennung von Strafurteilen der sowjetischen Besatzungszone in der Bundesrepublik* (About the Question of Recognizing Judgments of Criminal Courts of the Soviet Occupation Zone in the Federal

Republic of Germany), Yearbook for Eastern Law, I, 1960, p. 9 *passim,* and especially p. 18 *passim.*

[89] Federal Constitutional Court, No. 40, June 13, 1952, Vol. I, p. 332.

[90] This leaves also the problem unsolved which results from the fact that such a 'judgment' of a court in the Soviet Zone can be carried out in third-party states notwithstanding the rules laid down in paragraphs 2 and 15.

[91] Par. 2. sub-par. 1, 2, 3 V of the Law on Inner-German Mutual Assistance Between Criminal Courts and Public Authorities *(RAH),* of May 2, 1953, as amended on May 26, 1957.

[92] Guradze, *Zur Gültigkeit des Rechtshilfegesetzes* (On the Validity of *RAH),* in *Neue Juristische Wochenschrift (NJW),* 1958, p. 817.

[93] Also the decision of the Federal Supreme Court of July 15, 1960, follows this line of argument (BGHSt. 15, 72).

[94] Federal Constitutional Court, Vol. 11, pp. 150—158 *passim.*

[95] Federal Constitutional Court, Vol. 12, p. 62.

[96] Lange, *l. c.,* p. 14.

[97] *l. c.,* p. 14. The decision discussed on p. 12 of that article is not more closely identified by references.

[98] Decision of Oct. 24, 1958 (Ref. 2 S 182/58), published in '*Recht in Ost und West*' (Law in East and West), 1959, p. 74 *passim.*

[99] Lange, *l. c.,* p. 13.

[100] Readers should compare with this a newspaper commentary on the case of the Federal Attorney-General, Fränkel: —

'The terrible thing was that it was possible then to apply "the Law" of those days correctly and yet to become guilty... However, the most terrible disasters were caused by the fatal notion that statute law was always the same as justice — an equation which, in Germany, was supported by the legal positivists, through whose school far too many lawyers had gone... Overvaluation of ideas deriving from legal positivism gave to many lawyers an education in the wrong direction, so that they had become soulless technicians of the law, engineers of formal justice, who were no longer capable to distinguish the abysmal contrast between the "Law" that was applied by them and the will to justice...'

(D. Kramer in *Frankfurter Allgemeine Zeitung* of July 25, 1962).

[101] 'Publication of these guiding principles in the official periodical, *Neue Justiz* (1959, p. 469), proves that this is to-day's official programme for the control of the judicature.' (Lange. *l. c.,* p. 17).

[102] Lange, *l. c.,* p. 17.

[103] This *inner connection between the structure of the State and its criminal justice* is also emphasized by W. Sax in: *Grundsätze der Strafrechtspflege* (Principles of Criminal Jurisdiction), contained in Bettermann/Nipperdey/Scheuner, *Die Grundrechte* (Basic Rights), Vol. III/2, p. 967: 'The law of the criminal trial, in the last instance, is applied constitutional law.'

[104] Federal Constitutional Court, Vol. 4, No. 30, p. 331 *passim.*

[105] K. A. Bettermann, *Die Unabhängigkeit der Gerichte und der gesetzlichen Richter* (The Independence of the Courts and of Legally Appointed Judges), in: Bettermann/Nipperdey/Scheuner, *Die Grundrechte,* Vol. III/2, p. 523 *passim.*

[106] Eichenberger, *Die richterliche Unabhängigkeit als staatsrechtliches Problem* (The Independence of the Judges as a Problem in Public Law), Essays on Swiss Laws, New Series, No. 431, Berne 1960.

[107] Reut-Nicolussi, *Unparteilichkeit im Völkerrecht* (Impartiality in International Law), Innsbruck 1940, p. 66 *passim.*

[108] Prosper Feduzzi, *De l'Efficacité Extraterritoriale des Lois et des Actes de Droit Public; revue des Cours,* 1929 II (27), p. 145 *passim.* — See especially pp. 180, 183: '*Soutenir que l'attribution de valeur à des actes étrangers implique nécessairement attribution de valeur au droit étranger sous l'empire duquel ces actes ont été accomplis, ce qui veut dire en substance application du droit étranger, ne peut* être *que la conséquence d'une équivoque . . .*

Au point de vue logique autant que juridique, l'application directe d'une loi étrangère est bien autre chose que le fait de reconnaître les conséquences, traduites dans un acte juridique de l'application de la loi étrangère, qui s'est passé à l'étranger . . .

En effet, la fonction de notre ordre juridique n'est pas de s'approprier l'acte, mais d'attribuer à l'acte une efficacité quelconque.'

(Supporting the view that granting validity to foreign legal decisions implies necessarily also acknowledgment of validity of those foreign laws under whose rule such decisions were made — in other words, the substantial application of those foreign laws — can only be the effect of ambiguous thought . . .

Both from the standpoint of logic and from that of the lawyer, direct application of a foreign law is something quite different from recognition of the effects of the application of foreign law that takes the form of a legal decision under a law that has been enacted abroad . . .

As a matter of fact, it is not the task of our legal system to take over such a decision, but to grant such a decision some sort of efficacy).

[109] That all judgments passed in the Soviet Occupation Zone are based 'upon an alien and sovereign authority, and not on the constitutionality of the courts', has always been emphasized also by Günter Beitzke, who is widely known as a leading expert on the legal problems arising in the Federal Republic of Germany from the relations between the occupation zones; see, for example: Beitzke, *Zur Vollstreckung ostzonaler Titel* (On the Execution of Claims Established in the Soviet Zone), *Juristische Zeitschrift,* 1958, p. 53.; also in: *Mitteldeutsches Recht,* 1954, p. 321 *passim;* also in: *Familienrechtszeitschrift,* 1956, p. 36 *passim,* and *Juristische Zeitschrift,* 1957, p. 449 *passim.*

[110] In an interesting, and almost parallel, case, the *Generalstaatsanwalt* (General prosecutor) at the *Oberlandesgericht (Land* High Court) in Frankfurt issued a decree on Dec. 2, 1954, which denied a formal judgment passed by the *Landgericht* (District Court) at Chemnitz (now called, Karl-Marx-stadt, in the Soviet Zone) the essential character of a judgment under the Rule of Law. He argued that, in its outward form, this 'judgment' bore the form of a court finding, containing also a punishment decree, but it had been established that the 'judgment' had not been found in a properly conducted trial procedure under the *Strafprozessordnung* (Criminal Trial Rules). Furthermore, it had not been a definite criminal act of the applicant but his general political behaviour, which had become the subject of trial and verdict. 'This "judgment" has therefore not been passed either by a court nor has it imposed a penalty, so that the Law on Inner-German Mutual Assistance Between Courts, etc., of May 2, 1953, cannot be applied to it.' (*Neue Juristische Wochenschrift,* Vol. 8, 1955, p. 155).

[111] Decision of the *Kammergericht* (Berlin High Court) of March 15, 1954, *Neue Juristische Wochenschrift,* 1954, p. 1901 *passim.*

[112] *l. c.*

[113] *l. c.*

V

THE STASHINSKY TRIAL

ITS SIGNIFICANCE FOR THE CHARACTER OF THE SYSTEM OF SOVIET-COMMUNIST RULE

I.

Milovan Djilas has produced in two books his criticism, both comprehensive and thorough, of the system of Soviet-Communist rule. His outstanding analytical achievement has earned him a long term of imprisonment in his communist homeland[1]. In these books, he developed two statements which are highly relevant to the subject of our own investigation. The first of these statements[2] is that the changeover from Stalin's rule to collective leadership did not essentially alter the character of the Soviet system. Djilas provided evidence for his statement by supplying overwhelming proof from the theoretical foundations of the communist regime. He believes it to be impossible on principle that the views upon which all communist rule is based could be altered, because there will always remain an unbridgeable gulf between communist ideology and political reality under Communism, deriving from the communist-marxist views of the State.

His second statement is that the communist state, as long as the ruling party maintains its totalitarian claim to all-embracing power, and the basic ideology upon which that claim rests, can never transform itself into a Rule of Law, under which there would be a state government and a judicature independent of each other, the latter to administer laws whose validity would be independent of the ruling party. Djilas draws these conclusions from his discussion of the scientific value of Marx's views of the State. He allows that Marx discovered "*some* laws of social development", especially those governing the development of early capitalism. However, this achievement did nothing to justify "the assertion of modern Communists that Marx discovered *all* the laws of social reality."[3] The reason why the marxist doctrine survived is seen by him in the fact that the doctrine remains highly useful as a political instrument of social revolution, and not in its truth. 'Unless the political requirements of the European working class movements had called for a new and comprehensive ideology, the type of philosophy known as Marxism... would have been long forgotten... The power of marxist philosophy was not based upon its value as a social science but in its close connection with a mass movement, and especially upon its particular emphasis on the need and the aim to transform human society.'[4] But it was the basic teaching of Karl Marx, which was handed down by socialist tradition and which brought with it the unbridgeable contradiction between the theory of the State and its reality under Communism.

Djilas justly stresses that for theory and practice the question of the State is of focal importance for Communism. His investigations of present-day reality of Soviet-type communism — which are of particular significance for our own analysis — lead to the conclusion that, under Communism, the State lives in some sort of perpetual, latent civil war between government and governed populations. Political power is in the hands of the party oligarchy, which dominates the machinery of the state in all its ramifications (the police, the army, etc.), and 'Society and even the machinery of the State are in strong opposition to the ruling oligarchy, which endeavours to transform the latter into an instrument of brute and naked violence'[5].

The structure of Soviet society, the relations of its members to each other, are following to-day the trend of all 'naturally evolving societies'. It demonstrates the need of all its members for free activity, the untrammelled use of their human and basic qualities and faculties, unhindered criticism of the Party, etc. The Communist Party, on the other hand, basing its claims upon its dogmatic conviction, enforced by its hold upon power, that the Party alone knows the laws of social development, remains in irreconcilable opposition to this demand for human freedom.

Djilas reminds his readers that even such outstanding personalities as Lenin himself fell into almost inconceivable self-deception regarding social and political developments towards Communism. It was only nine months before the Russian October revolution that Lenin told a meeting of Swiss young socialists: 'We, the older generation, will perhaps not witness any more the decisive battles of approaching revolution. But I believe, I can express my hope with the fullest confidence, that youth... will have the great good luck... not only to fight during the approaching revolution but also to emerge victorious from it.'

That the victory of this revolution took place in a country which was, at the time, economically underdeveloped, was a blow in the face of basic marxist theory which postulated that the transformation would have to affect the societies that were most highly developed economically. Clever Trotsky then invented the substitute theory that the chain of Capitalism broke where it had its weakest link. Although the bolshevik revolution could not be explained either by the historical doctrines or by the philosophy of the state contained in Marxism but only through the actual social situation prevailing in Russia, marxist doctrine was accepted as their guiding light by the Soviets, yet they were forced to vacillate from one substitute construction to the next. Inspite of all this, they maintain their claim to total power to the present day with the 'assertion that they alone know the laws to which Society is subordinated' [6]. This is the point of departure for the Communists to the oversimplifying and unscientific conclusion that their alleged omniscience gives them the power and the exclusive right to change the face of society and to control its activities. This is the basic error of their system' [7].

This is the cause underlying the constant tension between State and Society in the communist Soviet system, which creates a situation of latent civil war. These conditions of social life under Communism lead Djilas to the following conclusion, which is of decisive importance for our own argument: 'Because of this contradiction, and because of the permanent need of the communists to use the state mainly as an instrument of power, the communist state can never grow into a Rule of Law, under which application of the State's law would be carried out independently of government, so that the individual statutes have actual force. The entire communist system militates against a state of this type. Even if the communist leaders had the ardent desire to build a state under the law, they would not be able to do so without endangering their totalitarian rule.

If jurisdiction was independent, and if the statutes had real force, it would be unavoidable that opposition would grow. For example, there is no law under Communism which forbids the free expression of one's opinions, or the right to form organizations. The statutes of the communist system guarantee all sorts of rights to the citizens, and they are based, in theory, on the principle of an independent judicature. But in practice, nothing of the kind exists.'

The communist Soviet system believes marxist doctrine to be the incontrovertible and scientifically precise synthesis of all absolutely valid laws of the entire development of society. This is the basis of its claim to total dominion [8].

If it could be shown that Marx's theories have no just claim to this high rank, the political claims of the Party fall likewise flat.

The trial against Bogdan Stashinsky has shown that, many years after the disappearance of Stalin, the Party and the leadership of the Soviet state are still determined, no matter whether this is lawful, to fight for the claims they have staked out, by any method that they think expeditious. This lends particular weight to that trial and to the facts unearthed by it.

II.

The trial against Stashinsky reveals a number of new facts of immense significance for a realistic description of contemporary communist Soviet rule. In the first instance, it can be shown that the notion of the 'Enemy of the State' is still of high importance for that system. In order to fight against enemies of the state, the system makes use of methods which are based on violence not only within the sovereign territory of the Soviet Power, but also abroad, not caring whether sovereign rights of other states are thereby violated. In other words, the Soviet system commits definite crimes under international law. In order to commit these crimes, the oligarchic party machinery uses also threats and browbeating of its own subjects, so that these are compelled to commit crimes that remain hidden to the eyes of the Soviet public.

And furthermore, the Soviet system clearly also uses systematic slandering and calumniation of persons and institutions known as, or believed to be, hostile to the Soviets.

The Stashinsky trial provided proof for all the three forms of state-promoted criminal activities, the evidence being partly direct, partly by inference.

The methods and circumstances of persuading the future murderer into joining the Soviet state security service provide proof for the use of violence on Soviet territory [9]. A special department of the MGB blackmails young Stashinsky, using as a pretext his own venial violation of Soviet Law, and threatening to do harm to his parents, forces him to join the ranks of the MGB.

The verdict of the German court [10] and the reasons given for it had to discuss the disorderly conditions prevailing in Stashinsky's Ukrainian homeland. Stashinsky was born in 1931 in a Western Ukrainian village near Lwow. The boy, whose home district was taken over (after the downfall of the Ukrainian State) by Poland subsequently to the First World War, first lives under Polish rule and among sharp national conflicts between Ukrainians and Poles. He was born into a Ukrainian family. The first foreign language he had to learn at school was Polish. After the dismemberment of Poland by Stalin and Hitler in 1939, Western Ukraine was incorporated into the Soviet state. That means that Stashinsky's school had to use Russian as the language of instruction, and he witnesses new violence in the struggle between Ukrainians, Russians, and Poles. In 1941, the Germans march in. Instead of Russian, he has now to learn German; the fight against Russians and Poles is replaced soon by the struggle against the Germans, because they deny the Ukrainians political sovereignty in a state of their own. After 1943, when the Germans left, the Soviets are returning, and the Ukrainians fight as partisans against the

Soviet invaders. Relatives of the defendant fought as partisans. Stashinsky managed to enter a teachers' training college at Lwow in 1948, and in 1950, on the railway journey home, the ticket collector found him travelling without a ticket. Under the Rule of Law, such a case would have ended with a stern warning, the offender being put on probation, or sentenced to payment of a double fare, or possibly a fine. Under the Soviet system, the young sinner was summoned to see the Transport Police, which is a sub-department of the MGB. Stashinsky is cross-examined by an officer. The interrogator is not at all interested in the actual reason for the interrogation — Stashinsky's journey without a ticket, but talks incessantly about Stashinsky's family and the conditions in his village. He goes on from there to talking about the Ukrainian resistance organisation (OUN). He indicates that he knows of anti-Soviet feelings among the members of Stashinsky's family. He describes the resistance movement as an organization of traitors; the leaders are said by him to be in the pay of the Americans. When Stashinsky spoke of his own development to the German Federal Court, he repeatedly emphasized that the Ukrainian resistance organization was described to him as an association of enemies of the state and of traitors against the Soviet people, and that he then believed this. In the end he was told that, if he decided to work for the MGB, he would not only serve the Soviet people, but he could thereby also protect his family against dire consequences, because all people, not only those who worked in the ranks of the OUN but even those who supported OUN, were sure to be eventually arrested, punished and deported. In the end he was moved by a mixture of Soviet patriotism and fear (through the threats against his nearest relatives) to join the MGB.

But the threats, wielded over Stashinsky's head by the omnipotent Party, continue. He is again being threatened on the occasion of carrying out his first assignement, to infiltrate himself into OUN, in order to report on the details of a murder committed on OUN's behalf: a Ukrainian writer had been killed. After having completed his mission, the OUN knows him as an informer, and he cannot return to his village and to his parents. He now accepts permanent employment with the MGB.

In 1952, the MGB transfers him to Kiev, where he receives training in the methods of the secret service. According to what is known about the practice of all secret services, Stashinsky's induction and special training remain within the usual framework. He is given a cover name and is told to learn German. In 1954, he is sent on a special training mission to Poland, using the maiden name of his mother, to obtain local knowledge of a number of places which are important in the life story of a man whose name he will be given later, when he is sent on killing missions into Germany. The second personality of the agent is that of a German formerly resident in Poland (a so-called "*Volksdeutscher*") whose date of birth is on November 4th, 1930 (Stashinsky's own birthday is on November 4th 1931), and whose name is Josef Lehmann. Stashinsky had to visit Lehmann's former places of residence and to learn all he could about them. Later, after he had already been sent to East Germany with an identity card bearing Josef Lehmann's name, he was employed in ordinary work for several months in Bautzen and Dresden. In 1956, he was given his first mission in the Federal Republic (West Germany). He is told to spy out the land with a view to kidnapping the Ukrainian leader, Rebet, or possibly to win him over to the Soviet cause. He also served as the distributor of money to other Soviet agents, and had to collect information on American military establishments in West Germany. His immediate superior is a Soviet citizen known as Sergei. In his talks with Sergei, an important theme is constantly being discussed. Sergei makes frequent remarks about the need to do away with the OUN leadership, if those types do not see reason'[11]. During the proceedings-in-chief against him, Stashinsky gave a vivid description of his own reaction: Through having been educated during his formative years under Soviet rule, reinforced by special political training which he received from the secret service, he found this attitude completely acceptable in the beginning: the Soviet people was thrown upon the defence against its enemies, and it was permissible and even mandatory to destroy them.

For the psychological motivation of Stashinsky's later behaviour, it is important to hear of the reasons which eventually undermined his belief in the Soviet system and his own willingness to do anything required of him in its alleged defence.

The first blow which cracked the rigid picture of black villains and white Soviet heroes, built up in his own mind through years of psychological drilling, was apparently caused by one of his talks with Sergei in 1957, when it became clear to him that the mission to investigate Rebet's habits actually only served the preparations for Rebet's assassination[12]. He was shown a novel type of weapon, which he had to use later, and it was tested in his presence and he was then given detailed instructions for the killing of Rebet by Sergei[13]. Stashinsky was now thrown into an inner struggle, of which he gave a graphic and credible description[14]. Rebet was killed on October 12, 1957, by Stashinsky pulling the trigger of the weapon, when Rebet, without suspecting anything, passed Stashinsky on the stairs of the house where he had his office. The post mortem on Rebet's body was made only forty-eight hours after the death, and nobody then suspected a crime. In 1958, Stashinsky was required to study the location and conditions of a flat inhabited by a certain H. S. Budeit in Dortmund, who had been born in Kassel in 1927. He was then given an identity card in Budeit's name in January, 1959, and was sent on his second assignment of murdering an 'enemy of the state'. To prepare for this, he had to study the place of residence and the habits of Stepan Bandera, the Ukrainian refugee leader living in Munich. Already in 1958, Stashinsky had been sent to Rotterdam to take part in a Ukrainian memorial service in a cemetery. The speaker during this celebration was recognized by him now in Munich; it had been Bandera. In April 1959, Stashinsky was called to Moscow. He had to report on the results of his investigations to a higher KGB officer, and this man told him of 'a decision made by supreme authority', which required Stashinsky to liquidate Bandera by the same method as he had killed Rebet[15]. Stashinsky apparently still suffered remorse because of his murder of Rebet, and he became frightened, but as he stated, he had learned to keep himself under control as an agent of KGB. It seems also that he was still dominated by the following reasoning: An order emanating from the supreme authority had to be carried out, even against severe pangs of his own conscience. In May 1959, he turned up again in Munich, and for a time he tried to evade his assignment.

In October 1959, the order was renewed, and Sergei emphasized again that the request for Bandera's liquidation had been received 'from the highest quarters in Moscow'. Using his identity card made out in the name of Budeit, Stashinsky now returned to Munich, and on October 15, 1959, he killed Bandera in the house where Bandera lived in Kreittmayerstrasse.

The repeated order issued "from the highest quarters" was now followed by a reward from the 'highest quarters'. In November, 1959, Stashinsky was called into the presence of a Soviet general at Karlshorst in East Berlin, and this superior officer told him that for carrying out an important government assignment, he had been decorated with the "Red Banner Combat Order". The decoration would be handed to him in Moscow. The general also requested Stashinsky to describe the assassination in detail. In December Stashinsky had to present himself to Sheliepin, then the chief of the Security Service. He read to him a document saying that he had been decorated with the order of the Red Banner by decree of the Supreme Soviet of November 6, 1959. He showed him also the document confirming the decoration, which was signed by Voroshilov, the then Soviet President, and of Voroshilov's secretary.

The highly interesting process of Stashinsky's complete change, which eventually led to his decision to flee (together with his wife) from the Soviet orbit, cannot be discussed in detail here. We will only enumerate its most important stages.

Comparing the contradictory impulses and motivations moving Stashinsky in those years, there are, on the one hand, a purely human form of reaction, on the other hand, a political motivation created by education and training. In the end, it was the human motivation which prevailed. Already the little dog which had been killed experimentally with the novel weapon had appeared to him as a symbol of a human being. He could not look at the dog when it sniffed at him, full of confidence and curiosity [16]. The severe inner conflicts created in Stashinsky by the order to kill Rebet mark the polarity of this two motivations with great clarity: He knew the commandment, 'Thou shalt not kill', and he simultaneously always remembered his duty of obedience and the learned formula, 'he is an enemy of the Soviet Union.' The Judgment of the German Court quotes Stashinsky's own words describing the constant reasoning moving between the two different extremes: —

In those days, Stashinsky suffered from a severe inner conflict. To-day, he describes his state as follows: 'It was like a nightmare to me that I was supposed to kill an unsuspecting person. I was running up and down as in a cage. *I was aware of the fact* that *I must not kill,* but *I was not able to rebel against the orders given by my superiors.* After all, I knew to which sort of organization I belonged. When I saw then a married couple walking along the street, I always imagined how it would be if the wife suddenly lost her husband. When I thought of that, I never believed that I could carry out such an order. But then I tried to justify such a killing. I remembered the violent deeds of OUN in my home country. And I said to myself that *Rebet, after all, was an enemy of the Soviet Union,* because he also *persuaded refugees against returning home* and thus shared the responsibility for their turning into foreign agents. I was at my wit's end. I convinced myself that *this was the same as in war,* when the aim sanctifies the means, and *orders have to be carried out against all resistance.*' Torn from one side to the other between such feelings and views without any result, he tried to calm down his conscience without succeeding in his endeavour [17].

In a state of such turmoil, he murdered Rebet; the crime seemed to him to be committed 'half-dreaming', 'almost automatically'. The same inner conflict was aroused by the assignment to kill Bandera. But in this case, still another factor apparently mitigated his responsibility. The senior Security officer, who spoke to him in Moscow, told him particularly that the order emanated *from supreme authority* [18]. This special pointer was repeated by Sergei. Thus, it is the specified origin of the order issued to him which transforms, in the beginning, even request to kill once again into an inescapable obligation, which does not admit of an individual rebellious conscience. However, when he makes his first attempt to kill Bandera, Stashinsky's human conscience suddenly revives, after it had been suppressed by political motives. He sees his intended victim stand in a garage, and this notion crossed his mind: —

'Death is on the way to him. Very soon, he will not live any more. But he has not done any harm to you. He, too, is a human being. I cannot do it.' Without thinking of the order 'to liquidate the enemies of the people, the traitors', and without thinking of the consequences for himself, he turned round under the influence of this overpowering picture in his imagination and ran away in the direction of the *Hofgarten* (Royal Court Park), where he reached the *Kögelmühlbach* (the mill stream). There, he held his weapon across the bannister of a bridge, pulled the trigger, and threw it into the water. For a short while now, he felt relieved. But after that, the automatism of the order received again got the better of him [19].

The political impulse behind his assignment remains victorious in the end, and he kills Bandera.

Then, the overpowering force of human sympathy, which had been mocked cynically by Sergei, his superior officer, gives him the final push for tearing himself free from the system that had made him its dependent slave and a murderer. By chance, he went to a cinema, where the newsreel showed pictures of Bandera's open catafalque: 'When he saw the dead man's face, convulsively distorted, it 'hit him like a blow with a hammer, a terrible shock', with "what he had loaded on his conscience". Deeply dismayed and disturbed, he cannot remember the main film, because he slumped deep down into his seat, and he soon left the cinema. He sought out Sergei, not caring whether he would lose Sergei's confidence, and craved his consolation.' [20] Apparently, he hoped for some human understanding from Sergei and talked to him also 'of the widow and the poor children.' — What was Sergei's reply? He made a 'cold and unmoved' impression on Stashinsky and remarked: 'Bandera's children would be deeply grateful later, after they have returned to the Soviet Union.' This answer amazed Stashinsky: 'To agree with this, I should have been a hundred and twenty per cent Communist. In this moment, I lost another part of my communist convictions [21].

The Judgment believes that it was the effect of these two completely opposed events, following each other in quick succession, that marked the turning point for Stashinsky's psychological development. The influence of his German fiancée helped to accelerate this process of change. He obtains permission to marry only with the greatest difficulty. The young couple is forced to live in Moscow under an assumed name. Their families are to be told that they are living in Warsaw. Their mail is censored. They discover a hidden microphone in their Moscow flat and thus know that their conversation is being overheard. For important communications, they can only use written notes, or must wait till they can take a walk in the streets together. After Mrs. Stashinsky became pregnant, they are given the choice of an abortion or of the permanent transfer of the baby to a children's home, and the young wife's joyful expectancy of the child is destroyed. Previously, they had been promised permission to move to East Berlin; this is now being evidently refused, as their application remains unanswered. Now, Stashinsky tells his wife everything, after having told her, shortly before, that he was in the employment of KGB but had still not talked of the two murders. Now they agree that they intend to flee, and they succeed through a combination of exceptionally favourable chance occurrences. This was the evening of August 12, 1961; next morning Berlin had been cut in two by the wall.

III.

The brief description under (II) follows the narrative contained in the first chapter of the Judgment. The Judgment accepts the defendant's own admissions, which are evaluated as 'credible, convincing, bare of unexplained gaps and contradictions'. [22]

The Judgment bases this general assessment in the first instance on the personal impression made by Stashinsky, whose description of the alleged facts had never shown contradictions either during the criminal investigation or during the trial itself but had remained, on the contrary, always the same even in remote details. Such complicated details could 'be reported with such precision and remain verifiable in so many points only by a person who has experienced them himself or had heard them directly from the actual murderer.' Regarding the inner struggle between orders and obligations, on the one hand, and Stashinsky's personal feelings, on the other hand, the Judgment says: 'The Senate (Judges' Bench) is convinced that these inner processes could only be experienced by the defendant himself.' This general evaluation is being supported in great detail by overwhelming and broad evidence, which comes under discussion in Chapter B I 2 of the Judgment. This chapter is divided into 35 paragraphs, which scrutinize even the smallest and seemingly most unimportant events that contribute proof. In their totality, they form a complete instrument for establishing the truth of Stashinsky's admissions.

For our own investigations, the paragraphs (y), (aa), (b), and (d) are of particular significance. These contain the Russian documents, which Stashinsky brought with him and handed to the Court. They were examined by experts, and have been shown to be all genuine. They establish the following facts: The so-called 'Scientific Institute, Post Office Box 946', is a camouflaged KGB department. The Director of this Department wrote a 'Service Characteristic' of Stashinsky, confirming that Stashinsky worked for this 'Institute' from March, 1951, to December, 1960. The report specially underlines the fact that, 'for successful activities in dealing with an important problem, he was decorated with the Order of the Red Banner by decree of the Presidium of the Supreme Soviet of the U.S.S.R. of November 6, 1959.' The Judgment comments that this tallies both with the statement made by Stashinsky that he worked for the Secret Service of the KGB from 1951 to the beginning of 1961, and with the report on having been decorated (for 'successful work on an important problem'), which was told him by the Soviet general in November, 1959, in Berlin-Karlshorst and by the KGB chief, Sheliepin, in December 1959 ('carrying out of an important assignment by the government').

IV.

For the judgment it was of special importance that it accepted the evidence produced, especially through the documents submitted, for the fact that Stashinsky had been given orders to commit murders (in the second case, the order emanated from the highest Soviet authority). This led to a qualified verdict on the criminal significance of the killings.

The Office of the Federal Prosecutor *(Bundesanwaltschaft)* had charged ('without giving detailed reasons') Stashinsky with murder. The Court did not accept the case of the prosecution and sentenced him only as an accessory to murder. (The term in German criminal law is '*Gehilfe*', i. e. helper or assistant.)

In the extended legal argument adduced for the verdict [23], it is of interest in this context, as a first consideration, that the Federal Court did not qualify the crime in this way for the first time but followed earlier precedents established by the Reich Court *(Reichsgericht)* of the Weimar Republic, and accepted by other Senates of the Federal Court. To decide the question whether a defendant has been an accessory (to murder or other felonies), these courts have found that it will be necessary to know whether he has collaborated, as an instrument, or as an assistant, in the commission of a third party's crime. Intent and attitude of the defendant will determine whether he was the originator of the felony, or only materially assisted in its commission. It is therefore possible that a felon may also be a person who causes the entire crime to be committed by third parties, and conversely, it is possible that an accessory carries out the entire criminal act himself. That a particular person has committed the felony himself, has the meaning only, for adjudicating the felony and participation in a felony, as an *indicium* (corroborative evidence). A principle that has been enounced by the Fifth Criminal Senate states that, "on principle, a murderer is the person who (under the conditions stated in the particular judgment) kills another person by the acts of his own hands", but at the same time admits of exceptions to that principle, and indicates the direction in which such exceptions can be found, e. g. in cases of a criminal superior order issued. In the particular case leading to its judgment, the Fifth Senate has argued that 'the inner attitude (of the defendant) towards his criminal act cannot be compared with that of a soldier who is supposed to carry out a criminal order of his superior officer as this officer's mere instrument or tool.'

The Judgment then discusses different legal doctrines (especially the doctrine of so-called 'material objectivity'). It rejects the 'material-objective' doctrine, mainly because this theory would prevent courts from taking cognizance of new and specific types of crimes and criminal motivations arising from contemporary political conditions.

Such a new contemporary crime is the one with which the court had to deal in the Stashinsky case. Therefore, the Judgment took it upon itself to examine the special structure of this new type of criminal event, which has hardly been subjected yet to careful criminological analysis. We believe that the Federal Court has succeeded in this difficult attempt, and thus has opened up important new legal territory.

In opposition to the 'material-objective' doctrine, the Judgment emphasizes the need for analysing and evaluating the special character of certain criminal motivations, notably such as evolve from contemporary closed systems of a unitary political and social creed. In doing so, the Judgment draws the attention of criminological science to the fact that the 'material-objective' doctrine is evidently ignorant of the fundamental differences in certain motivations, and therefore takes no heed of motivations that bear no comparison with those that have hitherto been commonly known to criminology. The new motivations do not derive from a 'common moral code of the community' and do not evolve from 'relatively stable political conditions within a state'. Among the crimes of this new type are political murders committed by persons who act simply in executing an order received, which means that such crimes that have been caused to be committed by public authorities do not carry with them traditionally known criminal or personal motivations as their causes. The Judgment admits that there have always been, from time to time, political assassinations. But the more or less common types of earlier political murders are fundamentally different from other political assassinations typical for our time. The Judgment states: —

> However, during recent times, certain modern states have decided, under the influence of extremist political creeds, in Germany that of national socialism, to plan systematically political assassinations and to issue orders for the execution of such bloody deeds. The recipients of such orders, when they commit officially required crimes, are not subject to criminologically scrutinized or similar personal criminal motivations. On the contrary, such tools of official crimes find themselves in a situation of moral confusion, from which there is often no way out: Their own State, which appears to many citizens *eo ipso* as an indubitable source of authority, which is reinforced by clever mass propaganda, directly commissions them to commit felonies. They then carry out such assignments under the influence of political propaganda, or of apparently supreme authority, or of similar influences emanating from their own government, of which they normally would justly expect the protection of Law and Order. These dangerous criminal motivations have their origin, not in the recipients of criminal orders, but in the holders of the state's authority, who brutally abuse their power. Such criminal orders are not even restricted to the territory of the criminal state. The proceedings-in-chief have provided proof that such criminal acts also occur in the international field[24].

The argument then continues to state that even the special conditions created by a public authority issuing orders for the commission of crimes do not exempt the executants from criminal responsibility, because man has the opportunity to determine its moral behaviour freely himself, so that he is capable of deciding for lawful and against unlawful behaviour. He who forces his conscience to become mute and adapts himself to third parties' criminal aims, so as to make them his own, shows that his thought and acts have become identical with those of the true instigators of the crimes — he has in general to be considered as a felon. The case is different with those who disagree with such criminal orders, try to resist them but still carry them out because of their human weakness, as they cannot cope with the superior power of the state, and have neither the courage to develop effective resistance nor the intelligence to evade the burden laid upon their shoulders.

This distinction between two types of political felons is, in our view, a pioneering contribution to the legal elucidation of important criminal facts of contemporary history. The Court has applied this distinction to the facts established during the Stashinsky trial, and has come to the following conclusions: —

> Stashinsky had not intended the crimes as his own;
>
> On the contrary, he submitted to the authority of his then political leadership;
>
> In none of the relevant details did he choose the form in which the crimes were carried out;
>
> He satisfied no material or political interest of his own in carrying out the crime;
>
> That he was decorated with a special order of merit surprised and repelled him;
>
> He was never truly convinced that Rebet and Bandera were enemies of the Soviet Union who must be liquidated;
>
> At the moment of the commission of felonies he, so-to-say, drugged himself with the political teachings he had received;
>
> But, above all, committing the felonies stirred up his conscience, and he offered himself up voluntarily to inexorable retribution, even risking his own life, after he had realized that he was to be abused and made a professional assassin.

The result, on the other hand, for the people who have issued the orders in the two cases, is the following: It has been they who determined that, and how, the felonies were to be carried out; they decided that there should be crimes; they chose the victims; they selected and tested the weapon and the poison; they picked out Stashinsky and gave him his orders, transformed him into their tool, and worked out all the details, where and when murders were to be committed.

The Judgment then deals with the objection that the internal state of the criminal's mind, as described, did not exist outside the writ of the

Soviet power, his employer, and rejects this proposition as unrealistic, as follows: —

> To believe that he only needed to make a clean breast to the western authorities means to misread the true situation. It can be believed if the defendant explains that he who, as an impressionable young man, has spent eleven years without interruption near the centre of the Soviet power machinery, where he was continually indoctrinated, experiences great difficulties in trying to understand the western way of life and thought, in finding his way there, in giving up for ever his homeland, his family and friends, and the territory where his own language is spoken, and in exchanging these for unknown conditions, risks, and influences, even though he had acquired new personal ties here. He also had not learnt a skill with which to make his living here. Because of the 'important government order' issued to him, it can also be believed that he was afraid to be under constant KGB supervision before and during the commission of his murder attempts in the West, where people are not worrying about such secret dangers, and to be exposed to the revenge of his employers as a 'traitor' after a possible defection. The composite picture offered by all the circumstances surrounding his crimes therefore does not show him as the felon himself. He had to be judged as an accessory, according to paragraph 49 of the German Criminal Code [25, 26].

The Judgment does not admit of the legal excuse that the defendant may have acted under duress, because he was not forced to commit his crimes by being threatened with 'present danger to life and body' of his own or his relations. Also his full criminal responsibility could not be denied. The Judgment goes on to take into account his spying out official secrets of the Federal Republic and military secrets of troops stationed on its territory. The penalty has been determined, keeping in mind his experiences in his youth, his forced entry into KGB services under threats, also that he was a reluctant tool of his employers, that he obviously showed active regret for his crimes that he made a full avowal, without keeping anything back, and without trying to whitewash himself in any way, and especially that he surrendered to the authorities out of his own free will, 'having before his eyes the certain possibility of a double murder charge, with all its consequences.' Qualifying his crimes in this way, it is an inescapable legal conclusion, logically to find that 'under the established circumstances the guilt of his employers was much more severe'.

Already when dealing with the doctrine of 'material objectivity', the Judgment had stated that the political murders typical for our time are not personally motivated, but 'rather originate in the holders of political power, who flatly abuse their power'. When giving the reasons for the length of the prison sentence against Stashinsky, the judges say: —

> Without any inhibitions, the Soviet Russian employers (of the defendant) thought it advisable to order the commission of two murders on the territory of the Federal Republic of Germany, and to have them carried out, thereby grossly violating international morality and their duties under international

law, as they emanate from correct diplomatic relations between two sovereign states. This responsibility of the actual felons in high position cannot be passed on to the defendant. On the other hand, Stashinsky, through his uninhibited admissions, has contributed to uncovering and exposing such criminal methods of the political struggle before the eyes of the public [27].

This leads to the further question of the legal qualification of the Stashinsky case under international law.

PROBLEMS IN INTERNATIONAL LAW ARISING FROM THE STASHINSKY CASE

What the Judgments Indicates

(1) The findings of the Federal Court of Law showed the significance of Stashinsky's criminal acts in the context of International Law. The two offences presented identical traits in a way that is important also from the point of view of international law — namely that the people who commissioned Stashinsky to commit those crimes 'fixed in advance the essential characteristics of these acts (victims, weapon, antidotes against the poison, the manner of using the weapon, the time when the crime was to be carried out, the place where the act was to be committed, the journeys to reach the aim of the assignment)' and therefore 'acted with criminal intent' [28]. The judgment continues to state [29] that the commission, i. e. the criminal motivation, was created 'by the holder of State power, which was thereby grossly abused.'

In the Bandera case, the holder of state authority also reveals himself. April, 1959, Stashinsky was informed, after he had done away with Rebet, that it was his duty now to liquidate Bandera, on the basis of a decision taken by 'supreme authority' [30]. Of course, this order did not name individually the persons representing the ‚supreme authority'. But the authority was now adequately, though not precisely, circumscribed. The judges believed Stashinsky's statement that he understood the order to come from a body belonging, at least, to the ranks of the government [31].

In October of the same year, the same order, its wording slightly altered, was passed on again to Stashinsky [32]. The government department that had issued the order became known later with greater precision when Stashinsky, after having murdered Bandera, reported to a Soviet general in the prohibited area of the Soviet Kommandantura in Berlin-Karlshorst (East Berlin), whom he believed to be the head of the KGB area command of East Berlin. This general, who was undoubtedly well informed, discussed with Stashinsky what he called 'an important government assignment' which required the murder of Bandera [33]. The same wording is repeated in the document investing Stashinsky with the 'Fighting Order of the Red Banner', which was handed to Stashinsky in Moscow by the Supreme Chief of the KGB. The investiture was based on a decision of the Presidium of the Supreme Soviet of November 6, 1959. Stashinsky was shown the document but it was not given him to keep; as the assignment and its execution had to remain secret, the document was put into his personal file. His attention was specially drawn to the signatures of Marshal Voroshilov, then Chairman of the Presidium, and of Goradse, its then secretary. This statement made by Stashinsky is, according to the text of the Judgment, reinforced beyond all doubt by the corroborative evidence through the Soviet documents taken away by Stashinsky and presented to the Court [34].

The Judgment then discusses the evidence and opinions presented by the expert witness, von Buttlar. Von Buttlar testified that orders to kill individuals and other acts of violence against Soviet citizens and other persons could only be issued from about 1956, according to well-founded information received by his department, by a committee consisting of several members of the Soviet government, and no longer by the KGB on its own responsibility. Killing a person without the formal verdict of a court, therefore, is still the practice of the Soviet state authorities to the present day, and the Soviet government still claims the right to carry out such acts [35].

(2) The results of the proceedings-in-chief and the Judgment accept the evidence produced as conclusive proof that the two murders were the results of orders issued by the named foreign government, and were carried out on the territory of the Federal Republic of Germany [36]. Also the reasons given for determining the length of the prison sentence contain the consideration that the defendant killed in the Federal Republic of Germany two persons, who could claim protection by the German authorities, as *a tool of foreign orders.* The text of the Judgment repeatedly underlines this fact.

(a) The discussion of the question who were the actual felons begins with the finding about the responsibility of the persons or government departments issuing the killing orders [37].

(b) Discussing the specific character of political murders under totalitarian systems, the Judgment states that, under these regimes, 'such perilous criminal motivations do not originate in the recipients of the orders but in the holders of State power'. Such motivations are not only restricted to the territory under totalitarian rule; during the proceedings-in-chief, it was proved that they occur also in the field of international politics. Determining the length of the prison sentence, the Court took into consideration that the defendant has killed two people in the

Federal Republic of Germany, acting under foreign orders. In this context, the Judgment continues that, through causing two political murders to be carried out, international morality was grossly violated and obligations under international law required by the maintenance of correct diplomatic relations between two states were broken. That the murders committed by Stashinsky are of great significance in international law has been established beyond all legal doubt by the Judgment, and it was not necessary to investigate this fact more thoroughly.

(3) It would lead beyond the scope of this investigation to extend the enquiry to all the details of the problems in international law created by the two murders. It is sufficient to indicate their main aspects.

The basis of discussion must be that the two murders committed by Stashinsky under orders given represent acts committed by a government department, acts which are forbidden under international law, on the territory of a foreign state.

Stashinsky acted as the authorized agent of a state. There is no doubt that the KGB is part and parcel of the state machinery of the U.S.S.R. When Stashinsky committed his crimes, the KGB was headed by a man who had been a member of the Central Committee of the Communist Party of the Soviet Union and of the Supreme Soviet since 1932, which means that he belonged to the highest and most select group of Soviet leaders. For the character of the crimes in international law, we need not investigate the question whether the relation of subordination, in which Stashinsky stood to the KGB as its employee, was of the same type as that of a soldier under his superior officers. This question has meaning only for deciding the individual criminal responsibility of the defendant.

What is relevant in this case under international law is the position of every single state within the community of international law, and in regard to the duties and obligations which a given state violates.

The Federal Republic of Germany is a sovereign state. The resumption of diplomatic relations between the Soviet Union and Germany was based on the recognition of German sovereignty [38].

The two states are at peace with each other. It is a tradition recognized unanimously in international law that a sovereign state wields on its territory exclusive jurisdiction and power, excluding interference by all third states [39]. Violation of state sovereignty therefore is a violation of international law.

In the case under review, a department of a foreign government caused the killing of two men on German territory. The two victims, though foreigners, were subject to the sovereign power of the Federal

Republic and, as the Judgment comments, 'could claim Federal German protection' [40].

Murders of this type are acts prohibited by international law and committed by a foreign power on the territory of the Federal Republic. The violation of German sovereignty was particularly grave as the act initiated by the foreign government for execution abroad is a felony (murder by order). A secret killing prevents the Federal Republic from carrying out its duty under international law to 'protect also the lives of foreigners against criminal assaults' [41], if these foreigners live on German territory.

All this goes to show that the Soviet Union has committed a threefold violation of international law: —

(a) It has violated internationally recognized Human Rights (the right of every human being to his own life; Principles of the Declaration on Human Rights of the United Nations; Article 3 and Article 1, paragraph 3, Charter of the United Nations [42].

(b) It has committed terroristic acts, which are condemned equally strongly by Soviet legal and state theory and doctrine. In 1937, the Soviet Union, together with others, signed in Geneva (but did not ratify later) a Convention for Preventing and Suppressing of Terrorism. In this convention, it is stated: 'Organisation or non-prevention by the organs of a state of terroristic acts directed against other states constitute violation of the fundamental principles of international law. Consistent application of the principle of state sovereignty and of non-interference in the inner affairs of other states obliges all states to oppose with all their power terrorism directed against foreign states . . .'. 'Examples of terroristic acts that had been prepared from abroad were the assassination of the German Ambassador von Mirbach in 1918 in Moscow and the murders of the Yugoslav King Alexander and the French Foreign Minister, Barthou, in 1934.' [43] It will be necessary to add to this list the names of Rebet and Bandera.

(c) According to Soviet doctrine, these murders are also cases of 'indirect aggression'. The Soviet Union submitted to the General Assembly of the United Nations a new draft definition of aggression [44]. In the first paragraph of this draft, the definitions are repeated as they appeared in treaties signed by the Soviet Union in 1933 [45], followed by a proposed new definition of 'indirect aggression', which is committed, according to this, by 'any state supporting and committing subversive activities against any other state'. Terroristic acts are specifically quoted as being among such acts of subversion.

FOOTNOTES

[1] Milovan Djilas, The New Class (German edition), 1962; M. Djilas, Talks With Stalin (German edition), 1962. (All further quotations from the German editions).

[2] Djilas, The New Class, p. 247.

[3] *l. c.*, p. 16.

[4] *l. c.*, p. 31.

[5] *l. c.*, p. 125.

[6] Djilas, *l. c.*, p. 17.

[7] Djilas, *l. c.*, p. 17.

[8] It goes far beyond the scope of our investigations to spin out the frequent proposition that Karl Marx's doctrine and the high rank ascribed to it by the communists reveals itself under closer examination as a new revelation, which must not be subjected to any critical scrutiny, which replaces Christian revelation and the doctrine of Man's destiny and his innermost self. Marxism is secularized theology. The demand voiced by the Communist Party that mankind must subordinate itself absolutely to the claim of communist dominion means subordination under the claims of an official state religion concentrated upon this terrestrial world. Djilas emphasizes (The New Class, p. 109) that Marxism has become a theory which may only be defined and interpreted by the party leaders, this only confirms this perversion: only communist believers are permitted to interprete this new creed and its axioms.

[9] The abbreviation for the name of the Soviet State Security Service used here is MGB (Ministry for State Security) till 1954, later, KGB (Committee for State Security under the Council of Ministers of the U.S.S.R.).

[10] German judgment, A I.

[11] Judgment, A IV 2.

[12] Judgment, A IV 2.

[13] *l. c.*

[14] Judgment, A IV 3.

[15] Judgment, A VI 2.

[16] Judgment, A IV 2.

[17] Judgment, A IV.

[18] Judgment, A VI 2.

[19] Judgment, A VI 3.

[20] Judgment, A VII.

[21] Judgment, A VII 1.

[22] Judgment, B I.

[23] Judgment, C II 2.

[24] Judgment, pp. 59, 60.

[25] Paragraph 49 of the Criminal Code: 'Punishable as an accessory to a felony or a misdemeanour is the person who renders important aid or assistance to the person committing a punishable felony or misdemeanour by his advice or actions in the commission of such punishable acts. Punishment of the accessory is to be found according to the law or statute which is applicable to the acts in whose commission the accessory materially assisted, but the penalty may be mitigated according to the principles applicable to attempted crimes.

[26] Judgment, pp. 63, 64.

[27] Judgment, p. 67 *passim*.

[28] Judgment, C II 1.

[29] Judgment, C II 2.

[30] *Cf.* Judgment, A VI 2: 'In this connection, senior officer of the KGB, Georgi Aksentevich ("Georgy") demanded a detailed report on the result of the defendant's enquiry in Munich. Following that, he told Stashinsky that the "highest authority" had decided that Stashinsky had the duty to do away with Bandera in the same way as with Rebet.'

[31] *Cf.* Judgment, *l. c.*: 'Now Stashinsky did not raise any more objections. He believed further protests to be useless, since for him as an agent of the KGB it seemed a matter of course that the "highest authority" represented at least a government department, whose orders had to be carried out unreservedly even inspite of the most severe pangs of his conscience.'

[32] Judgment, A VI 4.

[33] Judgment, A VII.

[34] Judgment, B II 2 y: 'The Russian documents taken away by Stashinsky and handed over to the Court, which according to the opinion of experts after scrutiny proved all genuine, are of particular value as corroborative evidence. In detail, they prove the following facts: (aa) The "Director of the Scientific Institute, Post Office Box 946" — which has been proved to be a camouflaged KGB department — issued a "Service Characteristic" on December 28, 1960, which mentions that "Comrade Stashinsky, Bogdan Nicolayevitch, born in 1931, was employed by this Research Institute between March, 1951, and December, 1960", and that he "proved to be an honest and conscientious collaborator . . ., who carried out all work with which he was charged . . ., punctually and successfully", also that "for successful work in dealing with an important problem, he was invested with the order of the Red Banner by decree of the Presidium of the Supreme Soviet of November 6, 1959." This confirms the statements of Stashinsky that he served the KGB altogether between 1951 and the beginning of 1961, until he started a course of foreign language studies, and that he was decorated with an order of merit. Their reasons given for his receiving a decoration ("successful activities in dealing with an important problem") agree essentially with the reasons quoted by Stashinsky, which the Soviet general allegedly communicated to him in Karlshorst in November 1959, and which the KGB chief, Sheliepin repeated to him in December 1959 in Moscow ("carrying out an important government assignment")'.

[35] Judgment, C II 1: '(1) Perpetration: Both murders were results of orders issued, according to the certain findings during the proceedings-in-chief, by government departments, to say the least, and Sheliepin, then Chairman of the Committee for State Security under the Council of Ministers of the U.S.S.R., took part in working out and passing on these orders. Proof for this assumption were the circumstances ascertained, especially the form in which the order was given, the investment of Stashinsky with an order of merit, and the document recording this investiture. The expert witness, von Buttlar, was able to convince the Court that after Stalin's death in 1953 government orders to kill or carry out other acts of violence against Soviet citizens and other persons, issued by the head of the KGB (previously called MGB, NKVD, GPU), became very frequent. After about 1956 (the year of the XXth Congress of the C.P.S.U.), von Buttlar's department received convincing informations that such orders could no longer be

issued by the KGB independently but only by a committee consisting of several members of the government. This information agrees with the detailed, completely consistent, unexaggerated oral evidence of the defendant about the manner how he received his assignments. Its truth is underlined by the fact that Stashinsky received the Fighting Order of the Red Banner for carrying out "an important assignment by the government" (*cf.* the talks of Stashinsky with the Soviet general in Karlshorst and with Sheliepin in Moscow), and by the text of the "Service Characteristic" issued by the KGB on December 28, 1960, which spoke of "dealing with an important problem" '.

[36] The relevant passage of the Judgment says: 'During the proceedings-in-chief, it has been proved that such ... (orders to commit crimes) occur also in the international field.'

[37] Judgment, C II 1: *cf.* also footnote (8), p. 190.

[38] It is true that when the Soviet Government and the German Federal Government resumed diplomatic relations fundamental differences emerged regarding what was to be defined as 'Germany'. The Federal Government, according to the position under international law, announced some reservations, stating that resumption of diplomatic relations did not entail recognition of the present territorial frontiers, and that the Federal Republic claimed authority to represent the entire German people in international questions (Proceedings of the Federal German Diet, Second Legislative Period, Cd. paper 1685, Appendix 2).

The Soviet government, on the other hand, maintained that there are two German states, but in the final sentence of its declaration it recognized beyond all doubt the sovereignty of the Federal Republic on its own territory.

[39] Soviet theory and practice strongly emphasize the importance of state sovereignty. *Cf.* 'International Law', published by the Academy of the Sciences of the U.S.S.R., p. 131: 'The principle of sovereignty is one of the most important principles of International Law, whose safeguarding is among the most important conditions of peaceful coexistence between the states of different economic structures.' — *Cf.* also the Western form of this definition: U.S. Supreme Court; Judgment, Oetyen vs. Central Leather Company (1918): 'Every sovereign State is bound to respect the independence of every other sovereign state.' — Stating the problems of the case under review with special clarity is the following commentary by Verdross: 'Political independence does not mean independence of all international law but independence of the power and authority of all other states to issue orders to it.'

[40] Judgment, C V.

[41] Verdross, *Völkerrecht* (International Law), IV, p. 292.

[42] This principle was given especially strong support by the Soviet Union, which even proposed the following addition to the Charter: 'Every direct or indirect violation or restriction of these rights constitutes a violation of this Declaration and is incompatible with the overriding principles proclaimed by the Charter of the U.N.' (International Law, published by the Academy of the Sciences of the U.S.S.R., p. 138.)

[43] *Völkerrecht, l. c.*

[44] Draft Resolution A/AC. 66/L. 2/Rev. 1 (Yearbook of the United Nations, 1951, p. 837).

[45] Text in 'Political Lectures', published by V. Bruns and G. V. Gretchaninov, 1936, Vol. I, p. 340.

APPENDIX: DOCUMENTS

The Appendix contains various forms of evidence (written statements by witnesses, some of the material results of official enquiries, letters sent to the West German authorities, etc.), which were incorporated in the files of the Investigation made under the Rule of Law. In the text of the Book, only extracts from them could be quoted, but their full value as evidence appears only if they are read in their entirety.

SELECTED PIECES OF EVIDENCE

I. THE NACHTIGALL UNIT

(1) Extracts from: —

Bolshevik Crimes against the Laws of War and against Humanity. Documents, collected by the German Foreign Office; 1st Series, Berlin 1941.

No. 7

Written and signed statements

Lwow, July 7, 1941

In the presence of:

Kriegsgerichtsrat (Court-Martial Counsellor) Möller,
Itinerant Army Judge, attached to
the Army High Command.

Schütze (Lance-Corporal) Berger,
Shorthand Writer.

The two persons named visited in her flat the widow, Josefa Soziada, née Bauer, aged 54 years, a Roman Catholic, resident at Lwow, 30 Wulecka Lane, who declares that she had been informed about the subject of the enquiry in progress, and admonished to speak the truth: —

'On Monday, June 30, 1941, I went to the NKVD prison in the morning between four and five o'clock, because I had heard that German troops were already entering the town. I first entered the courtyard of the prison and immediately saw several corpses lying there. There were among them three male bodies, with their skin already black, and the body of a completely naked woman. The view was so horrible that I could not bear to look at them for long. I then looked again through a window into the interior of the prison. Inside, I saw a table in a room covered with many corpses that had been slaughtered. The bodies gave the impression that the persons on and by the table had been beaten to a pulp. One dead man was seated in a chair, with a Russian bayonet sticking out of his mouth, that must have been pushed in by force. Hands and arms hung down in queer positions, as if they had been broken several times. Looking in through another window, I saw the dead body of a small girl, aged about eight years, hanging from the ceiling lamp. The body was unclothed, and the child had been hanged with a towel. The view was so terrible that I nearly fainted. Some people had to take me home. I have not yet been able to this day to calm myself from the impression made by these terrible views. What I saw there was too appalling.'

(signed) Möller (signed) Berger

(read to witness and signed by her:) Josefa Soziada

Solemnly admonished to say the truth, and informed about the meaning and sanctity of an oath, witness declared that she had spoken the truth and nothing but the truth, and could take an oath on her statement with a good conscience. The oath was administered to witness.

(signed) Möller (signed) Berger

Second Witness: —

Personal description: My name is Irene Loesch, née Kaczmar, my age is 24 years, I am a Greek Catholic, married, of Ukrainian nationality, resident at Lwow, Wulecka Lane.

Material evidence given: 'On Friday or Saturday, June 28 or 29, 1941, I went to the NKVD prison at about six o'clock in the evening to ask for my mother, who had been arrested about three months ago because of her religious belief. Being a parson's wife, she had once asked a member of her parish why he did not come to church any more. I entered the prison building, and already in the first cell, I saw many murdered persons, most of whom were mutilated. Among other bodies, I saw that of a woman, whose one breast had been cut off, whilst the second one was deeply lacerated. Another woman's abdomen had been cup open, she had been pregnant. From the open wound, the head of an unborn child stuck out. All the teeth had been broken from the mouth of a male corpse. A small girl was dressed on the upper part of her body, whilst the lower part was naked and smeared all over with blood, especially near her private parts, so that I had no doubt that a sexual crime had been committed against her. This cell was filled with the corpses of about thirty murdered persons, among them several women. All the women were naked. Almost all their bodies showed large spots that were suffused with blood, indicating that they had been badly maltreated. The view was so horrible that I gave up looking for my mother and left the prison. Already before that I had gone to the Zamartynow Prison to ask for my mother there. There I only cast a glimpse into a room from the outside, and this room was completely filled with corpses up to the ceiling. This gave me such a shock that I immediately left that prison.'

(signed) Möller (signed) Berger

(read to witness and signed by her:) Irene Loesch, née Kaczmar

Witness was interrogated with the assistance of the Grammar School Headmaster, Nestor Dobriansky, as an interpreter.

Solemnly admonished to say the truth, and informed about the meaning and sanctity of an oath, witness declared that she had spoken the truth and nothing but the truth and could take an oath on her statement with a good conscience. The oath was administered to witness.

(signed) Möller (signed) Berger

Witness Bogdan Kazanivsky: —

'I was taken to Lwow as a prisoner on March 23, 1940. During the first four months in Lwow, I was left in peace. Then I was called for an interrogation one night at ten o'clock before an examining magistrate. The interrogation started without any maltreatment. Later, the judge called in four other people, who seized me by the head, forced me to bend down, and threw me against the wall with my backside. Later, one of them held my head, the other my feet, and they threw me against the wall sideways. They did so several times, and at the third time I fainted. When coming to again, I noticed that they poured water over me, at the same time beating me incessantly. After that, I was again and again subjected to interrogation on about thirty occasions in the same prison. Only ten times, no violence was used during these cross-examinations. On March 11, 1941, I was transferred from this prison to that of the NKVD, where I remained until April 19, 1941, after which I was again sent to another jail, the Brigidki Prison, where I stayed up to the outbreak of war. On the second day of the war, I noticed that the forces guarding that prison had been reinforced, and we also got less to eat. During the following nights, groups of people were called from the cells and taken away without being permitted to dress. They were told that they would be taken to a very warm place. Soon after their departure, we heard muffled shots from the distance, and also cries and moans. On Tuesday, June 24, 1941, the NKVD guards left the prison temporarily. We broke down the cell doors and attempted to flee, but the courtyard was locked, and we could not escape. When we stood in the yard, sudden bursts of machine-gun fire were aimed at us. Several people were injured by them, and some died. We retreated again into the prison building. The NKVD guards returned and drove ninety of us into a single large cell. We were forced to lie on the floor face down, and to stay in this position the whole day. As I have mentioned before, groups of people were then called out every day, and after that we heard cries and shots. Of the ninety people in my cell, only twenty-two remained. They called me out, too, but I did not answer the calls. On June 28, prolonged shooting could be heard, sometimes at a distance, at other times nearer. During the day, NKVD guards entered our cell and told us that dogs deserved a dog's death. Suddenly, the shooting stopped, and after a while we saw that civilians had entered the prison to liberate us, as the NKVD guards had left the prison. I believe there were about 10,000 prisoners in the Brigidki Prison, and only between 600 and 800 left this jail still alive. I cannot say whether the NKVD guards perhaps dragged some prisoners with them on their flight.

When I returned to Brigidki Prison the next day, I walked round and entered several cells for solitary confinement near the blown-up prison chapel. In these cells, I saw bodies that had been squeezed into wooden boxes. The boxes were not coffins, but I believe that prisoners had been tortured in these boxes. Their corpses had a greenish-yellow colouring, their faces were distorted, and they seemed to have been burned on their chests.'

(signed) Möller (signed) Berger

(read to witness and signed by him:) Bogdan Kazanivsky

Solemnly admonished to say the truth and informed about the meaning and sanctity of an oath, witness declared that he had spoken the truth and nothing but the truth and could take his statement on oath with a good conscience. The oath was administered to witness.

Witness was interrogated in the presence of Nestor Dobriansky, who served as an interpreter.

(signed) Möller (signed) Berger

(2) Nachtigall Files: —

Nachtigall Files, Vol. II. Folio 183

Interrogation of F. W. H.

Defendant F. W. H. appeared on a summons and was informed about the subject of the interrogation. He stated: —

Personal Information: My name is F. W. H., publisher and author, born on May 5, 1889, in F./M., German, married, resident in B.

Material evidence given:

'On January 1, 1941, I took over the First Battalion of the Brandenburg Training Regiment for Special Purposes, No. 800. The regiment served under the immediate authority of the *Ausland-Abwehr* Department (Counter-Intelligence Abroad) of the Supreme Command of the Wehrmacht. It was in March or April, 1941, that the head of Division II of

Ausland-Abwehr, Colonel von Lahousen, informed me that a legionary unit, consisting of four companies of Western Ukrainian volunteers, had been in training at the army training grounds at Neuhammer in Silesia. The intention was to put this battalion under my command in case of war against The Soviet Union. The task envisaged for the battalion was not so much to fight but to serve as propaganda among the Ukrainian population by its mere existence.

Following this, I discussed the form of organization and the officers to be chosen for the Nachtigall unit with the officer commanding the Training Regiment, Colonel von Haehling, and with Colonel Stolze of Division II of Abwehr.

I influenced the appointment of officers in so far as I placed in command of the new battalion First Lieutenant Dr. Herzner, whom I knew well as an officer and privately as a friend. First Lieutenant Herzner was a member of the political circle round the magazine „*Der Nahe Osten*" (The Near East). He was an officer of the reserve in the Potsdam Infantry Regiment No. 9, and from the beginning of the war, he had worked in the Department *Ausland-Abwehr*. His character and political attitude were a sure guarantee for me that the Nachtigall Battalion would never do anything against the intentions and convictions of Admiral Canaris, Colonel von Lahousen, and myself. Dr. Albrecht Herzner was a practising christian, and as an officer, had been an active member of the resistance movement for many years. In September 1938, he had been a member of the special action unit formed in Berlin, which had been chosen to accompany Infantry General von Witzleben on his raid against Hitler, planned as a coup to prevent the Second World War.

I also arranged that one of the companies of the Nachtigall unit was placed under the command of one of my personal friends, the former Imperial Austrian *Rittmeister* (cavalry captain), Erwein Count von Thun und Hohenstein. Count Thun was an Austrian aristocrat in the best sense of the word.

In those days, I also regrouped my own personal staff so as to enable me to influence directly the manner of fighting and of treating the population in the eastern areas to be occupied.

My A.D.C. in the operational staff for the two battalions was Lieutenant Dr. B., in his civilian life a public prosecutor in S., and the officer in charge of the orderly service was Lieutenant Dr. Troebs, in his civilian life a theologian and *Oberregierungsrat* (Chief Government Counsellor) in the Ministry of Churches.

In May 1941, I visited the Nachtigall Battalion for the first time at the Neuhammer manoeuvre grounds. I had talks with the German and Ukrainian leaders, and as far as I can remember, I also met then for the first time

Professor Oberländer, who had been seconded to the battalion as a specialist at the request of Colonel Stolze (as far as I can recall). Professor Oberländer, who spoke Russian and Ukrainian, had been in the service of *Abwehr* already for some time. He was known as an expert on Eastern conditions, and his mission was twofold — to look after the Ukrainian volunteers politically, and to advise me on current Eastern problems. I may intersperse already here that, during all the time that Professor Oberländer served under me — that is between March or April, 1941, and the end of August, 1941, — I never heard him make an antisemitic remark, nor came it never to my knowledge that he overstepped my clear orders that prisoners and the civilian population were to be treated humanely and with regard to their human dignity.

When I addressed the German and German-speaking Ukrainians among the leaders of the battalion shortly before the beginning of the eastern campaign, I admonished and even begged and besought them to act with humanity always.

I remember the leader of one of the four companies, a lieutenant, named Middelhauve, who was a man with a keen interest in politics. Middelhauve talked to me and confirmed that he shared my political opinions.

I do not remember any of the other officers and Ukrainian leaders as individuals. I only remember the name of Lieutenant Schüler of the Brandenburg Regiment, who had also been seconded to the Nachtigall unit, but I do not recall any details about him.

The Nachtigall Battalion did not seem a highly desirable appendage to my own battalion. Nachtigall's state of motorization was exceedingly poor, and in modern warfare, it is virtually impossible to lead, and make proper use of fighting units whose one half is motorized, whilst the remainder has to march on foot. German non-commissioned officers had been used to strengthen the unit's skeleton staff. How exactly this skeleton staff was distributed over the companies has slipped my memory. I also arranged for the Brandenburg Regiment seconding Paymaster Meyer to the Nachtigall Battalion. Meyer was an evangelical parish priest, and I asked him to hold a joint religious service for both Brandenburg and Nachtigall. Nachtigall was armed, at most, for defensive infantry fighting. It did not possess any heavy arms, and it had never been trained to fight in association with other army units. However, I had the personal impression that the Ukrainian volunteers made quite good and disciplined soldiers, as they had been trained in the Polish army in peacetime.

Nobody in *Abwehr,* nor I myself, or the divisional staffs, etc., had any clear idea how to use Nachtigall. To only time when Nachtigall was used in action was during the fighting that ended with the capture of Vinnitsa.

First Brandenburg Battalion had been given the mission, when hostilities opened against the Soviet Union at 3.15 a. m. on June 22, 1941, to carry out a raid on the Soviet half of the town of Przemysl *. Whilst this mission was carried out, I kept Nachtigall in reserve. The battalion was stationed in a barracks in western Przemysl. During the night from June 22 to 23, First Brandenburg Battalion crossed the San river near Walawa, which lies north of Przemysl fortress that was still holding out. Its task was to attack the line of the Lwow fortifications from the north. In carrying out this fighting mission, I had taken parts of Nachtigall across the San river during the night. On the morning of June 23, Count Thun took Russian-speaking volunteers of Nachtigall on a reconnoitring mission, from which he returned with thirty prisoners. Some of the prisoners had been injured, and all of them were given the best medical attention. Fighting now started in earnest, but Nachtigall took no part in it; as far as I remember, I sent the battalion back behind the San river to the town of Radymno. After heavy fighting, which lasted several days, the First Battalion of Brandenburg, which had been in action under Lieutenant-General Marx with his 101st Light Division, was also withdrawn to Radymno. On June 24 or 25, my unit became attached to the First Mountain Division, which was led by Lieutenant-General, Ritter von Lanz. Together with one battalion of the Mountain Regiment No. 99, under Major Fleischmann, my unit was in the advance guard of First Mountain Division. We marched along the roads towards Lwow without encountering much resistance. We had been given the mission to break any resistance centered on Lwow, and to open up the way to Lwow for First Mountain Division.

Up to that time, there would have been no chance to treat the civilian population badly. During the night between June 29 and 30, our group and one battalion from Mountain Regiment No. 99 were spread out on both sides of the road leading to Lwow from the north-west, a few kilometres in front of the Lwow airfield. Soviet resistance had faded out during the day. The last firing of Soviet artillery was heard about 18.00 o'clock.

During the evening of June 29, 1941, I drove to Lieutenant-General von Lanz and suggested to him that we should take Lwow during the night, as the Soviets were obviously withdrawing their troops. General von Lanz rejected my proposal. He was afraid of a Soviet ambush. I could understand his standpoint, for the same division had been ambushed by the Poles near Lwow in September, 1939, and had suffered severe losses.

---

* The West Galician fortress town of Przemysl (to-day in Communist Poland) had been cut into a German-administered and a Soviet half when the Nazis and the Soviet Government, according to their secret accord, cut up Poland in 1939. The river San, flowing through the town, formed the frontier.

I returned to my staff and gave the order to the two battalions to be at rest. I was firmly convinced that First Mountain Division would not dare to enter Lwow before the late morning.

However, during the night I received reports that mass shootings had taken place in Lwow and were continuing. With my staff and an accompanying platoon in full fighting equipment, that was led by Sergeant-Major Moritz, I sat far in advance of my battalion near the first continuous row of houses that belonged to the town of Lwow. I am no longer able to reconstruct the facts — as to who really brought me the dispatches about the mass shootings in Lwow. Some of this information came through reconnaissance parties of the Nachtigall Battalion who had been sent into Lwow in mufti, and besides, the civilians living in the blocks of flats near the town boundary plied us with all sorts of rumours and horror tales.

About midnight, Major Fleischmann got in touch with me and told me that he would take his entire battalion forward to the actual border of the town of Lwow. As far as I remember, I then spoke to First Lieutenant Dr. Herzner. He confirmed that he had received a growing number of reports about mass shootings taking place in Lwow, so that it was easy to understand that the Ukrainian members of his battalion were deeply disturbed.

About midnight between June 29 and 30, I then decided for myself to occupy Lwow during the same night, in order to prevent further atrocities. I gave orders to alarm the two battalions which had gone to rest, and to assemble them for the march into Lwow. Major Fleischmann protested but decided not to pass on the information to Division that my unit would enter Lwow against divisional orders.

On the north-western boundary of Lwow, the companies of my unit, which had assembled, were given their fighting orders by me. Their missions were so-called object missions, which means that they had to occupy a number of key points in the town, e. g. the radio transmitter, the power station, the railway station, the citadel, etc. I remember distinctly that one company of Nachtigall was given orders to occupy the radio transmitter, and as Nachtigall possessed n.c.o.'s and men who knew the town well, Nachtigall units were also sent to the various prisons, which had been described by the rumours as the places where many people had been shot.

With the accompanying platoon, I drove across the town and occupied the buildings round the cathedral. The time was between 2 and 3 a.m. The roof of the cathedral was on fire. The men of my platoon entered the cathedral and liberated Cardinal Count Szepticki, the metropolitan of the Church of the Greek Union, who lay on the cathedral floor with his hands and feet tied with ropes.'

Witness was then shown the statement made by witness Dr. Hrynioch. Comment of witness: —

'I did not witness myself that the cardinal was found tied up with rope, but I was told this by Sergeant-Major Moritz. Perhaps it was the fact that the cardinal was paralysed that led to this report. I cannot remember to-day when the First Company of Nachtigall Battalion arrived at the cathedral.

During the following hours, reports came in from the companies of Nachtigall and Brandenburg which had been sent into action. My action headquarters remained in the cathedral till about 8 a.m., to be transferred later to the Lwow town hall. It is possible that a company of Nachtigall had already taken the town hall. I enlarged my action headquarters and gave orders to First Lieutenant Herzner to withdraw all the Nachtigall companies from the "objects" they had occupied, and to march them to the square in front of the town hall. In this square, many thousands of civilians had in the meantime assembled, mainly, as it seemed, Western Ukrainians but also a few Poles and Jews. I was asked, for example, by several Jews whether there would be a pogrom. When the Nachtigall company entered the town hall square, the civilians welcomed the soldiers with loud shouts, some of them going on their knees and praying. First Lieutenant Herzner reported to me and observed: "Well, this is worse than in Sudetenland." My own feelings, when the Nachtigall companies entered the market square, singing Ukrainian songs under the loud, cries of welcome by the civilians, were that I was deeply moved.

Towards noon, Captain Dr. Hartmann who led the First Brandenburg Company, came to me and reported that his company, on entering an NKVD prison, had found veritable mountains of corpses, all civilians who had been liquidated. When I heard that, I took Captain Hartmann, Lieutenant Dr. Troebs, and Dr. Benkelberg in my car to the prison. I cannot remember exactly to-day where this jail was situated and what it looked like. However, there must have been a fire in the prison, for I was repelled by the nauseous stench of corpses and of a fresh fire, and I could not force myself to enter the prison buildings myself. Without being quite certain about it now, I believe that the prison had been occupied by Brandenburg units. Lieutenants Troebs and Benkelberg, who had inspected the prison, later gave me written reports about all the details and the dead bodies that had been found. Later, more reports came in about mass shootings in other prisons. According to a personal arrangement I had made with admiral Canaris, I passed on all these dispatches directly to the Admiral by courier.

From about midday, the scene in Lwow was completely changed. All the streets were filled by troops marching through. I was very busy, and as far as I can remember, I withdrew during the same day or, at the latest, on the following morning, that is on July 1 — all the Brandenburg and Nachtigall companies from the occupied objects, as I expected to be told to take part in the further advance of First Mountain Division, as its advance guard.

The Brandenburg companies had been billetted in barracks. I do not remember where the various billets of Nachtigall companies were. It was then already that the double authority, to which Nachtigall was subject, proved a disadvantage. The *Abwehr* Branch at Breslau sent several of its officers, among them the then Major Ernst zu Eickern, and Professor Koch. Whilst the two battalions were stationed at Lwow, it became progressively less clear who was to give orders to them. However, the officer actually in command of Nachtigall, Dr. Herzner, reported to me at length every day. Herzner was the person who gave me the first information that civilians, mostly Jews, had been forced by the *Kommandantura* that had been set up in Lwow, but also by so-called Special Commandos *(Sonderkommandos)*, which appeared in the town, to clear away debris in the town and to bury the shot civilians. I thoroughly questioned Herzner whether men from his battalion had taken part in atrocities. He denied this strenuously, and during the day when I drove by car towards Tarnopol with my fighting staff (this may have been July 4 or 5, 1941) he made a report to me that the Nachtigall Battalion had not fired a single shot up to that time. I knew Herzner as an absolutely reliable man, and had no reason to doubt the truth of his report. I myself had sent *Rittmeister* Graf Thun, who in the meantime had joined my staff as my second orderly officer, and other officers of my staff, together with First Lieutenants Hollmann and Kürschner, through Lwow as patrols each day we stayed in Lwow. All these officers reported to me — with rising expressions of feeling revolted by it — that lawlessness was raging in parts of Lwow, and that the first of the so-called *Einsatzkommandos* (Special Action Groups of the *SD)* had started their "work". During those days, I sent my personal driver, Corporal F., who lives now in Hamburg as a jeweller, with reports to Admiral Canaris telling him about the chaos in Lwow, about the atrocities committed by these special staffs, and in some cases also by German troops. In this context, I should like to underline specially that also some German troops behaved with a complete lack of discipline towards civilians and their property. A Slovak unit, which passed through the town, behaved like rabble of pilfering bandits. The Austrian soldiers of the 4th Mountain Division, too, whose advance guard I joined on July 4 or 5, were especially rude to the civilian population, especially to the many Jews living in and near Tarnopol. Whilst at Tarnopol, for example, I heard that soldiers of the SS Wiking Division had murdered hundreds of Jews there, part of them by shooting, others by beating them to death.'

Answer to questions: —

'About the activities carried out by the Nachtigall Unit whilst in Lwow I have no clear picture in my memory. Nor can I say which individual billets were given to the companies of that unit. Never during the time whilst Nachtigall served under my orders did I give an instruction to the officer in command of the battalion, First Lieutenant Herzner, nor directly to sub-units of the battalion, permitting or ordering shootings, maltreatment of people, or pilfering. As far as it was in my power, I have done everything by continuous admonitions to prevent irregularities. I never received reports at any time about such irregularities having been committed. Whether individual members or whole units of Nachtigall ever took part in atrocities — which did indeed occur in Lwow after our occupation of the town — I cannot say. It is well known that after the capture of a big town like Lwow, when big army units passed through and *SD* and Party officials took over the administration, there was invariably a certain amount of chaos, which enabled forces determined to do so to commit acts of violence. According to reports made to me then by Professor Oberländer, some of the corpses found in the Lwow prisons were those of relations of Ukrainian Nachtigall soldiers.'

Nachtigall Files, Vol. II, Folio 96:

Interrogation of Count von B. *

On a summons to appear, witness Count von B. signified that he was prepared to testify. He was informed about the subject of the interrogation and that he was obliged to tell the truth and nothing but the truth.

Personal information: My name is Konstantin Count von B., at present a journalist. My age is 71 years, I am resident at Innsbruck. I am not related with the defendants by blood or marriage.

Material evidence given: 'I was born on January 3, 1889, at Dabki, District of Wyrzysk, Wojewodstwo (Province) of Pomorze (the former Prussian province of Posen). During the first world war, I served with the German Army, leading Red Cross units as a staff officer. After the defeat of Germany, I remained on my estate in the province of Posen. As is well known, Posen fell to Poland in 1918. I lived in the same place up to the outbreak of the second world war. When German troops entered the district, my estate came under artillery fire, and I withdrew eastward with the Polish Army. On September 20, 1939, I was taken prisoner by

* The witness is of Polish nationality.

Russian troops entering Poland from the east. I was put into prison. After about seven months of imprisonment, I was released and went to Lwow, as I had arranged with my family before the outbreak of war that we should all meet in Lwow. I lived under police surveillance, and until the German troops captured Lwow, I worked as a bookbinder. I lived in Ulicza Wlasna Strzecha in the southern part of Lwow. One of my daughters had joined me there. Two other daughters of mine had been deported by the Russians in March, 1940, when they organized the transfer of the population to Siberia. Immediately after the Russian occupation of Lwow, many people living in the town were arrested, and more arrests were carried out repeatedly afterwards. I myself believed that I might be arrested any day, and therefore I went into hiding every time I heard a Russian patrol approaching. Immediately after war broke out between Russia and Germany, when the first bombs were dropped on Lwow, Russian civilians were collected in police lorries according to prepared lists and evacuated from Lwow. I had been told that the Russians had also drawn up lists for a large deportation transport to Siberia. My name, too, was on one of these lists. My *Blockwart* (civil defence warden for a block of houses, also local police informer under Nazi and Soviet systems) had told me so; he warned me. The date for the deportation was fixed for June 27, 1941. As the Germans approached Lwow too swiftly, this project failed. Until the German troops took over Lwow, I went only once more to the centre of the town, in order to visit Professor Groer, the head of the children's hospital in Lwow, whom I had known well in Posen. As I lived in one of the southern suburbs of Lwow, it was naturally not possible for me to observe what exactly happened in the centre of the town during the last days before the German capture of Lwow. Therefore, I am unable to say whether a new wave of arrests was started by the Russians immediately after the outbreak of war. However, rumours of such new arrests reached me.

But during the last few days before the German troops marched in, members of the organised Ukrainian underground movement fired shots at the retreating Russian troops. During the last two days before the German troops took Lwow, it became common knowledge that the Russian NKVD had killed the prisoners in various prisons. Such killings took place especially in Brigidki Prison in Ulicza Kazimierzowska and in the NKVD jail in the bend of Ulicza Kopernika. I must add here that the NKVD usually employed Jewish citizens of Lwow to assist them in their arrests. Every NKVD agent and every Russian policeman was accompanied by a Jew. The Jews served as interpreters, and also through their knowledge of the locality. In contrast to the Poles, and later also to the Ukrainians, who were not very friendly to the Russians, the Jews, in the beginning, took a highly positive attitude towards the Russians. As I learnt later, these Jews who had been employed in the agencies and offices of the NKVD were also killed before the NKVD's and the Russian Police's retreat from Lwow. They were all shot in the backs of their necks. Part of the Jewish population of Lwow left the town in an easterly direction with the Russian Army.

I myself saw the prisons where the Russians had killed their prisoners only after the German troops had arrived. By chance, I found among the troops marching in an old friend and acquaintance, Count Erwein Thun-Hohenstein, who was then *Rittmeister* (cavalry captain) in an armoured company. It was with him that I went and looked at the places of execution in the above-mentioned prisons. People from Lwow had entered these prisons immediately after the Russians had left, to look for members of their families. In the two prisons, *Rittmeister* Count Thun took photographs of the murdered people. After he had developed his snapshots, he gave me quite a number of his copies, of which I have now still six in my possession. Some of the bodies had already been buried in mass graves. One of the photographs shows the reopening of one of these graves, when the corpses were taken out again. It is impossible that these people could have been the victims of a bloodbath caused by the troops marching in. (The said photographs have been presented by witness and were returned to him.) If the photographs are still needed, I am willing to submit them again.

After Lwow's capture by German troops — I have forgotten the exact date, but it must have been during the first week — I was myself involved in the following incident: One day I paid a visit to the flat of the above-mentioned Professor Groer (he lived in Ulicza Romanowicza.) Towards evening, I saw from the balcony of Professor Groer's flat that a closed police van stopped in front of the house opposite, where a Polish professor of surgery lived. Several men jumped out, ran into the house, and took away all its inhabitants. They all went away again with the police van. The escort of the police van were not members of the German Wehrmacht. The men did not wear uniforms of the German Wehrmacht but different ones, which I learnt later were those of the *SD* and the Gestapo, respectively. Upon this incident, I cut short my visit to Professor Groer and went home. Next day I was told that Professor Groer, too, had been arrested after the scene described by me. Again a few days later, I heard that about 30 professors of Polish nationality had been taken to prison in this raid. I was told that these arrests were made on the basis of a prepared list of names, and that was also the reason why Gestapo agents entered the flats of two professors, to arrest them, although these two men had already died of a natural death. Rumours were rife that the arrested men had been killed. Among those arrested was also Professor Bartel, whom I had known in Warsaw when he was Polish Prime Minister.

During these early days after the capture of Lwow, a Ukrainian militia was formed by members of the Ukrainian underground movement. In the beginning, these militia men wore civilian clothes but could be recognized by their yellow and blue armlets. The members of this militia carried out raids against the Jewish inhabitants of Lwow. I myself was dragged, at one occassion, from a queue in front of a food shop, and two milita men forced me to go with them, apparently because they suspected me to be a Jew for my better clothes. By chance, we passed some German soldiers whom I immediately accosted in German, asking them for assitance. The Germans chased away the two Ukrainian militia men and accompanied me to my house, after I had shown them documents to prove my membership of the Maltese Knights' Order (the Order of St. John). At the time, I knew nothing of the existence of a Ukrainian Nachtigall Battalion, nor did I ever notice any Ukrainian soldiers in the uniforms of the German Wehrmacht.

I can state quite confidently that the German troops behaved with absolute correctness towards the civilians during these first days. There was almost general fraternization between the people of Lwow and the German soldiers marching in. That situation changed only later, namely after the arrest and the murders of the Polish professors, and the measures taken by the *SD* units against the Jewish part of Lwow's population.'

Post scriptum: 'Professor Franziscus von Groer has now the following address: 17, Ulicza Kasprzaka, Warsaw (Institut Matki i Dziecka, i. e. Institute for Mothers and Children). My daughter exchanges letters with Professor Groer.'

II. THE BERGMANN UNIT

The Investigation carried out under the Rule of Law obtained its results from extensive enquiries. The main basis of the findings are statements made by witnesses. Among the great number of such witnesses and statements, there were four main groups: (1) former Caucasian members of the Bergmann Unit, of whom a large number live in France now; (2) voluntary statements made by Caucasian civilian refugees, who now live in other countries; (3) the results of cross-examinations made of more than 150 former German soldiers who had served in the Bergmann Unit; (4) the results of similar examinations of former members of the German Wehrmacht who, during their military service, had come in touch, or had to deal, with Professor Oberländer and/or the Bergmann Unit. In addition there were Professor Oberländer's war diary, and a great number of letters written by him to his wife from the war, of which some discuss the questions with which he had to deal in the field, and, finally, also Professor Oberländer's memoranda dealing with the fundamental problems of warfare in the East. (Extracts from these memoranda have been quoted in the main text of the book.) The following collection shows evidence presented and documents from all the above-mentioned groups. They give us a lively and instructive picture of the real conditions. Unfortunately, the Bergmann Files were not available to the author during proofreading, and that is the reason why a number of witnesses' depositions could not be given their full file reference. For the quotations on pages 264 — 274, therefore, the general indication 'From the Bergmann Files' has to suffice.

Bergmann Files, Vol. II, Folio 23

Paris 15e Paris, May 23, 1960
The Federal Chancellor,
Herr Dr. K. Adenauer,
Bonn.

Highly esteemed Mr. Federal Chancellor,

As charges have been made against Mr. Oberländer, federal minister, I beg to submit to you my statement as a witness, which you may use at your discretion. My father was a Social Democrat, and as a Georgian politician, he became a member of the national government of Georgia. The Russian bolsheviks shot him. I am also a Social Democrat. I have lived in

France from the time the Russians occupied my country. When France was occupied by the Germans, I volunteered to fight against the Russians. In the beginning, I was a member of the Tamara II Unit, and was later taken over by the Bergmann Unit, which, at that time, was set up by First Lieutenant Oberländer, a former professor of Prague University. I was then already the father of three children, and inspite of that, I volunteered for two reasons — to alleviate the fate of many Georgian, Caucasian, and other prisoners of war, and also to fight the enemy who had invaded my homeland, which had to suffer interminably under the alien yoke.

In the Stranz-Neuhammer camp, where the Bergmann Unit was formed, I was given several opportunities to attend the talks which Mr. Oberländer held with German officers and training staff. During all these conferences, I was always able to observe the great understanding and the willingness to give help both to prisoners of war and to the people of the countries through which the German Army had passed during its advance. He emphasized that such an attitude — apart from the fact that it was the most human one — was essential for securing the army's rear and its long routes of supply.

During the whole period we spent together, Mr. Oberländer showed himself always as a decided and clear opponent of that certain view which was based on the notion of 'subhumans', and which was very much favoured by the then political leadership.

It was due to Mr. Oberländer that we were able to inspect prisoner-of-war camps, and to help the prisoners, which meant that we preserved many of them from a terrible death.

Whilst we were at the Caucasian front, he helped in writing and editing a pamphlet for the German soldiers, which helped them to develop a better understanding of the people who had been robbed of their freedom. Oberländer always became active when it was necessary to save human lives who otherwise would have become victims of bureaucratic misunderstandings. During the withdrawal from the Caucasus, he repeatedly tried through his protests to draw the attention of the leadership in Berlin to the inhuman orders that had been given to kill all prisoners who could not keep pace with the withdrawing columns.

In the Crimea, he set up investigating commissions to find those who had been guilty of maltreating the local population. His understanding for the needs of his men and of the population went so far as to discuss the question whether to make Friday an official holiday, so as to show favour to the Moslem group in the population. Because of his numerous interventions and special decrees, he was recalled to Berlin in 1943 where he then was in disgrace. It was much later that I heard, to my great relief, that he had been spared liquidation, which seemed a miracle to me.

One of the best testimonials for Mr. Oberländer was the attitude and behaviour of the First (Georgian) Battalion of the Bergmann Unit, both regarding its fighting spirit and its contacts with the local population. I shall never forget the scene in the Crimea when our unit was given orders to march on Perekop. The entire population, often from miles around, came specially to line both sides of the road along which we were marching, in order to say a most touching farewell to us. Men, women, and children, with tears in their eyes, gave us presents and thanked us for the help we had been able to give them, because our soldiers had worked as cultivators after a terrible famine had raged in the area.

These people were later deported by the Russians, and any soldier who remained behind the Iron Curtain will be prevented from giving true testimonial as witnesses to-day. But, thank God, there were some who could escape, and who live now in many different places in the Free World. All of us are prepared to testify, in any free court, to the high regard we have for Mr. Oberländer who, for us, was always a man full of understanding, high ethical standards, and blameless morality — the model of a good German patriot.

We are living in a very depressing time, when hangmen usurp the office of the judge, and the real war criminals assume the features of apostles of peace. May fate guard all free men, to whose side you also belong, against falling into the traps which have been laid for them with method and indescribable lack of conscience by those who are planning their destruction.

With the expression of my deepest esteem, venerated
Mr. Federal Chancellor,
Yours etc.
V. H.

Above copy is an exact rendering of the original,
certified,
Bonn, June 11, 1960.
(signed) L. S., Government Inspector.

Bergmann Files, Vol. II, Folio 58:

G.C.G., Surgeon, M.D., F.I.C.S., residing Illinois, U.S.A., naturalized American citizen of Georgian extraction, duly sworn deposes and states that (the following in German):

I knew Professor Dr. Dr. Theodor Oberländer personally from April, 1942, when he was head of the Caucasian *Bergmann* Unit, which was then stationed for training at Mittenwald, Bavaria.

The following will give an idea of the circumstances which brought me together with Professor Oberländer: In 1921, my homeland, Georgia, was invaded by the troops of the Soviet Union without any warning, subdued in bitter fighting, and then forcibly incorporated in the Soviet Union. This was in flagrant violation both of International Law and of the *Treaty of Peace and Non-Aggression* that had been concluded a short time before between Georgia and the Soviet Union. The democratic government of Georgia, and a large number of Georgian citizens, went into exile to call for help from the Free World and the League of Nations. The Georgians remaining behind organized a long chain of revolts, of which that of 1924 was the most important. Apart from diplomatic protests, however, no help ever came from the democratic powers, which they had promised, and therefore all the desperate risings were drowned in the blood of the best Georgian patriots. Incidentally, there was again a rising in Georgia in March, 1956, during which more than 600 students were killed. (Report 7 of the Committee on Un-American Activities, House of Representatives, 86th Congress.) This makes it easy to understand that every power, or state, which is at war with the Soviet Union becomes a natural ally of the fighters for Georgian freedom. Such a situation obtained after the outbreak of war between Germany and the Soviet Union.

Furthermore, most Georgians kept fresh in their memory the help which they had received from the Germans in their struggle for freedom after the First World War, when General Kress von Kressenstein and Count von Schulenburg had been in their country. Therefore, many Georgian emigrants, who, earlier on, had fought on the side of the Polish and French Armies against Germany, under the changed circumstances decided to join the German Army in its fight against the Soviet Union. But that did not mean in the least that those people were in favour of the regime that then ruled over Germany. In addition, thousands of Georgians who had been called up for the Red Army went over to the Germans at the first opportunity, in most cases from the same motives *(Special Report No. 6 of the Select Committee on Communist Aggression, House of Representatives, 83rd Congress.)* To their deepest disappointment, they soon found out that they had been placed in a deplorable situation. Hitler's eastern policies led to cruel treatment both of the population in the occupied eastern territories, of prisoners of war, and even of the volunteers who had joined the Wehrmacht from the ranks of the Eastern peoples.

But there were also influential personalities in Germany who did not agree with Hitler's destructive policies, and who tried to oppose it frequently and with desperate determination. Only thanks to those men was it possible that Georgian emigrants could attempt to serve their true aims. Among them, I should like to name Count von Schulenburg, General

Kostring with many officers of his staff, Professor Gerhard von Mende and Professor Oberländer, with a great number of his collaborators.

I, incidentally, went to Germany in the autumn of 1941 — without knowing the situation there — desiring and planning to get in touch with the Georgian emigrants, and to join their national movement. Instead of doing that, I was more or less pressed into a German military unit but was soon expelled from it and sent to the penalcamp of Steinau near Hanau, for *criticism and non-recognition of German leadership* in the struggle. I found myself there in a rather desperate situation, but Professor Oberländer, in some way, had heard of my plight. Thanks to his intervention, both I and a large number of other men were released from the penal camp. I was deeply disappointed and much in doubt whether, under the circumstances prevailing, anything could be done regarding the Georgian question. But after long and exhaustive discussions with Walter von Kutzschenbach, who was then Oberländer's A.D.C., and who described to me the attitude, the plans, aims, and the spirit of the Bergmann Unit, I decided to talk to Professor Oberländer. After I had had long talks also with him, I hopefully joined his unit.

Already during my first conversation with him (April, 1942), I was astonished about the frankness with which Professor Oberländer discussed and criticized the graveness of German mistakes and German barbarities. He was in extreme opposition to Hitler's policies in the occupied eastern areas, and to those represented by *gauleiter* Koch. According to Oberländer's conviction, people there should have been treated quite differently without violating their human rights. It would have been necessary to abolish the collective farms, and to give the people self-government. The professor also stated that the treatment of prisoners of war would have to be changed drastically, and he advocated that the position of the volunteers in the German Army should be improved and altered. Professor Oberländer had the hope to be able to demonstrate with his *Bergmann* Unit to the Supreme Command and to other authorities the high potential value of such people as the Caucasians, and of all other people in the occupied eastern areas. He intended to reverse the disastrous course of German eastern policies.

As head of his military unit, the professor insisted that its Caucasian and German members had to be treated with exact equality and had equal rights. In the few cases of a different attitude shown by German members of his unit, he invariably insisted on their removal and transfer to other units.

When *Bergmann* later reached the Caucasian front — and proved its full and high value — Professor Oberländer prevailed upon the high military authorities that some Caucasian soldiers of the *Bergmann* Battalion were detailed for visiting most of the prisoner-of-war camps on the Caucasian front, and to serve as advisors to the camp commandants. This step, in fact, much improved the treatment of prisoners of war, and for many meant that their lives were saved.

If Professor Oberländer heard of objectionable conditions which he was not able to improve on the spot, he always went to visit his Army High Command. In most cases, he was able to remedy the situation.

During the withdrawal of the Army, Professor Oberländer fought an extremely hard personal battle to prevent the shootings of prisoners of war who could not keep pace physically with the march back during the hard winter of 1942/43. On his own responsibility, wherever he could, he gave orders to the escort units not to shoot down the exhausted prisoners but to allow them to rest in the villages along the road. Many of these people remained there until the last withdrawing columns had passed. Through his endeavours, Professor Oberländer personally ran great risks.

Professor Oberländer also always fought actively for the humane treatment of the civilian population — first in the occupied parts of the Caucasus, and later in the Crimea. He gave strict orders not to take away food or other property of the civilians. He often met local representatives of the population, talked things over with them, asked about their own difficulties, and always tried to assist them with his advice and help. In the Crimea, for example, he lent horses to the peasants, and also sent soldiers of his unit to help them with their work. He always respected the religion and customs of the people. In the Caucasus and in the Crimea, there was a wonderful spirit of friendship between the local people and Professor Oberländer and his *Bergmann* Unit. Because of this friendship, the Soviets later carried out brutal deportations and many shootings after their reoccupation of these areas.

Professor Oberländer also intervened personally to save the lives of many Caucasian Mountain Jews *. As he was the officer commanding the Caucasian unit, his authority in all Caucasian questions was uncontested, and his statement that these people were genuine Caucasians was believed, so that raids by the Security Head Office *(Reichssicherheitshauptamt,* i.e. the Gestapo) could be prevented. — Here I should like to add that we

---

* Caucasian Mountain Jews, known also as the 'Tat' tribe (as they call themselves), are an agricultural tribe of the Caucasus and its foothills, who have embraced the Jewish religion in the early Middle Ages. Their language is a Caucasian dialect. Some years ago, they became the subject of antisemitic slanders by the local Communist Party Secretary of Daghestan, who wrote that they were slaughtering Moslem children to use their blood for making the unleavened Passover bread.

Caucasians had saved the lives of all Jews of Georgian nationality, and of many other Jews, during the war. For this, some of my friends and I received a letter of thanks from Chief Rabbi Weil of Paris.

In the autumn of 1942, the Georgian Battalion No. 795 of the Georgian Legion was placed under the command of a German division and sent to the Caucasian front. Unfortunately, this was a unit which had been formed and trained under completely different circumstances by the Germans. They had a fundamentally different attitude to the people. The German staff maltreated the Georgian legionaries, and the situation was made even worse by the presence of a Georgian adviser, Shalva Maghlakelidze. This man Maghlakelidze was a refugee from Georgia who attempted later — about 1953 or 1954 — to recruit another Georgian for the Soviet secret service, and when this man informed on him to the C.I.C. (U.S. Central Intelligence Corps), he fled to the Soviet Zone (of Germany). Since that time, Maghlakelidze has become a valuable tool in the broadly based attempt of the Soviets to demoralize Georgian refugees by all the means at their disposal, and to undermine the prestige and the good name of their leading personalities and their friends. It has not yet been proved but, according to his earlier and recent behaviour it may be assumed that S. Maghlakelidze had been active as a Soviet agent already during the war, and perhaps even earlier. It can be incontrovertibly proved that he attempted to undermine the morale of the Georgians serving with No. 795 battalion. As soon as this battalion reached the front, many of the Georgians deserted and went over to the Red Army. The German divisional commander, upon hearing this, ordered the immediate disarmament of the remaining Georgian legionaries; it was also planned to have every tenth legionary shot as a punishment. Together with General Köstring, the Inspector-General of all volunteer units, Professor Oberländer requested the Army High Command to postpone the execution of this punishment, pending a thorough investigation of conditions in Battalion No. 795. Professor Oberländer dispatched a group from his Bergmann Unit to carry out the investigation. The group's report pointed to maltreatment of the legionaries by the German soldiers, and to their repeated psychological mistakes, as the true causes of desertion, because Communist agents were able to use these factors to the full. General Köstring and Professor Oberländer conducted very difficult negotiations with the High Command, but in the end they succeeded in obtaining permission to replace the shootings and other penalties by the transfer of part of the suspects to a road building company, whilst the soldiers who were under the gravest suspicion were handed over to *Bergmann*, where good treatment transformed them later, without exception, into reliable soldiers. The remainder of 795 Battalion was kept in existence under its own number.

Repeated interventions of a similar kind, and also his letters and memoranda, which he sent to influential German authorities to criticize the state of things severely, and to discuss German policies in Eastern areas, on the one hand made many people from the East love him, trust him, and consider him their friend, but in the end led to his removal from his post as officer commanding *Bergmann*, to his expulsion from the Wehrmacht, and to several cross-examinations by the Gestapo. With his brave, sincere, and humanistic bearing and actions in the Caucasus and in the Crimea, Professor Oberländer not only gained many personal friends but also proved to these people that there were still men in Germany who did not agree in the least with Hitler's and *gauleiter* Koch's inhuman eastern policies. Professor Oberländer thus gained many friends for the real Germany. I may add here that it was Hitler's and Koch's disastrous policy in the East which did more than anything else to help the Kremlin win the war.

As a highly active Minister for Refugee and Expellee Questions, who is also a deeply experienced expert on the Soviet system and its uncompromising opponent, Professor Oberländer became the target of a widespread propaganda offensive for the Soviets. I have no doubt that Shalva Maghlakelidze, who could never forgive Professor Oberländer his successful intervention in the affairs of 795 Battalion, also takes part very actively in this propaganda campaign. And the so-called *priest*, Alexander Demetrashvili, who probably is one of Maghlakelidze's agents in Germany, has exactly the same aims.

I saw the pamphlet that was published in East Germany against Professor Oberländer, and read there about his alleged brutalities in the Caucasus. I am able to state emphatically that such accusations are pure lies.

As my mother is still living in Georgia — I heard of it only recently — and as I have also other relations there, I ask you very earnestly not to disclose my name to the press and to keep it strictly confidential.

Eight inclosures with the letter. (signed) G.C.G., M.D.

Sworn and subscribed to before me this 25th day of October 1960,

(signed) Notary Public

Witness H., Georgian nationality, at present resident at Paris: —

Regarding the assertion that Caucasian prisoners of war were forced to fight on the German side by threats, especially threats to let them die from hunger: —

'I should like to answer that allegation by pointing out that the question itself incorporates a Soviet propaganda phrase. I was myself in a number of German p.o.w. camps. I have never seen any Caucasian having been forced to join the German Wehrmacht by threats. On the contrary, many came to me and offered to serve in the Wehrmacht as volunteers. To tell the truth, I wish to emphasize that, of course, not all of them who volunteered and offered to serve in the German Wehrmacht did so from pure fighting spirit but in some cases also in order to escape from the status of prisoner of war. The volunteers among the Caucasians were so numerous that the most suitable ones had to be selected. Selection naturally was made according to their military usefulness.'

Question: Is it true that the officer in command, Oberländer, was very brutal and feared by everybody?

'This statement is completely false. Oberländer's attitude towards the Caucasians was always full of understanding. He invariably took a very active interest in the requirements of the soldiers, regarding their food supplies, their medical care, their training, etc. The Caucasian members of the unit had completely equal rights with the German skeleton staff. I should even like to state that Professor Oberländer sometimes was harder to the German soldiers when they did not show the necessary spirit of understanding for the Caucasian members of the unit. Oberländer gave lectures, on the one hand to the German trainers, and on the other hand, to German and Caucasian soldiers, in which he drew the attention of the Germans to the Caucasian nationality problem, asking all the members of his unit to show correct behaviour towards the civilian population.'

Question: Is it true that Oberländer ordered his men to treat the Caucasian population with cruelty, and to destroy the partisans? Did he permit pilfering and fireraising by the unit, and did he take a prominent part in this?

Answer: 'As I have already stated, Oberländer gave very strict instructions to treat the Caucasian population decently. Pilfering and requisitioning were strictly forbidden. By and large, the soldiers heeded the prohibition of pilfering. There were a few cases of illegal requisitioning, but in every case that became known, the guilty parties were punished. I still remember a case of a member of First Company, who had stolen. He was punished by the company leader and sent to a p.o.w. camp. Oberländer pointed out repeatedly the imperative need for maintaining good relations with the population, not only because it was humane but as also military necessity demanded it, since the extremely long supply routes went through the settlements of the civilians. Oberländer tried to inform all German authorities of the absolute necessity for showing understanding for the needs of the population. During positional warfare in the Crimea, he formed several commissions for investigating infringements of the rights of the civilian population by German soldiers in general, and by German administrative authorities, in order to suppress them. I know that he wrote a number of memoranda on the problems of how to treat the civilian population, which he sent to higher German authorities.'

Witness had the opportunity to inform Oberländer about several important points for his memoranda.

Question: Is it true that Professor Oberländer and the Bergmann Unit took part in the mass extermination of Jews and Communists in Naltchik district?

Answer: 'This is the first time that I hear of that accusation. There is no doubt that I should have heard of it at the time if the allegation were correct. There were relatively few Jews in the Caucasus. In one of the p.o.w. camps, prisoners once told me that Jewish prisoners of war were sent to a separate part of the camp, where they were probably liquidated. The Bergmann Unit and its commander never had anything to do with such things. I should like to mention that there were even some Jews serving with the Bergmann Unit — I myself knew three of them. They had the same position as all other men of the unit. I must assume that Oberländer also knew of them.'

Question: Do you know anything about Oberländer having given orders to beat to death three prisoners of war, whom he believed to be Jewish?

Answer: 'I know nothing of this. And I do not believe that Oberländer would have been capable of this.'

Question: Is it true that Oberländer ordered the shooting of a man of German nationality (a *Volksdeutscher*), who had been made Chief Constable?

Answer: 'Neither do I know of such an event. Such behaviour would have been in flat contradiction to his character. If he had noticed any breach of duty, he would have reported it to the proper quarters for prosecution and judgment by a court.'

Answer to Question: 'Nor do I know anything about shooting a communist named Vody. What I have said about the previous case applies also this question.'

Comment of witness upon being told of certain allegations: 'I have never heard of such an incident in Piatigorsk prison. I believe these accusations to be fairy tales. As I know, Oberländer has generally been very moderate as a drinker, perhaps in contrast to other officers of the unit. Nor did Oberländer ever assault a member of the unit physically. On the contrary he punished one of the trainers, who had seized a Georgian by his uniform and had shaken him, with three days of c.b. Oberländer had not witnessed the incident himself; it had been reported to him. In the Bergmann Unit, it was strictly prohibited to beat any man. If such things happened contrary to orders, the guilty person was immediately reported for punishment.

I simply cannot believe that Herr Oberländer would have been able to do such things as are alleged against him in the Piatigorsk prison.'

Question: Is it true that prisoners of war who could not follow the columns retreating from the Caucasus were shot by members of the Bergmann Unit forming the rearguard, by order of its commander, Oberländer?

Answer: 'There is no doubt that prisoners of war have been shot during the withdrawal. But it was Oberländer who always protested strenuously against such practices, both in Berlin and to Kleist (the field marshal). The Bergmann Unit had never anything to do with escorting prisoners of war, nor did any other marching troops. The prisoners were chased back by the guard units of the p.o.w. camps, and it were these guards who shot or beat to death prisoners who were no longer able to walk. In many cases, soldiers of the rearguard attempted to prevent shootings of the prisoners of war who were unable to continue the march. When we got into trouble for that, it was always Oberländer who stood by our side and shielded us. I was myself sentenced to death by a field court-martial, together with five of my comrades, because I had tried to prevent such shootings. We were to be shot, because Oberländer was away then. Some other comrades, who had heard of our situation, liberated us, and Oberländer later protected us. I should like again to add that Oberländer wrote numerous letters in order to suppress these shootings. I also believe that his representations were successful, as soon after only a few prisoners were still being shot.'

Comment of witness, after being told of further allegations: 'The companies of the Bergmann Battalion were never given orders to blow up and destroy, during our retreat, settlements, production units, or factories. They did not have the necessary equipment. It is certainly true that objects of military importance were blown up by German units during the withdrawal. But it is completely untrue that Oberländer gave orders to blow up a water tower at the cossack settlement of Timoshevskaya, and that these orders were carried out before the eyes of First Company. As I have stated, First Company had the task to act as a rearguard, that means it would not even have been able to carry out such destruction. In the same way, I have never heard of an army hospital at Kislovodsk being blown up.'

Statement made by a Georgian national, now resident in France:

Witness had been an officer in the Soviet merchant marine. He jumped ship and went to France as a refugee in 1928. After the outbreak of the German—Soviet war, witness volunteered to fight against the Soviet Union. He emphasized that none of the Georgians who came from France was willing to take the oath on Hitler. He read about the accusations against Oberländer in French newspapers, and voluntarily offered to testify.

Verbatim: —

'From my own experience, I can state that the accusations are completely untrue. It is not true that Oberländer treated the Caucasian members of the battalion cruelly, on the contrary, all Caucasian soldiers of the battalion trusted Oberländer completely. I would not have stayed with the unit if I had lacked confidence in him. It is absolutely untrue that Bergmann Battalion committed any war crimes against the civilian population of the Caucasus during its advance or on its retreat. Professor Oberländer harangued the battalion several times, and each time he emphasized that the battalion must treat the civilian population decently. He addressed the Caucasian volunteers directly and told them that they were now in their fatherland, and therefore ought to do their best for its civilian population. From my talks with Caucasian civilians I knew that the civilian population esteemed Dr. Oberländer highly and honoured him greatly. He asked the battalion to serve as an example to other German troops by its behaviour towards the civilian population. During my stay in the Caucasus, I have not witnessed any important measures being taken against the local population by other German units. It is completely true that individual Germans behaved badly against members of the local population. But I have never witnessed the killing of any civilian.'

Answer to questions: —

'Never at any time was it the task of Bergmann Unit to guard prisoners of war, also not as escorting troops during the retreat. As I have stated before, our squadron belonged to the rearguard. It is true that we saw, during our march back, many dead prisoners of war lying on both sides of the road, singly or in small groups. We heard then that the escorting units who took the prisoners back (partly Ukrainians and some Russians under a German skeleton staff) shot down prisoners who could no longer walk. If any members of our unit had taken part in these shootings, I myself would have shot them upon seeing it. I did not witness it myself, but was later told by other Caucasians of the Bergmann Unit that Doctor Oberländer, on the contrary, tried to save stragglers among the prisoners from death by shooting by handing them over to the mayor of a village, who had to feed them up until they were able to continue their march.'

Bergmann Files.

B., a Caucasian witness, of Azerbaidjani nationality:

'I have read about the allegations against Oberländer. I can only state that they are very different from the true facts. On the contrary, I must say that Oberländer was extremely popular with his unit, precisely because he had its members' interests at heart. I knew that he addressed a letter of complaint to the Führer's headquarters, in which he protested sharply against the treatment which national socialist governors meted out to the population of the liberated eastern areas.'

Witness comments on the charges made by Caucasian witnesses during the trial held in the Soviet Zone and says that such statements could never have been made by them from their own free will. He assumes that such statements were made under Russian, or Communist, pressure.

Bergmann Files, Vol. II, Folio 75

Examination of witness.

Ministerialdirektor (head of department in a ministry) R. W., 52 years old, resident in Bonn (gives his official address), appears on a summons and states that he is not related to defendant either by blood or by marriage. He was informed about the subject of the interrogation, and admonished to tell the truth.

Material evidence given: 'During the second half of 1942, I held the regular commission of a First Lieutenant and served as orderly officer in XLth Panzer Corps. I was Third Orderly Officer in Department Ic (administration), and later deputized for the First Orderly Officer, *Rittmeister* (cavalry captain) von Hassell, in the Ia Department (operational planning).

XLth Panzer Corps had advanced from Kharkov to the Caucasus, and during the last days of August, 1942, it had set up its Operational HQ. in a small settlement called Rusky 1, north of the town of Mozdok on the river Terek. I remember that, one day, Captain Oberländer reported there to the Command Headquarters of our general, as on officer commanding a unit composed of various nationalities oppressed by the Soviets. I also recall that we had a talk with Captain Oberländer in the evening, during which he vividly explained to us, what he thought about German policies in the East. Such a policy, in his view, was only possible on the basis of partnership with the various peoples of which the Soviet Union consists. It was completely impossible to replace the Soviet commissar simply by a new German commissar. He directed particularly keen criticism against German occupation policies in the Soviet Ukraine. He then talked of his memoranda, or he may even have handed them to us. The language he used in these memoranda was so strong that I, for my part, was sometimes afraid that he might have personally to suffer for it. After the German offensive against the Caucasus had come to a halt, I was given leave and went away. I did not return to the Terek river before November, 1942. At the time, I used my letters from the field to my mother to report to her about occasional meetings with Captain Oberländer, as everything he said then made a deep impression on me. I herewith hand over extracts from these letters for the files.

Read by witness, agreed to, and signed,

(signature) (signature)

Extracts from letters written by above witness, then First Lieutenant W., Orderly Officer in the Staff of XLth Armoured Corps, stationed in the Caucasus, to his mother: —

31st August, 1942.

The night before yesterday, an interesting conversation. A certain Captain Oberländer is visiting us. He is the officer commanding a battalion formed of Circassians, Daghestanis, etc. who were trained in Germany. O. had once been a soybean grower here, later became Dean of the Law Faculty in the University of Prague, but he also worked once in the Ford motor works. Subject of the talk: How to treat the subjected or liberated Slavonic nations (Poles, Russians, Ukrainians, Caucasians), the prisoners, and what else there is. Point of departure for talk: Oberländer's memoranda to Wehrmacht and Reich Chancellery. Present, apart from Kandutsch & Buxhoeveden, also my colleague, who speaks Russian, of the Berlin Panzer Division (Third P.D.), which has been attached to Corps. He is Lieutenant Count Dohna. All that under Caucasian sky with an easygoing Caucasian red wine. End of argument: How, and with whom, do we want to build Europe?

21st November, 1942.

(After return from leave). Here everything o.k., only . . . necessities pointed out by Oberländer if we want to occupy and keep the area prove to be true in a frightening manner. You could really v . . . Herr Major . . .!

Witness E., Director of Trading Company, Munich.

'I knew nothing about the methods of recruitment but I cannot believe that pressure was used for it. When the volunteers arrived at Neuhammer, they made an enthusiastic, confident, and contented impression. In conversations with them, I was told repeatedly that they did not feel as Russians, because Caucasians were something quite different from Russians — as their homeland was practically subjugated by Russia —, that they believed it to be an honour to join hands with German soldiers fighting for the liberation of their homeland. I never heard anything from the mouths of these volunteers about reprisals or other methods of pressure. It is true that, without exception, p.o.w. camps for Soviet soldiers were probably bad, as supplies could not be sent to all these camps in sufficient quantities for the enormous number of prisoners. To hold Oberländer responsible for these conditions, or to pretend that he had produced such conditions intentionally, is completely impossible and absolutely untrue. It appears utterly impossible that a lowly First Lieutenant could have been responsible for conditions in camps holding millions of prisoners.'

About the alleged killings of Jews: —

'Shortly before we gave up the Caucasus, a higher SS leader came to us in Naltchik and reported to Oberländer that he and his men arrested about 1,000 Jews. He asked Oberländer to let our unit shoot these Jews. He was informed that these Jews were so-called Mountain Jews, i.e. a Caucasian tribe who accepted the religion of Moses. Oberländer had to bring into play all his arts of persuasion to convince the SS leaders that these people were no true Jews. Oberländer's intervention saved these Jews from being shot, and as far as I know, all these Jews later came again under Soviet rule. I know nothing of shootings having taken place in the panzer ditch at Naltchik. As I was stationed in the town all the time during the occupation, it would have been a miracle if I did not know of such things.'

Regarding the incident in Piatigorsk prison: —

'Oberländer never took part in drinking parties. Neither in Piatigorsk nor elsewhere was there any carousing. I know nothing of incidents in the Piatigorsk jail.'

From the Bergmann Files, without reference: —

Statement made by witness B., sales agent: —

'The officer commanding the Bergmann Battalion, Oberländer, decidedly took the side of the foreign nationals who served as soldiers. For example, he threatened us, the German soldiers in the battalion, with punishment if foreign soldiers should have just reason to complain about one of us. There were such cases, namely German soldiers were punished because they had apparently discriminated against Georgians in the issue of food. It was Professor Oberländer's guiding rule that these people stood under great psychological pressure, as they had no families in the occupied areas or in Germany, so that they needed moral support. That was also the reason why our unit did not use the full gamut of drill and the usual tone of command of the German Wehrmacht. That there was never any compulsion used against these foreign soldiers can also be seen from the fact that they were given leave like Germans. Professor Oberländer saw to it that the Georgians were able to spend their leave in a holiday home in Ruhpolding, Bavaria. Georgian soldiers received the same pay as the Germans, and they were also treated as equals in the distribution of food and army issue tobacco, etc. What the Soviets say about alleged methods of shanghaiing Caucasians for our unit flatly contradicts Oberländer's general attitude. Nor did I ever hear anything of soldiers who had to be invalided out for health reasons being liquidated. I have never heard of a single case of killing a foreign soldier with or without due process of court.'

Bergmann Files, without reference: —

Witness B., photographer, of Sonthofen: —

'I have never seen or heard that Oberländer was much feared and brutal. As dispatch rider and courier, I had frequent dealings with him. He was extremely kind and just to the Caucasians. I might even say, he treated them with kid gloves. He was stricter against German soldiers, but never unjust.'

Bergmann Files,without reference: —

Witness B., of Hindelang: —

'If anybody tells me that Oberländer was brutal and much feared, I can only laugh. With a completely clear conscience, I am able to state that exactly the opposite is true of Oberländer. I have never seen Oberländer behaving brutally, or indulging in alcohol.

Regarding allegations about Piatigorsk prison: —

'That Oberländer shot a Soviet woman teacher, when under the influence of drink, is completely unknown to me. I simply cannot believe that Oberländer should be capable of such a crime.'

Regarding the allegations of mass extermination raids in Naltchik:

'I have never heard of mass exterminations of Jews by members of the Bergmann Unit. Even if I had not personally taken part in such a raid, my German comrades would certainly have told me of mass executions later. Nor have I ever heard of a mass execution called *Taufe* (Code word, 'Baptism'). I can state with absolute certainty that my company never took part in any such mass murders. Nor do I believe that any other company ever took part in such atrocities.'

Bergmann Files, without reference: —

Witness D., farmer, Rural District of Rosenheim: —

Finally, witness was told of the accusations raised against Oberländer. He comments: These accusations and the crimes and atrocities allegedly committed against prisoners of war and civilians are pure figments of the imagination. Most of the witnesses for the prosecution named in the verdict passed by the Soviet Zone Court are known to witness.

'These so-called witnesses returned to their homes when the war was over, and later. They were all arrested by the Russians, and it is clear why they were forced to give such evidence under pressure consisting of deliberate lies.'

'When Bergmann Battalion was engaged in action in the Northern Caucasus, it never plundered, or murdered anybody. Besides, Oberländer would have rather put a German in prison than harm any Soviet prisoner of war.'

Bergmann Files, Vol. I, Folio 250.

Paris, 27 décembre, 1960.

M. le Procureur

Me trouvant dans l'impossibilité de me présenter et déposer personellement devant vous dans l'affaire de M. le Ministre Oberländer, je considère de mon devoir de vous adresser le témoignage suivant.

Par la presse d'abord et par mes amis ensuite, j'ai appris les calomnies répandues sur le compte du bataillon Bergmann et de son chef M. Oberländer.

J'ai eu l'honneur de servir dans ce bataillon sous les ordres du Hauptmann Oberländer et j'affirme que les faits reprochés tant à cette unité qu'à son chef sont le fruit d'une imagination criminelle, me peinent profondement et me révoltent.

Je suis fier d'avoir appartenu à un bataillon composé d'hommes qui combattaient pour la liberté de leur patrie et avec une notable avance sur tout le monde, pour la liberté tout court. Non seulement le bataillon Bergmann n'a commis aucune atrocité, mais au contraire a fait énormement de bien et les populations qui'il a cotoyées n'ont jamais manqué de lui témoigner toute leur sympathie et toute leur reconnaissance. N'étaient-ce pas les hommes de cette unité qui partageaient leurs maigres rations avec les enfants des villages privés de toute nourriture par la guerre qui aidaient à labourer les femmes, dont les maris étaient absents et qui leur apportaient de quoi se chauffer. Les médecins et infirmiens soignaient les malades et les faisaient transporter en cas de necessité dans les infirmeries et hôpitaux militaires. Des divertissements étaient organisés au profit des ces populations qui y participaient spontanément dans l'espoir d'oublier, ne fût ce qu'un moment, les vicissitudes de la guerre. Le bataillon Bergmann avait reçu l'empreinte de la forte personalité de Hauptmann Oberländer, qui personnifiait la bonté et la plus grande compréhension. N'était-ce pas lui, encore, qui nous aidait à libérer des camps allemands les prisoniers géorgiens et nous conseillait de refaire de ces pauvres gens opprimés par un régime inhumain de Géorgiens libres ayant recouvré leur dignité d'hommes.

Tous les anciens du bataillon Bergmann qui vivent actuellement dans les pays où règne la liberté et d'où la terreur et le chantage sont bannis n'auront pas peur de témoigner et de confirmer la vérité. J'éspère Mr. le Procureur, que la justice triomphera et que les hommes qui sont tombés au champ d'honneur en faisaient leur devoir, ainsi que le chef qui les commandait, seront lavés des horribles accusations lancées contre eux par les ennemis du monde libre.

I am, etc.
(signed) (A.D.)

LIST OF JUDGMENTS AND COURT DECISIONS USED IN THE TEXT OF THE BOOK

Judgment of the International Military Tribunal, Nuremberg, of Oct. 1, 1946 (Chief War Criminals).

Judgment of the American Military Court No. XII, of Oct. 27 and 28, 1948 *(OKW* Trial).

Judgment of the Federal Constitutional Court of June 13, 1952 (BVerfGE 1,332).

Decision of the Federal Constitutional Court of Nov. 9, 1955 (BVerfGE 4, 331).

Decision of the Federal Constitutional Court of May 31, 1960 (BVerfGE 11, 150).

Decision of the Federal Constitutional Court of Jan. 17, 1961 (BVerfGE 12, 63).

Judgment of the Federal Supreme Court (BGHSt) of May 9, 1956.

Decision of the Federal Supreme Court of July 15, 1960 (BGHSt 15, 72).

Decision of the *Kammergericht* (Berlin High Court) of March 15, 1954. *Neue Juristische Wochenschrift,* 1954, p. 1901 *passim.*

Decision of the *Oberlandesgericht* (Land High Court) at Cologne of Oct. 24, 1958; *Recht in Ost und West,* 1959, p. 74 *passim.*

Judgment of the Supreme Court of the so-called German Democratic Republic, File No. 1 Zst (I), 1/60; Supplement to the magazine, *Neue Justiz,* 1960, No. 10 (The Oberländer Judgment).

Decision of the Public Prosecutor at the *Landgericht* (District Court) at Bonn not to proceed with the prosecution in the Nachtigall case, Sept. 26, 1960; File No. 8 Js 393, p. 43.

Decision of the Public Prosecutor at the *Landgericht* at Bonn not to proceed with the prosecution in the Bergmann case, March 3, 1961; File No. 8 Js 359/60 — 8 Js 134/61.

LIST OF SENTENCES, DECISIONS, STATUTES, AND TREATIES QUOTED IN THE BOOK

Sentence of the IMT, Nuremberg, of Oct. 1, 1946 (main war criminals)

Sentence of the American Military Tribunal, Nr. XII, of Oct. 27/28, 1948 (High Command trial)

Sentence of the American Military Tribunal ("Wilhelmstrassen-trial")

Sentence of the American Military Tribunal of Sept. 8 and April 10, 1948 (IX, pp. 6851—7129 — induction group trial)

Sentence of the Bundesverfassungsgericht (Federal Constitution Court) of June 13, 1952, BVerfGE (decisions of the Bundesverfassungsgericht) 1, 332

Sentence of the Bundesverfassungsgericht of Aug. 17, 1956, BVerfGE 5, 85 f. (sentence upon the German communist party)

Sentence of the Federal Supreme Court of May 9, 1956

Sentence of the Federal Supreme Court of Oct. 19, 1962, BGHSt 18, 87 f. (sentence on Stashinsky)

Sentence of the East German Supreme Court, reference number 1 Zst (I) 1/60, enclosure to the magazine "Neue Justiz" (new justice), 1960, No. 10 ("sentence" on Oberländer)

"Waldheim sentences", quoted in: Beschluss des Kammergerichts Berlin vom 15. März 1954, NJW 1954, pp. 1901 f.

Decision of the Bundesverfassungsgericht of Nov. 9, 1955, BVerfGE 4, 331

Decision of the Bundesverfassungsgericht of May 31, 1960, BVerfGE 11, 150

Decision of the Bundesverfassungsgericht of Jan. 17, 1961, BVerfGE 12, 62

Decision of the Federal Supreme Court of July 15, 1960, BGHSt 15, 72

Decision of the "Kammergericht" (highest court of appeal) of March 15, 1954, "Neue Juristische Wochenschrift", 1954, pp. 1901 f.

Decision of the "Oberlandesgericht" (Supreme District Court) Cologne of Oct. 24, 1958, in: Recht in Ost und West, 1959, pp. 74 f.

Dispositional act of abolition by the attorney at the District Court, Bonn, of March 3, 1961, 8 Js 359/60 — 8 Js 134/61 (Bergmann)

Dispositional act of abolition by the attorney at the District Court, Bonn, of Sept. 29, 1960, reference number 8 Js 393/60, p. 43 ("Nightingale")

Grundgesetz (Constitution) of the Federal Republic of Germany of May 23, 1949

Weimarer Verfassung (Constitution of the German Reich) of Aug. 11, 1919, RGBl (bulletin of Reich statutes) 1919, p. 1383

"DDR"-Verfassung (Constitution of the so-called German Democratic Republic) of Oct. 7, 1949, GBl 1949, 5

East German Statute for the protection of the inter-German commerce of April 21, 1950, GBl 1950, 327 f.

Rule of procedure of the "Staatsgerichtshof" (state court) of the Freie Hansestadt Bremen of March 17, 1956, GBl 1956, p. 35

East German statute on the state attorneyship of May 23, 1952

Statute on inter-German juridical and administrative assistance in criminal cases of May 2, 1953 (version of May 26, 1957)

"Kontrollratsgesetz" No. 10

Statute upon the constitution of the East German Courts of Oct. 2, 1952, GBl 1952, p. 983

StPO (code of criminal procedure) of Febr. 1, 1877, in version of Sept. 12, 1950, BGBl 1950, 629

StGB (criminal code) of May 15, 1871, in version of Aug. 25, 1953, BGBl 1953, 1083

Covenant of the League of Nations

Charter of the United Nations

Agreement upon the treatment of prisoners of war (convention of Genève) of July 27, 1929

London Agreement by the Big Four of Aug. 8, 1945

German-Russian treaty on frontiers and friendship of Sept. 28, 1939, RGBl 1940, II, p. 4

Briand-Kellogg-Pact of Aug. 27, 1928

European Convention for the Defence of Human Rights and Freedom of Nov. 4, 1950, BGBl 1952, II, p. 685

Moscow Declaration of Oct. 30, 1943

Statute of the International Court of Justice

Statute of the International Military Tribunal of Tokyo

Statute of the Nuremberg Military Tribunal

Index

DATE DUE
APR 16 19